Not Dead Yet
so plan your estate

AN ESTATE-PLANNING HANDBOOK and GRAPHIC NOVEL
by
ERIC G. MATLIN, ATTORNEY AT LAW
ndy@ericmatlin.com

Interior Illustrations,
Graphic Novel Illustrated and Co-Written
by Troy Locker Palmer
Troy Locker Palmer troy@phgindustries.com

Graphic Novel Layout, Lettering, and Inking
by gabo (a/k/a Gabriel Bautista)
gabo@galvosaur.com

Cover Art and Text Content Design
by Lena Norberg
lenasdi@aol.com

©2017

What people are saying about
Not Deat Yet so plan your estate (NDY)

Natalie Choate
Attorney and author of Life & Death Planning for Retirement Benefits
(Ataxplan Publications, 2011 or later edition):

> *"This engaging book should help lots of people get up to speed fast on the importance and nuts and bolts of estate planning. Lots of useful info, but the cartoons are the best part – funny, scary, and (sadly) all too realistic."*

Tim Kazurinsky
Screenwriter/Actor/Saturday Night Live alum:

> *"The Problem: How to make a complicated subject easier to understand. The Solution: (NDY) includes a graphic novel book-within-a-book that convincingly illustrates why estate planning matters to everyone. Brilliant!"*

Jane Bryant Quinn
Personal finance columnist and author of How to Make Your Money Last: The Indispensable Retirement Guide:

> *"I love this book. The cartoon stories bring home the critical importance of estate planning, in ways that will reach both the old and the young with assets to leave."*

Stephen Sayadian
Cult filmmaker and recovering corpse:
> *"The information here is of gargantuan proportions, yet it always entertains and enlightens. Read it while you still can!"*

Michael Rabiger
Author and Documentary Filmmaker:
> *"(NDY) is absolutely excellent, both as reference guide and as a narrative (en)lightening a task most people find grim."*

Larry Kopald
Kopald/Stranger, Los Angeles, CA:
> *"(NDY) is a tour de force of insight, encouragement, and entertainment all rolled together into a very approachable and immensely helpful book."*

Stuart C. Bear
Attorney, Chestnut Cambrone, Minneapolis, MN:
> *"(NDY) is absolutely excellent! It addresses very in-depth, substantive matters in a straightforward but whimsical way, if death and taxes can ever be whimsical or light-hearted! In all, it captures, I believe, the best qualities brought to an estate planning matter by an estate planning lawyer, the qualities of intellect, humor and emotional intelligence."*

Not Dead Yet
so plan your estate
ISBN #978-0-9912462-2-9
Library of Congress Preassigned Control Number (PCN) 2016913300

Publisher's Note

This publication is designed to provide entertainment, along with accurate and authoritative information in regard to the subject matter covered. It is sold with the understanding that the publisher is not engaged in rendering legal, accounting, or other professional services. If you require legal advice or other expert assistance, you should seek the services of a competent professional.

All characters appearing in the graphic novel portion of this work, with the exception of those identified by name in 'TDR's Estate Tax Tour' preceding Chapter 20, are fictitious. Except as stated, any resemblance to real persons, living or dead, is purely coincidental.

Acknowledgements

Troy Palmer-Hughes

You took my sketchy vision of an estate-planning book that would include a graphic novel with alternate realities, all stemming from a broken promise, and you ran with it. You helped me develop the graphic novel story and conceived/drew all the characters, as well as the famous people featured in the text. You also helped me re-chunk and edit the overall text. I could not have done this without you.

gabo (a/k/a Gabriel Bautista)

I was lucky enough to meet you at the Wizard World comic convention. You saw the merit in this project and helped me develop the graphic novel to its full potential with your sense of style and color.

Lena Norberg

Since the beginning of my law practice, around 1990, you and the great Arnie Press helped me in countless ways. Your design work is amazing, and your critical analysis enabled me to bring NDY to a higher level.

Kathryn Gooss

Yes, you gave me creative input on NDY, but, most important, you have been extraordinarily dedicated to keeping keeping Matlin Law Group, P.C. running efficiently.

Julie A. Kolodziej, Johannah K. Hebl, Mary E. Vanek, Ryan S. Smith, and Michael A. Goldberg

My partner, Julie, and my associates, JoJo, Mary and Ryan, who, besides helping me with estate planning, provide legal counsel to trustees, executors, and beneficiaries when estate plans "mature" or are non-existent, working with families to navigate the legal issues caused by death and incapacity. Ryan, you helped me immeasurably with your millennial perspective, editing, research, and attention to detail.

Jason S. Ornduff

Attorney and partner in the downtown Chicago office of Harrison & Held, LLC, who concentrates a significant part of his practice on complex estate planning, proofread and tweaked some of the thornier concepts presented in this book.

Patti Waldygo

Your eye for grammatical style and detail enabled me to finish the text in accordance with the Chicago Manual of Style (including the use of contractions!).

Early readers/tweakers Ernesto Mestre-Reed, Chris Adano, Carol McKibben, Chris Loeffler, and Nancy Traver all helped me get NDY off the ground.

Kudos to the rest of my awesome staff: Ashley Wiloff, Sara Ramirez, Lee Schneider, Melissa Chamberlin and Helen Youkhana.

Thanks also to my dear friend Randi Fiat for your steady collaborative guidance.

Dedicated to Glo.

As always, the love of my life.

Preface

The best book to help you learn about estate planning is one you will actually read. *Not Dead Yet* (NDY) explains estate planning in a way that anyone can understand. It features a fully illustrated graphic novel that functions as a book within a book. Though NDY necessarily touches on arcane legal topics, it does not dwell on techniques that affect only a tiny percentage of the population.

My attempt to create an antithesis to more typical estate-planning books led me to present certain aspects of the subject in a minimalist fashion that may not answer all of your questions, particularly if a complicated situation affects you directly. There are exceptions within exceptions (ad nauseum) in all legal fields, and NDY certainly does not address them all. By no means is NDY intended to be the final word or the definitive textbook on estate planning.

Why Read NDY?

Whether you are obsessed with death or hardly give it a thought, are 18 or 88 years old, are healthy or on your deathbed, you need an estate plan.

The road you take to "get your affairs in order" may be fraught with angst or just another chore. It can be mundane, twisted, or even fun, depending on your life, the issues, and the people involved. Yet difficult or not, if you put off planning for the inevitable, you might leave behind a myriad of horrific messes and/or miss out on a stellar opportunity to enhance the totality of your existence.

Although the core of estate planning includes distributing assets, minimizing taxes, and ameliorating or avoiding probate at death, there is much more. In fact, there is something in it for just about everyone.

The odds are reasonably high that you have an estate. It may be a large one, or it might be running on empty. Regardless of its size, the motion of the ocean, and whether you are carefree or fatalistic, there are reasons to pay heed.

If you are an estate-planning novice,
I'm talking to you.

If you are already schooled in estate planning,
I'm talking to you.

If you are an estate-planning professional who can benefit from a way to reach clients and make your job easier,
I'm talking to you.

Even if you believe that the plug will soon be pulled on civilization as we know it,
I'm talking to you.

Ultimately, NDY and estate planning are more about life than death. Though estate planning is a serious subject, it doesn't have to be entirely dreary. Black comedy, irony, satire, and love all play a role.

Don,
the hero of
our story

Eric,
the Estate Planning
Mojo Man

How to Read NDY

Each of NDY's twenty-four chapters is preceded by a comic book–style vignette, often relating to the text chapter that follows. Together, they tell the story of Don, his family, and his friends and why estate planning is important, even to those who cannot fathom why they would need it, now or ever. You'll recognize parts of Don's story in yourself or in people you've known. You may even come to realize the urgency of putting your wishes to paper.

If certain chapters, subchapters, or other chunks of text are completely irrelevant to you, skim to sections that apply to you. Some portions are relevant only if you have big bucks or a very specific need. It is not quantum physics, but some convoluted thinking is necessary. Even if you just look at the pictures early on, without reading the good-mojo text—let alone the snoozier elements of estate planning for the very wealthy in later chapters—you'll find that estate planning doesn't have to be a total drag. The return on your investment, in both time and effort, will amply make up for any discomfort the subject causes you.

If you are young, have a tiny estate, and read only one chapter of NDY, let it be Chapter 8, because whether you're young or old, rich or poor, healthy or frail, it is universal. If you have wealth to spread around and read only one chapter of this book, choose Chapter 18, which views estate planning as a singular opportunity to do something for the greater good.

Conventions Used in NDY

Similar to a dining guide listing prices in a restaurant, chapters have **$** signs, with a single **$** signifying that you should read this text even if you have a tiny estate, while **$$$$** means that the chapter mostly concerns readers whose wealth is measured in many millions. One chapter is marked **¢** — which is for everyone, because it just makes good sense.

Boxed Definitions Shaded Yellow	Used in some spots, so that the legalese doesn't throw you off track. All defined words also appear in the Glossary.
Blue shades	Things I think are funny, ironic, interesting, or extraordinarily tragic are sprinkled throughout NDY.
Dead Celebrities and Their Estates...	Symbolized by vultures instead of little birdies, these blurbs are limited to 140 characters. If celebrities interest you, there is plenty more about their estates online.
IN THIS CHAPTER...	At the beginning of each chapter is a brief overview.
Pearls of Wisdom...	At the end of each chapter is some sort of conclusion, being the minimum you should walk away with.
The Blue Gradient Edges	The edges of the graphic novel pages make it easy to read the full comic story arc before you tackle the regular text.
Glossary	If you come across a legal term you don't understand, which may have been explained earlier in NDY but you don't want to search for it, there's a good chance you'll find it in the GLOSSARY (page 280).

Chapter 1: Tie Up Loose Ends, While You Can Still Make A Knot   5

$
Practically everyone needs estate planning, whether major or minor.
What brought you here?

Chapter 2: Estate-Planning Mojo   18

$
More than just the forms—an estate plan can be about substance,
personality, and legacy.

Chapter 3: Probate And Intestacy   28

$$
Unfortunately, not everyone has an estate plan. What then?
What happens in probate court?

Chapter 4: Tangible Personal Property   39

$
Antique or high-tech, meaningless junk or priceless heirloom,
you can't take it with you.

Chapter 5: Other Assets That Make Up Your Estate   46

$
What else do you have that others may covet?
Know the nature and extent of your bounty.

Chapter 6: Getting Started   54

$
Now is as good a time as any for a first step—you must
have picked up this book for a reason, right?

Chapter 7: The Will   69

$$
The hammer of estate planning: No toolbox is complete without it.

Chapter 8: Health Care And Financial Powers Of Attorney,   79
Living Will, And HIPAA Authorization

¢
The baseline threshold for estate planning.
What every legal adult needs and why.

Chapter 9: Living Trusts—Revocable And Irrevocable   95

$$
Introducing the estate-planning Swiss army knife: The Trust.
It slices, it dices, it does just about everything.

Chapter 10: Testamentary Trusts—Control From The Grave, Part 1   108

$$
They kick in when you kick it. They give direction to the trustee
and determine the extent of beneficiaries' control via powers
of appointment.

Chapter 11: Testamentary Trusts—Control From The Grave, Part 2   119

$$
Immature beneficiaries? Blended family? Avoid outright gifts.
Provide a binding road map.

Chapter 12: Planning For Couples—Shelter Trusts And Marital Trusts   126

$$$
You've done it together. Plan for the unit, instead of just the individual.

Chapter 13: GST (Generation-Skipping Transfer) Tax Exempt Trusts   139

$$$
Creditors and taxes: Protect your family's inheritance
from outsiders, those who want to take a slice.

Chapter 14: Trusts Funded By Disclaimers   144
$$$
    Anticipate the need for your family to do postmortem planning.

Chapter 15: Special-Needs Trusts   151
$$
    Your special beneficiaries need that social safety net.
    Don't disqualify them from government help.

Chapter 16: Pet Trusts   164
$$
    For dog, cat, horse, reptile and bird (+) owners/parents. Make sure
    your non-human companion is well cared for.

Chapter 17: Estate-Planning Potpourri   172
$$
    Everyone has a junk drawer, full of this, that, and the
    other thing. It's all-important, and it's all useful.

Chapter 18: What's For Charity? Part 1   188
$$
    Charity begins at home but does not end there.
    How far will your legacy reach?

Chapter 19: Special Asset Planning Challenges—Life Insurance, Real   200
$$ Estate, Family Businesses, and Retirement Plans
    Unique assets require appropriate attention.
    Give yours the treatment they need.

Chapter 20: Estate, Gift, And Generation-Skipping Taxes   220
$$$
    Taxes on the wealthy, and the political/historical figures
    who have influenced them.

Chapter 21: Lifetime Gifting And Other Ways To Reduce   239
$$$ Your Taxable Estate
    Give it away now, or give it to Uncle Sam later.

Chapter 22: More Aggressive Estate Tax Reductions And Freezes (Brrrr)   252
$$$$
    Mega-complex strategies for people worth mega-millions of bucks.

Chapter 23: What's For Charity? Part 2   260
$$$$
    Gifting strategies that are wins for both you and your chosen
    charities, with benefits lasting for years.

Chapter 24: At Last   276
    The end.

Glossary   Don't understand a word? Look it up.   280

Index   288

Bibliography And Recommended Reading   294
    The author relies on experts to learn more.

About the Author   295

Eric Says

NDY's graphic novel is a tool to engage more readers, setting it apart from ALL other estate planning books. You may not need the graphic novel hook to be interested in the text, as the content speaks for itself, but if you do read the comic, I would suggest first reading it in its entirety, eased along by the gradient blue edges of those pages. Though the first 20 graphic novel vignettes relate directly to the text chapters that follow, some readers have found that by alternating the graphic novel and text, it is easy to lose the thread of the story and get bogged down. Just a suggestion, but it may work better for you to alternate text/comic on the second or third reading!

Unfortunately, I do not own a working crystal ball, so I cannot see the future, but, as Bob Dylan once said "The Times They Are a-Changin'." It may be that President Donald Trump, as promised, will deliver a death knell to the federal estate tax (death tax). One possibility being tossed about is that federal estate taxes will be eliminated as part of overall tax reform. Speculation also centers on axing basis step-up so that more revenue is raised with capital gains taxes. For more information on estate planning and changes in estate and capital gains tax laws, please visit www.notdeadyetbook.net.

Grandma Rose's promise was no secret, but she died without a will. Her belongings were divided between her daughters. Aunt Joanne and Sophie stayed in Grandma Rose's home. Don and his mom moved to another state where she finished college. The ring remained behind, packed away in the attic.

Thanks for letting me leave my stuff here. The car is already packed to the gills.

Of course, sis! I'll hold onto everything for you.

SOPHIE, DON'T TORMENT YOUR COUSIN!

Mom, meet Coach Henderson!

For a while, it was how Don preferred it, just him and his mom. Don met his best friend Derek, whose dad coached little league. When Mom met Coach, it was love at first sight.

Sarah & Coach married. Doug came along later, joining Derek and his sister Mara, her dogs and me. A happy, hectic blended family.

Sarah and Coach met with a lawyer to organize their affairs.

Guardians for the kids... instructions for the house and cars... pretty basic Will. Anything else?

Make a list, and we'll do a codicil.

My mom left me some nice china and jewelry.

It's at her old house with my niece, who still lives there.

$

Chapter 1

Tie up Loose Ends,
While You Can Still Make a Knot

No one here gets out alive
- from Five to One, Jim Morrison/The Doors -

In This Chapter...
we examine the proposition that practically everyone
needs estate planning.

The Twists and Turns of Life

Why should you plan for death—beyond reckoning with the metaphysical/religious side of it, which is a matter best taken up between you and your higher power?

Our lives
move in only
one direction.

The road may
twist and turn,
but each individual journey
meets a corporeal end.

That knowledge may tend
to make you more sad than happy,
but it is an undeniable truth.

No matter who you are, the end of life approaches.

The more carefully and thoughtfully you plan today, the less angst your loved ones will experience tomorrow. Putting your affairs in order casts your spirit in a way that perpetuates your life path and sharpens the focus of your legacy. Yet if you do nothing, your inaction can compound the grief and burden put on others and may ultimately diminish your life's work.

The Big Roulette Wheel

Estate planning is the most concrete step you can take toward achieving goals that can only be met in your amorphous future. At its most basic, an estate plan simplifies the transition from life to death and aims to circumvent any foreseeable problems. Now is the time to contemplate your relationships with friends and family and envision the consequences of failing to plan.

Imagine that unexpected events suddenly render you nonexistent or a shadow of your former self. Visualize your last brush with disaster. Was it crossing the street, oblivious to a car streaking out from a blind side? Stumbling off a ladder without a spotter? Or one of the countless other, often forgotten, narrow escapes littering the game of life?

Even if none of this seems relevant now, it makes no sense to ignore a shared common denominator: Your final epochal moment may be lurking just around the corner. And wearing blinders will not prevent it.

The truth is that no one lives forever. Some of us are cut down in our prime. I may be dead already, but you are not there (yet). The roulette wheel of life eventually spins its last for the most powerful athlete, the wealthiest miser, the wisest sage, and the most precious child.

Whether you die two weeks from Thursday on a treadmill at the gym or decades from now, peacefully and surrounded by family love, you have many reasons not to neglect the legal aspects of death. Leaving grief-stricken family and loved ones scrambling to adapt can cause immense damage and add layers of emotional stress to an already disquieting time.

If you wish to be remembered for the mess you inadvertently left behind, you may be one of the millions of American zombies trapped in a rapid-paced, celebrity-obsessed, over-consumptive lifestyle that leaves little room for the type of critical thinking you need to plan your estate.

Yet if you manage to squeeze ESTATE PLAN into your overflowing schedule, you may discover a therapeutic exercise that leads to mental clarity in a critically neglected area of self-analysis. Planning while you can still analyze the impact of your death on your supporting cast of characters will not trigger an unhealthy death fixation, unless you already have one. It is simply an honest acknowledgment. This is not about the when or the how, let alone the why. If you are fearful, it is but one more way to transcend some of the pain and fear associated with both reality and the unknown.

Estate Planning? Do I Even Have an "Estate"?

It's likely that you do have an estate, modest though it may be. Your car, your furniture, clothes, this book, hopefully a bank account or two, and real estate, even if it's worth less than the amount you owe. Who gets what? Who takes control of your empire, such as it is? Whether you are bursting at the seams or running on empty in the material world, estate planning also requires selecting someone to make your most intimate medical and personal decisions when you lose your voice.

Revocable RMD Funding Irrevocable
Spendthrift Blended Family Settlor
Grantor Trustee **Trust** Double Power of Attorney for Health Care
Contingencies Guardian

Estate Planning

Q-tip **HIPAA** Will Beneficiary **Probate** Immature Beneficiaries
Testamentary
Intestacy Durable Power of Attorney for Property Springing Power
Gift **Heir** Fiduciary **Agent** Executor
Deed Rule Against Perpetuities
Joint Tenancy

Do I need an estate plan?

Answer the following questions, yes or no:

YES	NO	I am a legal adult, responsible for myself and my actions in the eyes of the state where I live.
YES	NO	I am conventionally married—I have a wife or husband, two and one-half children and a dog, etc.
YES	NO	My spouse and I have formed a blended family. We each have children from prior relationships and one together.
YES	NO	I have a life partner to whom I am not legally married under applicable state law.
YES	NO	I am single and do not mind playing favorites among my family.
YES	NO	I have young or elderly dependents.
YES	NO	I care for and/or am the guardian of someone with special needs.
YES	NO	I love someone who is immature when it comes to handling money.
YES	NO	I have assets large enough to know I must be aware of tax issues.
YES	NO	I prefer to select the person who will make personal decisions with regard to my care and finances if I am ever incapacitated or when I die, rather than have that selection made for me.
YES	NO	I want some of my money to go to charity.
YES	NO	I want to add a little panache in giving away my personal treasures.

If You Answered YES to Any of These Questions, You NEED an Estate Plan

Unintended Consequences That May Be Avoided by Estate Planning:

1. A nasty fight over "stuff," in which an undeserving or distant relation ends up with a personal item, contrary to all reasonable expectations.

2. The IRS receives a tidy sum that relatively simple planning could have prevented.

3. A loved one withers away in misery, unable to communicate his or her personal-care wishes to others.

4. Though legally correct and in accordance with applicable statutes, judges or jurors adhering to the letter of the law without regard for individual circumstances commit a grievous wrong. The noble spirit of the law is fine and dandy, but when pitted against the letter of the law, the letter nearly always wins.

5. A probate battle breaks out, and lawyers take center stage in an expensive family drama played out in a public forum. Heirs feel as if they were run over by a legal dump truck.

6. Various parties squabble over guardianship of you or an incapacitated parent, sibling, or child.

7. Loved ones scramble to make sense of an estate that was not properly planned.

What Documents Do I Need?

Estate planning is nothing more than turning your thoughts into action by legally putting your wishes into writing and structuring your assets so that they flow in sync with the documents. Basic documents include:

WILL – Instructions on who should receive your possessions and other assets after your death, plus directions for the care of your minor or disabled children and disposition of your remains, all in a format the court will recognize and accept.

HIPAA AUTHORIZATION – Allows designated people access to your health-care information.

POWER OF ATTORNEY FOR HEALTH CARE – Appoints an agent (a proxy) to make personal and medical decisions on your behalf, should you become incapacitated.

POWER OF ATTORNEY FOR FINANCES OR PROPERTY – Appoints an agent (a proxy) to manage your finances, should you become incapacitated.

REVOCABLE LIVING TRUST – A Trust established by the grantor (its creator) during his or her lifetime, with terms that can be amended (changed) or revoked (canceled) at any time during the grantor's life.

IRREVOCABLE TRUST – A Trust that cannot be amended or revoked by its grantor, either because of its terms or because the grantor has died.

Estate Plan Quickie-Quiz

1. Who will my children live with when I'm dead?

2. Who will care for my pets?

3. Who will get my cash, real estate, business, and insurance-related assets? Under what conditions?

4. Who will get my tangible stuff? What is the fairest way to divide it up? Maximize its value?

5. What will be left for charities? Which organizations do I support?

6. Who will make personal, medical, and financial decisions for me, if I am unable to communicate?

7. Should my viable organs be donated for use by someone who is in need?

8. Cremation or burial?

Neil Young

In a 1975 interview with Rolling Stone magazine, Neil Young said, "When I'm gone, there's just going to be those records. Let the lawyers fight about the business. The records matter." While those records amount to a gigantic legacy, their value could be greatly magnified if he specifies the way they should benefit his family, friends, and/or favorite charitable causes.

Neil Young's current views on his legacy may differ from those he held in 1975. I would guess that the Canadian rocker, who strictly prohibits his music from being used for commercial purposes, probably now has an estate plan that prohibits a trustee from licensing his intellectual property to sell products and provides directions regarding other musicians covering his music to benefit his favorite causes. Because the future revenue his estate will generate likely exceeds some countries' gross national product, these are important considerations that impact both his family and any number of potential charities.

You might not be a rock star, but the only difference between your estate and Neil Young's may be one of scale. Make sure your assets end up in the right hands, so they are fully valued, rather than misused or misappropriated.

Tying It Together

Whether prioritizing estate planning is an easy detour for you, induces mild apprehension, or brings on a bout of projectile vomiting, think of the relief and satisfaction you'll feel when you check this vital piece of unfinished business off your mental "to do" list. You will feel more secure in the face of an uncertain future, helping loved ones avert the kind of nightmares that destroy families and undermine your achievements. If you cannot eliminate family feuds, good estate planning can at least mitigate the damage.

It is really not that hard.

Up.
    Loop.
        Over.
            Under.
                Across.

Affairs in order.

Contingency Planning: The "What Ifs…"

Occasionally, someone will tell me that his or her estate is so simple that a formal plan is unnecessary. After hearing about the structural steps taken to ensure a smooth transition, such as the use of joint tenancies or payable-on-death beneficiary designations, I may ask, "But what if . . . ?"

Quality estate planning involves contingency planning. For instance, what happens if someone dies "out of order" or otherwise unexpectedly? Although you can't foresee every potential future disaster or fork lying in the road ahead, you may wish to anticipate a few possibilities.

Pearls of Wisdom

Tying up some of the few loose ends of my life now, while I can still make a knot, can be relatively easy.

Difficult or easy, if I put off planning for the inevitable, I might leave behind a myriad of horrific messes and/or miss out on a stellar opportunity to enhance the totality of my existence.

When I am dead, it's impossible.

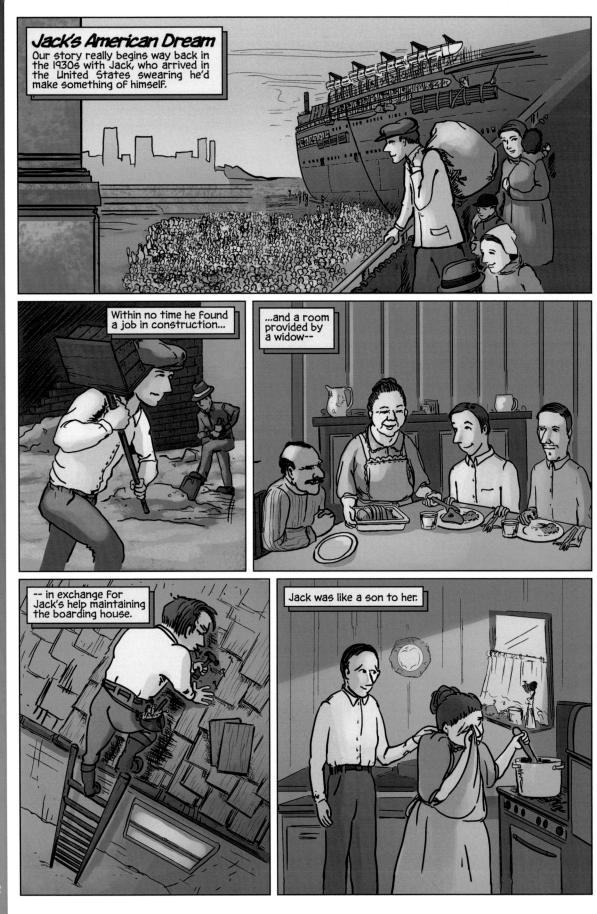

Jack's American Dream
Our story really begins way back in the 1930s with Jack, who arrived in the United States swearing he'd make something of himself.

Within no time he found a job in construction...

...and a room provided by a widow--

-- in exchange for Jack's help maintaining the boarding house.

Jack was like a son to her.

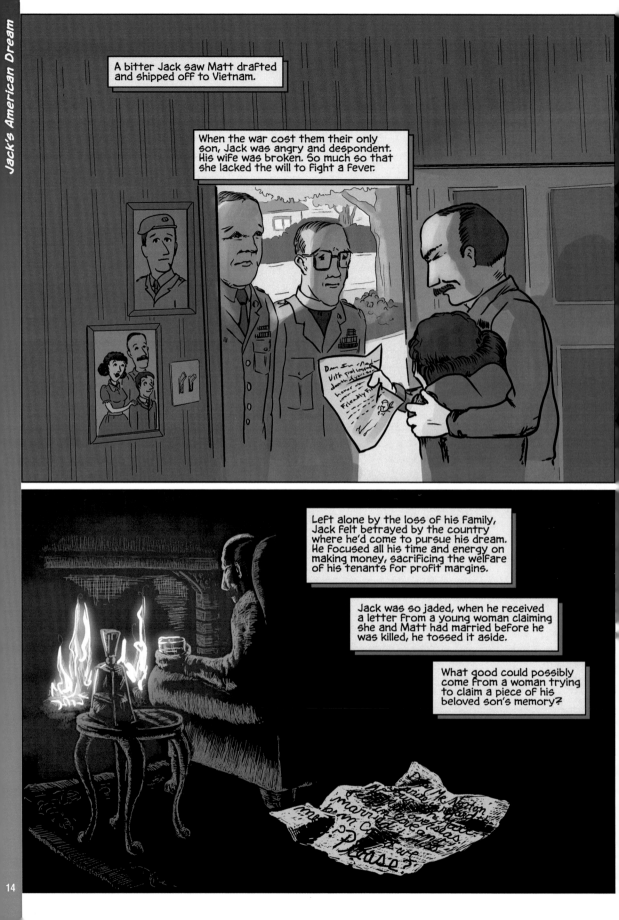

A bitter Jack saw Matt drafted and shipped off to Vietnam.

When the war cost them their only son, Jack was angry and despondent. His wife was broken. So much so that she lacked the will to fight a fever.

Left alone by the loss of his family, Jack felt betrayed by the country where he'd come to pursue his dream. He focused all his time and energy on making money, sacrificing the welfare of his tenants for profit margins.

Jack was so jaded, when he received a letter from a young woman claiming she and Matt had married before he was killed, he tossed it aside.

What good could possibly come from a woman trying to claim a piece of his beloved son's memory?

Family Tree

Libby Parker

Tammi

Ethan Parker

Jeff Parker

Rob

Cheryl Parker

Olivia

Phil Parker

Susan

Edward Parker

Linda & Sam Parker

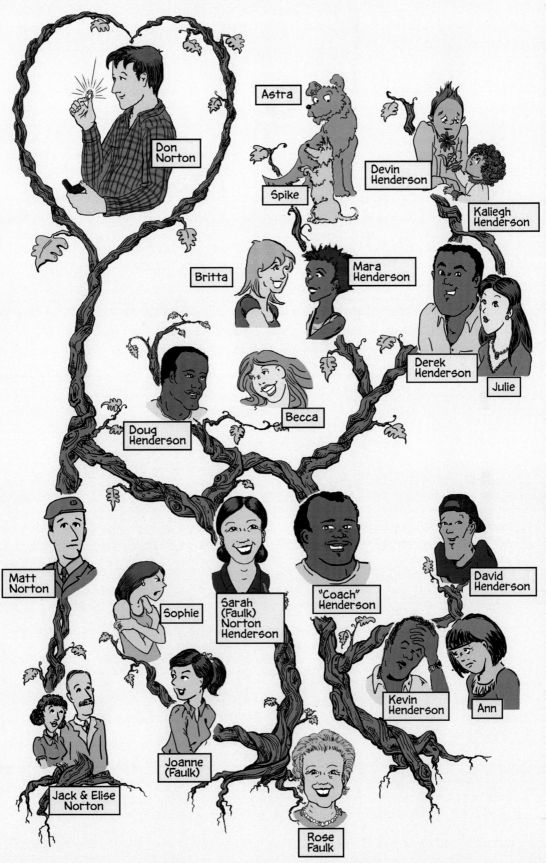

Chapter 2

$

Estate Planning Mojo

We only die once, and for such a long time!
- Moliere -

In This Chapter...

you'll find a few concrete ideas to add substance and personality to your estate plan.
Contribute to the mountain of benefits that comes from sharpening your legacy,
and wield your estate-planning mojo like a Sakura samurai.

EP Mojo

Originally a voodoo term, mojo typifies the magical charm of Muddy Waters and other blues greats. Despite having permeated pop culture, mojo—even at its most watered-down—is a good thing to have.

Estate planning (EP) mojo means using your heart—and not simply your head—to spread your own brand of magic in unique ways. Though EP mojo cannot be quantified, its value is unmistakable. Think of it as an extra ingredient to amplify your positive karma, regardless of your place in the universe.

Mojo-enhanced estate planning adds luster to your legacy, even if you have limited resources. Write your own obituary. Leave detailed personal bequests of your belongings, accompanied by stories about their importance to those you care about. Compose a message to be read aloud during your funeral service, and let your friends expand on it, publicly eulogizing your many virtues before a captive audience. Make a list of psalms or poems you would like sung or read during the service. Develop a music list to accompany your memorial ceremony or to be played during a wake, a shiva, or a farewell party. Use your send-off as another opportunity to inspire, honor, and delight those you leave behind.

If you have a few extra bucks, make a list of out-of-town people who may enjoy an all-expense-paid trip to attend your funeral or memorial service.

If you search for your EP mojo, you will find it. It may be tiny, fleeting, ephemeral, or incorporeal, but that doesn't mean it isn't real. It can be the cornerstone and embodiment of your own priceless legacy, belonging to you and people you've shared your life with. EP mojo may not add heat to your love life—but you can't rule that out, either.

Your EP mojo lies in the peace of mind you'll feel when you have carefully mapped out the inevitable division of your assets (i.e., real property, money, record collections, jewelry, etc.). EP mojo may not be voodoo, but it is definitely magical. I can't tell you what your mojo looks like, but just maybe I can point you in the right direction.

Dean Smith. February 28, 1931 – February 7, 2015

Classy Tar Heel hoops head coach: 879 wins, 2 Championships, 96% graduation rate. Added to great legacy by leaving each former player $200 for "Dinner out on Coach."

Complete the Following Statement:

"Estate planning is not something I'm doing for myself. I'm doing it for

_____

_____

_____."

No matter your situation or motivation, you have the power to perpetuate your values and to right a few wrongs. After your final bills have been paid, careful planning ensures that whatever is left serves your particular purpose.

Everyone Leaves a Legacy

Your legacy is the story of your life, the sum of your influence on those with whom you have had direct or indirect contact. Every day, your actions, both large and small, affect the lives of others. The people most obviously influenced are those closest to you, but the threads of your legacy affect people you don't even know. Estate planning presents a last opportunity to write your life story's final chapter.

Your estate plan can enhance your legacy by inspiring and delighting those around you or nurturing future generations. It can also defray inevitable problems and help family and loved ones bypass petty squabbles, minimize strife, and avoid costly court battles. By diffusing a host of potentially unhealthy situations, it can serve as an antidote to toxic power struggles and unfair outcomes.

You may simply want to ease the transition for your own family by making practical pre-death decisions. You may have friends and acquaintances whose lives you would like to improve by sharing what is a relatively small sum of money to you but manna from heaven to them. Beyond that, many local and global communities can benefit from your generosity.

Once completed, your estate plan is an extension and a continuation of everything you have done for loved ones and the greater community during your lifetime. Each decision you make and action you take is another thread in the tapestry you have woven into the fabric of your being. The sum total of your legacy affects other people in ways impossible to fully comprehend. It neither begins nor ends when you die. A piece of you will always live on.

Ethical Wills: Your Legacy Letter

"Ethical Wills" are non-legal media that vary from person to person. They generally express love, impart wisdom, or provide guidance to close relations. Some professional videographers specialize in taping final, parting messages from the terminally ill to their loved ones. The productions can accompany related memorial services. Young parents with debilitating or fatal illnesses have found audiovisual ethical Wills to be a priceless way to pass loving wisdom and meaningful mojo on to their children.

When Mixing in EP Mojo, Consider:

1. Did I work hard my whole life to acquire these things—with little or no outside help?

2. Did I inherit what I have and later realize that it robbed me of certain adversities that could have helped me develop a higher moral character?

3. Did I benefit from the generosity of someone who owed me nothing, but who helped me get ahead—for example, with a scholarship?

4. However I acquired my assets, do I want to pass them on only to immediate family members, or is there someone else I would like to recognize?

5. Are there zombies in my family, who, if they suddenly find themselves in possession of copious resources, may not be able to escape the lure of an idle, unfocused lifestyle?

6. Are there vampires in my family who may suck the essence out of my estate, if it is not protected?

7. Would it kill me now to picture some particular in-laws or step-relations plowing through my money?

8. Can I avert any obvious conflicts brewing on the horizon?

Although your EP hot buttons may not be particularly complex, you probably have at least one issue that deserves urgent consideration. Estate planning is an opportunity to preemptively address those potentially problematic situations. By managing and dividing your assets clearly, you can also stay one step ahead of the intestate gamble (see Chapter 3). What could be better than imparting a value system and promoting positive karma? At the same time, you'll accomplish more practical goals—for example, avoiding unnecessary drains on your estate and navigating potential craters in your family's future.

When you craft a written estate plan, it enriches your life both financially and spiritually. You will thoughtfully distribute your money and possessions to the loved ones who survive you, and your legacy will continue to touch the lives of countless others. Consider the impact you have made already and the effect you can still have once you are gone. While you're living, you have choices. Once you're dead, they evaporate.

Final Resting Places of a World Traveler

Marge liked to travel the world. A month or two after she was cremated, Marge's daughters held a memorial service for her. Attendees were able to take one or more envelopes addressed to one of the daughters, which contained very small zip-lock bags, each holding about a half-teaspoon of Marge's ashes. If you took an envelope with ashes, you were encouraged to bring it with you on a trip, sprinkle the ashes at your destination, and then mail the envelopes from your exotic locale. The daughters received envelopes from all over the world, adding mojo to Marge's legacy as world traveler.

Are there special people you wish to include in your plan? Some may be blood relatives and others may not—godchildren, for example. Dictionaries define godchildren as "people for whom one becomes a sponsor at baptism." My EP definition is much broader and includes anyone who should get a share of your estate. Do you want to remember a favorite relation or friend with a special gift? Perhaps a grocery clerk who goes beyond the call of duty? A local hero whose selflessness or courage inspires you? Your estate plan is the perfect place to recognize people who do the right thing. In turn, you can be their angel.

A Baker's Dozen: Fresh Ideas for Mojo-Infused Giving

1. Unexpectedly sweeten someone's life by making his or her wishes come true.

2. Fund a party at your favorite local restaurant or tavern for all of the familiar faces.

3. A spoonful of sugar always helps: pay travel costs for unsuspecting out-of-towners to be at your final resting spot or memorial service.

4. Spice up your friends' lives and treat them to a weekend spa or a poker retreat in celebration of your life.

5. Provide a school lunch or a student activity program with the key ingredient it needs to thrive.

7. Foot the bill for a much-needed renovation project at your house of worship or retreat.

8. Boost a community organization's ability to cook up food, provide shelter or clothing, and so on, for those in need.

9. Add your own dash of culture to a library or a museum of your choosing by donating your collection of books, music, or precious objects d'art for members of your community to appreciate.

10. Donate funds to your alma mater, with the stipulation that the school put a stone bench out front that reads: "From the Class of '98."

11. Sprinkle some magic on the life of a deserving child with a gift of unused airline miles/hotel points so the family can visit Disneyworld.

12. Establish a family fund/party stash to finance family reunions and gifts for family members on their birthdays, at holidays, and so on.

13. Surprise a loyal employee or coworker who has helped you in countless ways with a well-deserved windfall.

Let Your Special Send-Off Set Off a Tradition

"Mac" McKenzie allocated a few thousand dollars for a memorial party at the beach, complete with bagpipes. His trustee (by direction of his Trust) paid for transportation, food, drink, and lodging. In later years, it became an annual affair for a select few. Mac's spirit lived on more intensely than it otherwise would have, thanks to his thoughtful planning.

You may not believe you have much to give, but the simple act of placing a treasured item in the hands of someone who will cherish it allows you to impart an invaluable loving vibration. That act lives on beyond your physical expiration date and projects an influence that does not perish with your final breath. It adds a shine to what you have already done to make the world a better place and magnifies your place in it. Deliberate planning can do extraordinary things after you die, so that your name lives on in accordance with your passions and beliefs.

Take the mental voyage that bridges the present to the unknowable future, and consider ways your giving spirit can continue on. Dream about the legacy your estate plan can help sustain and the good it can do for others, as a tool you use to perpetuate your quintessential self. Devise strategies to turn today's deepest desires and wishes into future realities.

Your estate-planning issues might be simple or routine, or your thoughts may drift to the lasting impact your assets can have on the world. In either case, fresh insight comes when you get the process rolling. That alone makes estate planning worth the effort.

Pearls of Wisdom

Simple or complex, it is my life, my mojo, and my legacy.
My EP is an extension of me and therefore deserves
careful consideration.

Mara, Britta, Astra and Spike

Mara and Brita met cute.

27

Chapter 3

$$ \$\ \$ $$

Probate and Intestacy

Death is not the end. There remains the litigation over the estate.
- Ambrose Bierce -

In This Chapter...
you'll discover what probate is all about
and what happens to your assets without a Will.

Without a Will,
Probate Assets Pass at Death to Intestate Heirs.

WILL
A legal document written in accordance with state law that directs the distribution of your probate assets, including personal effects, after your death. Appoints an executor to administer your estate according to its terms. (For more details about what makes a Will valid, see Chapter 7.)

PROBATE ASSETS
Everything you own individually. Does not include assets owned jointly or in partnership with someone else, or assets that, via contractual arrangement, are payable to another person or persons at the time of your death.

INTESTATE
Dying without a valid Will.

INTESTATE HEIRS
Those persons, usually next of kin, who inherit your probate assets if you do not have a Will. Each state has its own intestacy formula for determining heirs.

JOINT TENANCY WITH RIGHT OF SURVIVORSHIP (JTWROS)
A shared ownership between two or more people, with the survivor(s) owning the property after the death of one or more fellow joint tenants.

Do I Own Probate Assets?

You do if you own assets titled with a financial institution or government agency and all of these three statements are TRUE with respect to them at the time of your death:

1. There is no surviving joint tenant. Joint tenancy delays but does not ultimately eliminate an asset from the probate asset category, because the surviving joint tenant will eventually die as well. You might say, "That's someone else's problem." Yet if you take a long view of your assets, it is your concern as well.

2. There is no effective beneficiary designation on file with your insurance company or other financial institution. Most banks, brokerage firms, and mutual fund companies allow for beneficiary designations that avoid probate if the beneficiary survives you, but require them to be relatively simple, such as, "100% to my spouse if he or she survives me; otherwise, 50/50 between my surviving children."

3. The assets in question do not pass by Trust or other contractual arrangement.

In many instances, tangible personal property—"modest stuff," as discussed in Chapter 4— can be transferred without probate unless it is titled, such as a car or a boat. This is because beneficiaries can use and sell your stuff without any change in registration from a financial institution or a government agency.

BENEFICIARY
The person, the entity, or the charity that receives a gift from you when you die, either as an intestate heir; as a legatee of a Will; having been named in a Trust; or through a contractual designation (payable or transferable on death) in an insurance policy, a qualified plan, an annuity, or another financial account.

LEGATEE
A beneficiary to whom you leave assets in your Will.

TRUST
A written legal agreement in which one or more persons or companies—"trustees"—hold and manage assets for the benefit of one or more beneficiaries under a fiduciary relationship.

FIDUCIARY
An individual, a corporation, or an association in a position of trust and responsibility and to whom property or power is assigned to be managed for the benefit of another person or entity. If this fiduciary accepts the appointment, the person, organization, or association is required to comply with the terms of the appointing document and is held to heightened legal and ethical standards. Fiduciaries include, among others, trustees, executors, guardians, and agents.

DEATH PROBATE
A court action connecting a dead person's probate assets to the beneficiaries of those assets.

Time Sheets: Watch the Clock

If you are acting in a fiduciary capacity, always keep track of your time in writing. Even if you begin acting with no intention of being paid, having a basic journal may come in handy later on. Sometimes a fiduciary embarks down a simple road that turns into a time vacuum, for which he or she would rightly want to charge the estate, presenting problems when a beneficiary objects if there is no time substantiation.

What Is Probate?

Most commonly, probate is the in-court process of legally validating a Will and carrying out its terms. It links a dead person's probate assets with the living beneficiaries who will eventually receive them. It can add significant legal expenses and delay the transfer of assets to your beneficiaries.

If there is no Will, the probate process is essentially the same as if there is one, but the court selects the personal representative and determines the beneficiaries in accordance with the laws of intestacy in the state where the probate case is filed. Under court control, assets are collected, bills are paid, and assets are retitled and eventually distributed to beneficiaries before closing the estate. Sometimes the legal costs of probate exceed the value of the assets, leaving beneficiaries no choice but to simply walk away from the probate assets.

Probate procedures vary by state, but all types in every state can be substantially avoided and costs minimized though proper estate planning. This includes "living" probate, also referred to as a guardianship (see Chapter 8).

How a Will Helps

With a valid Will: Your Will determines to whom your estate is transferred and the executor who controls the process.

Without a valid Will: (Dying intestate) State law specifies who gets what from your estate, and the court selects the person who controls the process.

Think of probate as the script that guides the orderly transfer of your estate, linking you after death with your beneficiaries. The procedures vary by jurisdiction (state to state, and sometimes county to county), but most are recognizable in their various iterations.

Selecting a Personal Representative

In your Will, you name the individual (or the bank) you want to be your personal representative or executor (terms often used interchangeably), the person in charge of your estate after you die. A petition initiates probate, asking the court to appoint the executor and validate the Will. The probate court requires other forms and procedures that can be found by searching the Internet for "probate forms" and the name of the state or the county where the deceased resided.

The court picks the personal representative for your estate if:

- You die without a Will.

- Your Will does not specify who you want to be your personal representative.

- The person you selected has died or for some reason cannot serve—and you did
  not provide a contingency to replace your original choice.

Absent a valid executor selection, usually your spouse or an adult family member files the petition and requests that the court appoint him or her or another appropriate choice as the personal representative of your estate.

Once the representative is chosen and the Will is ruled to be valid, the court will issue Letters of Office, Letters Testamentary, or Letters of Administration to the representative. These "Letters" officially grant authority to a personal representative to act on behalf of the estate after swearing an oath to perform the duties to which the court entrusts the representative. A dead person cannot sign checks or legal documents, and "Letters" give someone the authority to deal with such business. With "Letters" in hand, the representative can liquidate existing accounts, open one or more estate accounts, sell real estate, and take other steps toward distributing and closing the estate.

In the absence of a Will, the court will order the personal representative to pay a bond premium to an insurance company for a policy that guarantees he, she, or it will not steal funds or violate fiduciary duties. A Will may waive the bond requirement to save the estate an extra expense, although a bond premium is money well spent if the personal representative turns out to be a thief.

King Lear. Late 16th – Early 17th Centuries

Death knocking, Shakespearian Monarch giveth his kingdom to daughters based on their most insincere flattery. When riches corrupt, an old fool they make of Dad..

Notifying Heirs, Creditors, and the Public of Your Death

In addition to notifying known creditors and heirs in writing, most states require your personal representative to publish a death notice in a local newspaper. This serves as public notice of your estate's probate and enables those who think they have an interest in the estate, such as unknown heirs and creditors, to file a claim against it within a specified time period.

Inventorying Your Assets

One of the personal representative's jobs is to inventory all of your assets to determine the estate's value. The representative must also pay valid debts. If the value of the estate is insufficient to cover all of the debts, including legal, accounting, and personal representative costs, then your beneficiaries may get nothing at all.

The personal representative must "marshal" (collect and protect) estate assets to make sure all of the property is available for distribution at the end of the probate process. If the decedent's property goes missing, the personal representative may face probate hell. For example, if your Will specifies the distribution of an item that you no longer own at the time of your death, the executor should note that early on, so that the beginning inventory reconciles with the inventory at closing.

Paying Bills and Taxes and Distributing the Estate

The estate must pay administration costs (legal notices, appraisal fees, personal representative fees, attorney and accounting fees, etc.), taxes, and other debts, such as medical bills, utilities, and credit cards. Most states require family allowances, modest stipends paid to any surviving spouse and dependent children. If probate proceeds according to plan and all notices and communications are properly handled, the personal representative and the estate are usually personally protected against any subsequent, late-arriving claims.

After all valid claims and family allowances have been paid, whatever is left gets distributed to the beneficiaries named in the Will. If there is no Will, the state's intestacy laws determine who gets what.

Public Forum

Some probates are relatively straightforward. Others can be particularly complicated, making it difficult to map a timeline in advance. In general, the simplest estates may close six months after both filing the petition and publishing notice to unknown creditors (and heirs, if there is no Will). If there are any complexities, such as a dispute among beneficiaries or problems in determining the heirs, or if the validity of the Will is at issue, all bets are off. Preposterously litigious probates can take years. "Ancillary"—or secondary—probates are also required in every state where you own real estate.

Probate often provides a needlessly public forum for people wishing to stick their grubby little fingers into your postmortem business to be seen and heard. Anyone can examine your probate file by visiting the court and asking for it. That means seeing an inventory of your probate assets, along with the names and addresses of the beneficiaries and their respective shares.

In other words, probate files serve up ready-made suckers for whatever probate vampires are selling. Picture a financial services peddler calling a naive beneficiary who just inherited $100,000, informing him or her of the "perfect investment opportunity." Nosy neighbors can join the vampires and rifle through your probate file out of macabre curiosity. At the very least, personal representatives and probate beneficiaries can expect an increase in junk mail.

Probate is often the least convenient and most public method through which your assets flow to your beneficiaries, a true mojo killer. It can be avoided, and assets often protected from your creditors, through contractual payable-on-death transfers (if persons or organization named survive you), funded revocable living Trusts (see Chapter 9) and joint tenancies (if another joint tenant survives you).

Despite the negative aspects of probate, it does have a few advantages, which are discussed in Chapter 9.

Small Estates May Not Need Court

Less valuable estates can sometimes be transferred without opening a full-blown probate and simply require a small estate affidavit. However, not all states provide this expedited procedure, and court approval may still be required. In most cases, the affidavit process cannot transfer real estate. Most often, it's used to transfer automobiles.

AFFIDAVIT   A formal signed and sworn statement of fact, signed by an affiant, who is making the assertion, usually witnessed by a notary public.

The definition of a "small" estate varies by state, usually qualified as those with a maximum aggregate value of $10,000 at the low end and $100,000 at the high end. This is typically a net equity value after subtracting liens and encumbrances, basically the value of your assets (see Chapter 5 about these items) minus any loans or other financial debts. As with a full probate, there is usually a requirement to pay all bills and family allowances prior to distribution to any beneficiary.

Some states prohibit the use of a small estate affidavit until a certain time has elapsed after death. A spouse or a child making the claim may face different rules than a distant relative. To learn more about the rules in your state, search the Internet for "small estate affidavit" plus the name of your state.

Intestacy: Who Gets Your Probate Assets If You Don't Have a Valid Will?

Without a valid Will, your estate is considered to be "intestate," and the laws of intestate succession in the state where you lived determine who gets your probate estate when you die. State legislatures write these intestate succession laws, and the courts carry them out.

Intestate distribution varies from state to state but operates purely by formula. Usually, when a spouse and children survive you, then no other people participate in the distribution of your intestate estate. If you leave either a spouse or children, but not both, your spouse or children may have to share your assets with your parents. If your only survivors are parents and siblings, then either your parents have priority or your parents and siblings all participate. If only one parent survives you, that parent sometimes gets your deceased parent's share as well. If a sibling is deceased, then usually that sibling's descendants step into that person's shoes.

If no spouse, descendant, parent, sibling, nephew, niece, great nephew, or great niece survives, your personal intestacy tree may reach as far as your dead great-grandparents and their descendants to include aunts, uncles, and cousins of varying degrees. In a few states, a deceased spouse's family may also be entitled to something. Most states treat half-brothers and half-sisters as full siblings. That status may also extend to other "half" relatives (sharing an ancestor) but rarely includes "step" relations (where the only connection is through marriage). At the time of your death, persons conceived but not born are often considered the same as already-born heirs.

Sometimes the division between your spouse and children will be affected by whether you or your spouse had children with a prior partner. In some states, the length of your marriage is a factor.

If you have never been married and have no family descending from common ancestry going as far back as your great-grandparents (and you don't live in one of the few states where your spouse's family would participate as intestate heirs), your estate will likely "escheat." In other words, your estate will be transferred to the government of the state in which you lived—with real estate ownership going to the county in which it is located. Escheats are pretty rare, but they happen. It takes a tiny family for there to be a complete absence of intestate heirs.

Money Falling from the Sky… with a Price

Heir finders are companies that search for distant relatives who are intestate heirs of probate estates. When the companies find these long-lost heirs, they require the individuals to sign a contingency agreement, usually for a percentage of the eventual inheritance, prior to giving the heirs any information.

Some state intestacy laws distinguish between personal property and real estate. Others give automobiles special treatment. If you die in one of the nine community property states (Arizona, California, Idaho, Louisiana, Nevada, New Mexico, Texas, Washington, and Wisconsin—see "Community property" in the Glossary) and leave a surviving spouse, the law usually distinguishes between community property assets and separate property assets in making intestate distributions.

You can easily obtain additional information on intestacy online by searching for the name of the state in question and "law of intestacy."

Intestacy laws are written for the masses, so they don't always result in fairness. The law makes no distinction among your children, so your devoted daughter and the son you haven't seen in ten years will receive equal portions.

Pearls of Wisdom

I learned what probate means, both as a type of asset and as a court process.

If I want my assets at death distributed to anyone other than to my intestate heirs, selected purely by formula, I must either:

1. Put my wishes in a Will (which may still be subject to probate);

2. Retitle the assets in joint tenancies (provided the joint tenant survives me);

3. Own the assets in Trust;

4. Specify beneficiaries with the financial institution (bank, broker, mutual fund, insurance company, IRA custodian, etc.) through "payable on death" (POD) or "transferable on death" (TOD) designations; or

4. Designate beneficiaries by contractual agreement, such as a buy/sell agreement.

Absent one or more of the above, my beneficiaries may not receive the share of structures, or if intestate distribution works for me, I must consider what happens if someone dies out of order. Incomplete contingency planning can destroy my vision of the future.

Chapter 4

$

Tangible Personal Property

A house is just a place to keep your stuff while you go out and get more stuff.
- George Carlin -

In This Chapter...

*you'll find a few ideas on how you can ensure fair distribution of your valuable,
useful, and sentimental things. Whether it is meaningful junk, automobiles,
furniture, dishes, artwork, or fine jewelry, you probably have stuff that other people would
appreciate. The distribution details can be handled in your Will under the control
of your executor (see Chapter 7) or as part of your Trust under the control
of your trustee (see Chapter 8), but either way, it should be in writing.*

You can't take it with you! The old adage is true. Without planning, some of your favorite stuff may go to family and friends, while other treasures may end up in thrift shops or dumpsters. Planning gives you a voice in redistributing your possessions. You worked for them, you may have spent countless hours mall shopping or antiquing to find them, or maybe you inherited them yourself. Why shouldn't you say what happens to them?

One of the first legal concepts kids learn is that "possession is 9/10ths of the law." Whoever gets to the house or the safe deposit box first may keep its contents. If you are disturbed by the thought of your children racing to claim your stuff before they even bury you, plan to keep things fair and prevent that scenario.

Be as Specific as You Wish

Divide your wine cellar among several friends, giving them bottles to savor on special occasions; portion out your crystal collection among your grandchildren; bestow your jewelry on your nieces. Pass on your tastes and personality by giving special items to those who will cherish them.

Truly valuable objects may deserve special treatment, even if their only worth is sentimental. Make sure things wind up in the right hands. A single item may dominate your thoughts, so put your mind at ease by making the trustee or the executor and the beneficiaries aware of important possessions. If you fear something may fall through the cracks or be handled incorrectly, you may want to hire estate sale specialists or other experts to oversee the process.

Reduce Conflict

In our hearts, most of us agree that personal relationships are the true gems of our lives. Yet our consumer-crazed society often warps our perspective, leading us to get emotionally wrapped up in our stuff. In the aftermath of death, the bestowal of that stuff—even seemingly inconsequential possessions—can cause gigantic, knockdown, drag-out fights.

Making everyone happy, though a lofty goal, may not be possible. Yet if you create a plan to divide your things reasonably and intelligently, it will help your heirs and legatees avoid painful disputes. Obviously, you cannot divide a house full of furniture with precision, but you can provide guidance if multiple beneficiaries have an equal claim to something that cannot be divided.

Keep It Clean

If there's perhaps a side of you that you would prefer your family not know about, choose someone to sanitize your stuff after you're gone—maybe delete computer files or discreetly get rid of that sex toy at the back of the underwear drawer.

One way to deal with your stuff is by making gifts during your lifetime. Would you enjoy seeing a favorite niece wear your antique pendant or a nephew ride your backup Harley while you're still alive? Lifetime gifts not only prevent fights at your wake, but you get to see your loved ones enjoy your prized possessions. On the flip side, leave directions that the person who gave you a gift during your lifetime gets first dibs on it when you are gone.

Whether you want to gift some of these valuables now or hold onto everything until you are gone, you can allow current and future beneficiaries to select items they covet. Add a new dimension to Thanksgiving get-togethers by letting family members choose what is important to them, a token to remind them of you when you're not around. Be aware, this may have drawbacks, depending on the dynamics of your family: one daughter wants everything; another, who finds the whole exercise morbid, refuses to pick anything. You may not want to introduce a divisive element into already tenuous relationships any earlier than necessary.

With or without input from your beneficiaries, you can eliminate uncertainty by providing specific instructions, as detailed as you wish, in writing, photos, or videos, and dictating who gets what. Moderation is advisable, as it is in all things. Trying to account for every item down to the last paperclip can drive you crazy.

 Marilyn Monroe. June 1, 1926 – August 5, 1962

Famed actress leaves all personal effects to Lee Strasberg (GF's Hyman Roth). Expresses desire for friends to get stuff but Lee's widow sells it & pockets millions.

A gift of tangible personal property to someone, other than an outright gift without any strings attached, requires a testamentary Trust (see Chapters 10–11). A simple example of a gift in Trust is:

"My diamond engagement ring to my granddaughter Ruby, to be given to her when she is married. Until Ruby marries or attains age 28, whichever occurs first, my daughter-in-law Jane shall possess the ring, provided . . ."

There are better ways to distribute your things, but for some families, the old school method works best: marking items with stickers. If you decide to stickerize your stuff, be sure to use stickers large enough to contain a hand-written item description, because tags can easily be switched, leading to allegations or perceptions of misdeed.

Scrapbooking

Sally added meaning to her stuff by taking digital pictures of about 150 items. She printed the 5" X 7" pictures and attached them to 8½" X 11" sheets of paper in a binder, along with notes describing why each item had meaning, including its history: Great-granddad's pipe and pocket-knife, her mom's favorite 1960s vintage dress with matching hat and gloves, and so on. She even put pieces of fabric in the book, along with pressed flowers from the family cottage.

Provide a Path for Resolution

After specifying particular items, divide your tangible personal property residuary—what is left after specific bequests are made—among classes of people. You can batch your stuff according to the categories of people entitled to it: "my surviving children will divide everything else in substantially equal shares" or "my jewelry to my daughters; my tools to my sons." If multiple beneficiaries want the same indivisible item, provide for a way to resolve disagreements. In most cases, the distribution of an item claimed by more than one person is left to the trustee or the executor or an independent third party.

A Few Tips for the Living

As the trustee or the executor involved in distributing tangible personal property, you should keep a record of who takes what and how the decisions were made. Your notes may come in handy if disputes arise later.

If you are inheriting stuff, comb through it carefully. Take the drawers out of Grandma's dresser, and maybe you will find the $1,000 Grandpa taped to the back of the drawer and forgot about. People often hide things so well that even they cannot find them.

Going through Grandpa's backyard with a metal detector before selling his home of sixty years isn't a bad idea either.

What if your kids don't get along, under even the best circumstances? A decision maker who is also a beneficiary may be a source of friction. If your ultimate decider has a reputation for fairness, it may help to talk with this individual and make sure he or she does not mind the potential heat.

A number of conflict-resolution techniques can ease the process and take some of the pressure off the trustee/executor: direct that the kids draw in order by age, and then continue to draw by reversing the order each time, or use games of chance, roll the dice, draw cards, or play "rock, paper, scissors."

Whoever is in charge, usually the trustee, must rise to the occasion when a complex, intense, or contentious issue arises regarding any or all of your personal property. To fairly break a deadlock, consider more formal means of dispute resolution. Leave the decision to a disinterested third party, or choose a committee (of siblings, for instance) to decide by majority. For intractable problems, you can provide for outside mediation or arbitration. If your stuff is fabulous but hard to divide, or your beneficiaries squabble, estate sale professionals can simply sell the belongings and distribute the proceeds.

Specify what happens if a beneficiary has not survived you or if a particular item is not part of your estate, perhaps because you already gave it to its recipient, you lost it, or it was stolen. If the fate of the item is a mystery to the intended inheritor, it can lead to big problems.

Leona, Part I

Leona Helmsley, a billionaire New York City hotel operator and investor, died in 2007. She was a flamboyant personality and had a reputation for tyrannical behavior that earned her the nickname "Queen of Mean." Among the wacky terms in her Will was a bequest of $12 million to a Trust for the benefit of her dog (see Chapter 16 for "Leona, Part 2," and more on pet Trusts) and a yearly payment equal to 10 percent of a separate $5 million Trust to certain grandchildren, with the sole requirement of payment being that they must visit their dead father's cemetery site at least once during that year.

She also directed that she be interred wearing her wedding band, "never to be removed from my finger," a thoughtful sign of devotion to her late husband, Harry. She did not show much sentimentality, however, in directing her executor to sell all of the rest of her "furniture, furnishings, books, paintings and other objects of art, wearing apparel, jewelry, automobiles, and all other tangible personal property."

Pearls of Wisdom

Why I must take a look at the full scope of my stuff; techniques that my stuff goes to the right people; how I can prevent a free-for-all over my stuff; and ways to ensure that the true value of my stuff is not overlooked.

Chapter 5

$$\$\ \$$$

Other Assets That Make Up Your Estate

Being of sound mind, I spent it all.
- Leon Jaworski, referring to the shortest Will on record -

In This Chapter...
you'll categorize and tally the value of your assets. Some of your fortune may have readily identifiable cash value, while other financially significant aspects may be more difficult to measure. Understanding the nature and extent of your bounty is essential for proper planning. Know what you have before you figure out what to do with it.

Chapter 6 contains a Checklist/Questionnaire to help you identify and organize your asset information.

Different Asset Types Present a Variety of Particular Issues

Liquid portfolios include publicly traded stocks, bonds, mutual funds, bank accounts, CDs, money markets, and green cash. These assets are the easiest to understand, count, divide, and distribute to beneficiaries or use to pay debts and final expenses. IRAs and other retirement plan assets and annuities with complex tax issues must be considered separately. Retirement plans, especially the intricacies of naming beneficiaries, are touched on later in this chapter and at length in Chapter 19.

Covered in Chapter 4, tangible personal property consists of things you can touch, move, and enjoy.

Life insurance proceeds ("death benefits") paid when you die are basically the same as cash. To determine ahead of time how much cash will actually end up going to your beneficiaries, consider whether the insurance policy will be in force when you die and whether the death benefit you currently expect will be the amount paid. Insurance is more fully discussed in Chapter 19.

Real estate includes your principal residence, vacation residences, deeded time-shares (which sometimes nobody wants), and any investment properties. Compared to cash (including life insurance payouts) and portfolio assets, real estate is challenging for beneficiaries because each piece is unique and requires some degree of hands-on management. Its value is usually not readily ascertainable until sold. Carrying costs can put pressure on the beneficiaries of an illiquid estate. Emotions and personalities may also complicate how the beneficiaries calculate value, especially for a family residence.

Keep in mind that by the time you die, the value of your real estate may be significantly different than it was when you originally planned your estate. You can roughly estimate what a building, a farm, or a vacant parcel is worth based on the sale price of comparable properties. There are numerous websites that list property for sale.

Banks and the IRS have varied but specific standards for what they consider comparable properties. Their valuation may differ from yours. If you or your beneficiaries need valuations that will withstand scrutiny, you may have to spend a few hundred dollars to hire an appraiser to professionally solidify a value. Still, an appraisal is only an estimated value. Like any unique commodity, actual property values fluctuate and require a willing buyer.

Unlike liquid portfolio assets, you must actively manage, maintain, and repair real estate. Rent has to be collected, and property taxes, insurance, and utilities must be paid. An empty or neglected building can be an enormous cash drain. Make sure someone will take control of your properties.

Other special considerations for real estate are covered in Chapter 19.

Keep an Eye on the Real Estate

I had one group of fighting adult children who were co-trustees, none of whom lived near Mom's Chicago residence. Owned free and clear, the house was half the value of the estate. Nobody wanted to take responsibility for maintaining it after she died, and they couldn't agree on a sale price or a real estate agent.

As the house sat vacant, they ignored the electric and gas bills. Nobody paid casualty insurance or property taxes. They finally paid the gas bill before the pipes could freeze in winter, paid the property taxes before the government could sell it, and paid the fire/casualty insurance just in case. Even the squabbling sibs were able to put their differences aside long enough to take the actions necessary to avert disaster.

A *family business* is usually a private company not traded on the public markets. It can be a sole proprietorship, a corporation, a limited liability company, or a partnership. Regardless of form, many family companies have no readily ascertainable market value. Like real estate and tangible personal property, each family business is unique and is worth only what a qualified buyer is willing to pay.

If your business is to be sold after your death, the trustee (or whoever else is responsible for the sale) must understand its value. A shareholder agreement should provide a valuation formula on the death of a minority- or majority-interest shareholder. Different types of businesses use different valuation techniques; some relatively easy, others rather difficult. Value can consist of complex variables tied to earnings, profit margins, or nebulous goodwill. Your key advisors (CPA, corporate attorney, or others) will likely be involved in the sale process and should help lay the groundwork during your estate planning.

If your business is based entirely on the talents or the production of a single person—you—its postmortem value may consist solely of accounts receivable, inventory, used equipment, and cash on hand, minus payables. If that is the case, it is virtually worthless without you and does not present much of an estate-planning challenge.

If you wish for your business to stay in your family, then serious planning is often needed. For more on business succession planning, see Chapter 19.

Retirement plans, including individual retirement accounts (IRAs), are a huge component of many Americans' savings. According to the Investment Company Institute, IRAs in 2013 totaled more than $5 trillion. In some ways, IRAs are the same as cash, but the tax considerations of naming the right beneficiary can be a mind-bogglingly complex maze of challenges.

The best-known advantage of an IRA is the deferral of income tax. The financial-planning theory is that during the accumulation phase, when you are young, you contribute pre-tax dollars. Then during the deferral phase, your IRA investments grow without any income tax on earnings or growth. At retirement age, you withdraw your savings and pay tax, possibly at a lower rate. If you don't need the money, you should try to hold off (defer) IRA withdrawals for as long as possible. Depending on how you name your beneficiaries, they may also defer income taxes on inherited IRAs. See Chapter 19 for much more about retirement plan beneficiary considerations.

If any of the assets contemplated in this chapter are subject to testamentary Trusts over which you have partial or no control, as explained in Chapters 10 through 15, that will be a factor when considering ultimate disposition.

A Life Online

Several states have laws that recognize digital assets as an important part of a deceased person's estate. Generally, these laws empower estate representatives with the authority to assess, delete, and administer online accounts. Some of the laws specify email accounts, micro-blogging, and social networking websites as areas within the scope of the deceased person's estate.

Your estate plan can specify the manner in which you want your digital assets handled. It is more than helpful to leave your online passwords in a safe but accessible place.

Pearls of Wisdom

I learned the broad asset categories, besides my "stuff,"

that I must consider when planning my estate.

Phil had had some success, played with some well-known musicians and made some recordings.

Y'know, there'll be royalties from these, you got a manager to help you with the contracts and stuff?

Nah, never needed one.

No worries, my guy'll take care of you.

Cool. Me and O here are heading off to Vegas, I'll catch you after.

Success didn't happen fast enough for Olivia, who took off with another musician about 6 months after Vegas

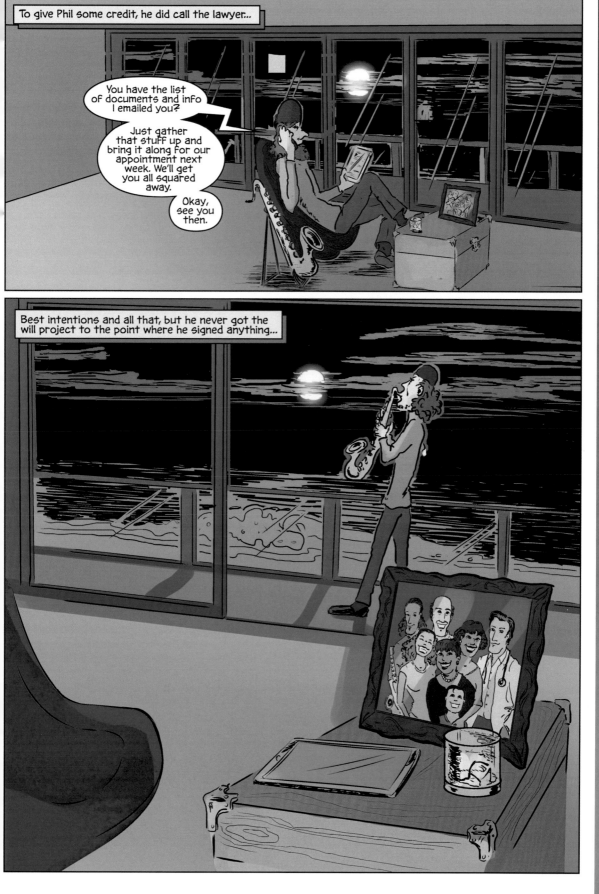

Chapter 6

$

Getting Started

Tomorrow is often the busiest day of the week.
- Spanish proverb -

In This Chapter...
Take action to turn your estate plan
from a vague yearning into a concrete reality.

What's Stopping You?

Ideally, you can use estate planning as a perfect catalyst to get organized. The more you know about everything you own, the more complete your estate plan will be. Organizing your paperwork and your mind may seem like a daunting task, but the relief and satisfaction that come with it make the effort worthwhile, from not only a practical but a psychological and emotional standpoint.

Maybe you have an aversion to lawyers and arcane legal documents or even a crippling case of papyrophobia (fear of paper). A serious paperectomy may do you good. If you can't muster up the energy to organize things, consider hiring someone else or seek the help of a professional, a friend, or a grandchild. You will find it worth the effort and any related expense. Don't wait for a wake-up call—you may not get one.

If the mere thought of getting organized triggers panic, the questionnaire in this chapter may get you on the road. If plowing through such a detailed questionnaire is a big hurdle, and you're meeting with a lawyer for the first time, ask the lawyer what he or she needs for a get-acquainted meeting. You may be able to accomplish a lot without too much advance preparation.

BENEFICIARY – A person, a company, or an organization that receives a gift from you or will receive one upon your death.

FIDUCIARY – A person to whom property or authority is entrusted for the benefit of another, subject to heightened legal and ethical standards.

COMPETENCY – Knowing the general nature and extent of your assets is a basic requirement for the ability to write a legally binding Will or Trust. Allegations of incapacity, along with undue influence, are the main reasons to challenge a legally executed estate plan.

What to Bring for an Initial Consultation with a Lawyer

In a perfect world, every client would walk into his or her lawyer's office with all necessary information ready to go, in the preferred format. Yet if the thought of gathering detailed information makes you want to abandon the whole project, there are usually only three or four things you really need to get the ball rolling at a first meeting:

1. Your address book or electronic database (e.g., your smartphone) with the contact information of the beneficiaries and the fiduciaries. Personally, I do not ask for or even want these people's social security numbers until they are needed.

2. A general understanding of your assets. While a spreadsheet is great, a rough idea of net worth is sufficient in most cases, especially at a first meeting.

3   If you want, make a list of bank, retirement, and investment accounts and any real estate and business holdings, with an estimated value of each one (rounded to the nearest hundred or multiples of thousands, depending on what seems reasonable). Include the death benefits of any life insurance policies you own. I rarely need account numbers at this stage, unless there is a rush to retitle assets.

4. Prior Wills or other estate plan documents may or may not be needed. An old Will to be superseded by a new one is not usually crucial, though it may instruct on a previous trend, such as favoring or disinheriting a certain beneficiary. Nevertheless, it's very important to bring any operating Trusts of which you are a beneficiary or if you have the means to control the Trust's terms in any way, especially if you plan to integrate it into future planning.

5. Prenuptial agreements, buy-sell shareholder agreements, or other contractual arrangements often require a certain disposition of assets. Inconsistencies between those documents and your estate plan must be acknowledged.

*I give you the non-commercial right to copy the following questionnaire,
divided mainly into three parts:
Personal Data, Financial Data, and Fiduciary Data.*

*I suggest making a photocopy and attaching the answers on a separate sheet of
paper or, even better, find it on my website (ericmatlin.com), copy it to a Word
document, and electronically add the information below each numbered paragraph.*

Beyond that, all rights are reserved.

ESTATE PLAN QUESTIONNAIRE

PART I
YOU AND YOUR BENEFICIARIES

1. List your name and any previous or other names by which you are or have been known. If married or in a civil union, list the spouse's name and all of the same information. Make a note if you or your spouse are not U.S. citizens. If you have a relationship with a significant other that is not legally recognized, but you want that person to receive assets or continue a living arrangement, provide that information as well.

2. List all contact information: address, telephone numbers (home, work, and cell), and email addresses.

3. If you or your spouse has previously been married, list all relevant information, including previous spouses' names, when either of you were divorced, or when previous spouses died. If there is anything in a marital settlement agreement (MSA) that may affect your estate plan, bring the MSA to your estate-planning meeting. If you and your spouse have a prenuptial agreement, bring the prenuptial agreement to your estate-planning meeting. When answering the beneficiary questions listed below, if you and your spouse have separate families, indicate who belongs to whom (his, hers, or ours).

4. Do you have children? List names, dates of birth, addresses, telephone numbers, and any special needs they may have. Are any children being disinherited or otherwise treated differently? If so, provide some details.

5. Do you have grandchildren or great-grandchildren? If so, list their names, who their parents are (both biological and by marriage or adoption), dates of birth, and any special needs they may have. Are any grandchildren or great-grandchildren being disinherited or otherwise treated differently? If so, provide some details. Do you want to make gifts to any grandchildren or great-grandchildren, independently of the gifts being made to your children?

6. Do you have parents, siblings, stepchildren, or other relatives or friends whom you wish to be included in your estate plans? If so, list their names, addresses, and any special needs they may have, even if they are not intended beneficiaries or fiduciaries.

7. Is there any person you wish to exclude from your estate plan? Is there any person whom you fear may try to thwart your wishes? If so, provide some details.

8. Are there control issues regarding your beneficiaries? If any beneficiary is a minor, postponement of possession is assumed. If there are adult beneficiaries whose control you wish to limit, be prepared to discuss how much control you want them to have and some of your thoughts. Control may be withheld or given incrementally at certain ages or times.

9. Do you wish to include charitable organizations as beneficiaries? If so, indicate the names and the EIN numbers (comparable to the social security number of an entity), if known. If you know what you wish to leave them or have special requests or limitations as to how the money shall be used, indicate this also.

PART II
YOUR ASSETS AND LIABILITIES

If your assets are not all owned individually, please distinguish between his (individually or in a Trust), hers (individually or in a Trust), and theirs (usually, but not always, joint tenancy assets).

10. Do you own a residence and/or other real estate? Provide addresses. How is title being held to each property? What is the value of each property? What percentage of the total value do you own (if there are partners or other people owning an interest)? If you own vacation timeshares, list those and note whether they are deeded or by agreement.

11. Do you have life insurance? If so, what type? (Term, whole life, etc.?) Who are the beneficiary and the contingent beneficiary? If you own whole life or universal, what is the cash value? If term, how many years are left on the level term? If you have an irrevocable life insurance Trust, have you followed all steps required to make it function effectively?

12. List your financial assets/accounts, including stocks, bonds, mutual funds, bank accounts, CDs and money markets, credit union accounts, private notes receivable, mortgages owned, business interests (including their form: C corporation, S corporation, partnership, LLC, etc.), annuities, IRAs, 401Ks, 403Bs, SEP, and other "qualified" retirement plans. For all of the annuity and retirement plan assets, list the beneficiary and the contingent beneficiary, if any. Don't get too bogged down with this part. Generally, ballpark numbers are sufficient, and no account numbers are needed at this stage.

13. List patents, trademarks, copyrights, trade secrets and other intellectual property you own as inventor, author, artist and the like, including all intangible assets from which your estate may derive future royalties and similar earnings.

14. List all of your "special" personal property (collections, antiques, jewelry, etc.) and the value of each. If you have a special beneficiary for any piece of personal property, indicate that as well. Also, titled personal property, such as cars, boats, airplanes, and so on, and odds and ends, such as airline mileage rewards, a prepaid cemetery plot or prepaid funeral expenses, and sports ticket licenses.

15. Are you or do you fear becoming a part of any lawsuit? If so, provide some details.

16. Do you anticipate that you will be inheriting money or other assets? If your answer is yes, please indicate (if you know) an estimate of the inheritance amount and how the inheritance will be transferred to you. For example, is there a Trust restricting your control, or will the property pass outright to you? Tip: If you have a high net worth, you may want to coordinate your estate plan with that of your parents and/or your children, if they are adults (particularly if any of the players have high net worth or engage in an occupation carrying a high risk of liability).

17. List all liabilities, including mortgage and home equity loan balances, student loans, car loans, credit card balances, notes payable, margin balance in brokerage accounts, lawsuits in which you are a defendant, and other monies owed. Do you fear a lawsuit because of your occupation or business or because you own real estate that is rented to third parties?

18. Have you made any significant gifts and/or filed any gift tax returns during your lifetime? If yes, provide details.

PART III
YOUR FIDUCIARIES, ADVISORS, ACCESS, FINAL DISPOSITION, OR SPECIAL WISHES

19. Who do you want to be your fiduciaries and contingent fiduciaries (they're needed in the event that your first choice cannot act) with respect to guardian for minor or disabled children, agent under power of attorney for health care, agent under power of attorney for financial matters, executor of the Will, and trustee of a Trust? Various fiduciary jobs can list the same or different people.

20. Do you have a CPA, a financial planner, or a corporate lawyer who advises you? If yes, who are they? List their contact information.

21. Final arrangements? Burial . . . cremation . . . funeral . . . memorial/party . . . unique finishing touches? Any out-of-towners for whom you'd like to pay expenses to attend your funeral or memorial?

22. Where do you keep your estate plan and other important paperwork? Who has access?

23. Is there anything else you deem important to your estate-planning needs, or do you have any other concerns that should be considered? Who will take care of your pets?

Now That You're Organized (!?)

Consider your potential continuum of thought and action. On one end of the spectrum is the attitude you have already left behind: "I'll be dead, so why should I care?" On the other lies an inspirational journey that leads to the big questions about sharpening your legacy and spreading your mojo.

More Than the Forms

Estate planning has two major arms: (1) document preparation/execution; and (2) the proper structure of assets, which may involve changes of ownership and beneficiary designations. The effectiveness of the first arm often depends on the follow-up of the second.

Though you may be able to plan your own estate using resources available on the Internet, if you decide to use the more traditional route with a lawyer, Chapter 17 discusses the process of finding and hiring the right one.

Chances are high that you require at least one departure from ready-made estate-planning templates and guidance. It is your legacy at stake, not that of the people who wrote a set of generic forms. You may have a blended family or be involved in other nonlinear relationships; you might own a family business or a collection with great sentimental value; or there could be a horrendous in-law or some other person or situation that requires careful attention.

Perhaps you witnessed or heard about a terrible situation involving the loved ones of a person who did not plan, and you want to ensure that your family doesn't suffer a similar fate. Beyond powers of attorney and a simple Will, your needs depend on your particular goals, concerns, and complications.

Warren Burger. September 17, 1907 – June 25, 1995

Supreme Ct. judge DIY will shows why you should get a pro to help you with estate planning. His probate case wasted money on taxes & legal fees that he could have avoided.

Don't Get Hung Up

If weird circumstances or family dynamics present major challenges, focus on the big picture first, then tackle the thornier issues. Get them out of the way at least partly. Don't seek perfection. That will drive you insane. Resolve to identify and pursue the best overall course of action today and avoid familial complications and confusion later.

By starting and following through, you may put to rest issues you have struggled with for years. If you find yourself facing a proverbial brick wall or are stuck in estate-planning mud, remember that life's complexities are often best worked though one at a time. New opportunities and ideas may sprout from your willingness to address the most anxiety-provoking issues.

Your own nature and circumstances may conspire to yank you away from the matter prior to completion. Sometimes (or maybe all the time) you cannot even plan for what is happening now, let alone the future. It's impossible to take everyone and everything into account, so do your best to achieve satisfactory solutions. Accept that you probably won't see the results of your planning. Know that you put forth your best and noblest effort in charting a course for others to follow.

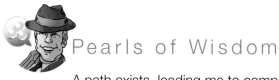 Pearls of Wisdom

A path exists, leading me to completion of my estate plan.

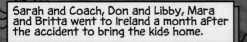

Sarah and Coach, Don and Libby, Mara and Britta went to Ireland a month after the accident to bring the kids home.

We hadn't planned to spend our retirement raising kids, but our grandchildren need us, especially Devon.

He's been cutting school and getting into trouble. And little Kayleigh... I'll just be glad when we're all on that plane tomorrow.

DEREK & JULIE HENDERS
BELOVED PARENTS
of
DEVON + KALIEGH

Chapter 7

The Will

A man who dies without a Will has lawyers for his heirs.
- Anonymous -

In This Chapter...

you'll learn about the importance of a Will to distribute probate assets upon death, nominate a guardian for minor or disabled children, name an executor to act as personal representative of the probate estate, and provide guidance regarding funeral wishes.

If you die without a Will, your probate assets will be distributed purely by a relationship formula, governed by your state's intestacy laws. Probate and intestacy are featured in Chapter 5.

WILL – A legal document completed in accordance with state law that distributes your probate assets upon your death. The Will appoints an executor to administer your estate according to its terms.

TESTATOR – The person making a Will.

PROBATE ASSETS – Everything you own individually.

HEIR – Someone who inherits or would inherit as next-of-kin under intestacy.

LEGATEE – A beneficiary to whom you leave assets in your Will.

BEQUEST – A gift made in a Will to a legatee.

Basic Elements of a Will

Each state has specific requirements to create a valid Will. In general, the testator must have the mental capacity to create it—the often heard "of sound mind" (rather than the "of sound mind and body" you may hear in old movies). To be of sound mind, you must understand generally what you own, to whom it is being left, and that you are creating a binding document to dispose of your estate at the time of your death.

A Will must be written, signed (or marked in the event of physical disability) by you, and witnessed by at least two non-interested people (requirements vary state to state). Heirs and beneficiaries should not be witnesses. A Will often contains a notarized affidavit, lending more authenticity to its execution. If the Will is filed with a "self-proving affidavit," witnesses do not have to testify in court that they were present when you signed it competently and under no duress.

You can change your Will at any time, because it goes into effect only upon your death. A Will usually revokes any previous Wills, so that at your death it is, in fact, your *Last* Will and Testament. Any previously signed Wills have no legal status. Their only value may be to establish your thought process should anyone challenge your last Will. A "codicil" is an amendment to a Will and must follow the same formalities.

Given certain circumstances, a few states recognize oral Wills, but never involving real estate. Handwritten or "holographic" Wills are generally valid in any state, if signed and witnessed properly, but only about half recognize unwitnessed holographic Wills.

All Wills name the legatees to receive your assets. You can leave specific assets to specific people. You can also leave assets to a class of people, such as to "all my nieces and nephews in equal shares."

Most Wills contain some amount of contingency planning, directing the consequences of what happens if a legatee does not survive you. Does a deceased nephew's share go to his or her children or does it lapse, to be spread among the shares of other legatees? Is there any special bequest for your favorite niece, or does she get the same as her siblings and cousins? Are you leaving anything for charity?

Anna Nicole Smith, November 28, 1967 - February 8, 2007

26 y/o marries big $ 89 y/o. Her will: all to son-disinherits future kids. Has daughter, son dies 3 days later while visiting mom & baby ½ sis in hospital. ANS dies.

Disinheriting

Some states give your surviving spouse the right to a portion of your estate, but few require you to include or exclude any other individual.

Your Will or Trust may intentionally leave someone off the list of heirs and legatees because you don't want that person to inherit from you. If the disinherited person goes unmentioned among a class of similarly situated people, he or she might argue that you simply made a mistake. It's better to clearly and explicitly exclude that person as a beneficiary, so there is no confusion.

You may want to include your reasons for disinheriting someone, but it's best to do so briefly and unemotionally, lest you commit libel. This is not the time to tell people what you really think of them. You don't want a beneficiary to come in through the back door of your estate as a plaintiff, if you say that this person is not getting any of your money because he or she is a thief. "I have intentionally excluded Bob as a beneficiary" suffices. There is also no need to leave Bob $1, as good as that might feel. Uncooperative beneficiaries of such nominal bequests can be a pain in the butt for your executor or trustee.

Disinheriting a close family member is a big decision and not one to be made spontaneously or on a whim, but you may dispose of assets as you wish, regardless of hurt feelings.

Rather than completely disinherit someone, try giving a lesser beneficiary enough money so that when faced with a non-contest (in terrorem) clause, the beneficiary is less likely to challenge your wishes. Even if this beneficiary's siblings each get $25,000 while he or she gets only $5,000, the beneficiary may hesitate to contest the Will if it risks that $5,000. With nothing to lose, this person may be more inclined to, in effect, extort money from the estate. Though non-contest clauses don't always stand up in court, to a contester with a bequest he or she would prefer not to lose, they can be like garlic, holy water, and crosses to a vampire.

Watch Your Step

Mary, bitter toward her ex-husband, wanted her executor to hire someone to pick up all of her dog's excrement in the back yard, put it into a plastic bag, wrap the bag in a gift box, put the box into a nice bag, and present it to her ex. Creativity and a bit of humor are great, but never direct anything that might subject your estate to a lawsuit.

Executor

Your Will names an executor to act as personal representative of your estate, stepping into your shoes to take care of your finances after death.

The court will usually approve your nominee, but not if this person has a legal disability. Provide for an alternate, in the event the executor you name is unable or unwilling to act. Except in the case of small estates, as discussed in Chapter 3, the person nominated is not actually the executor of your probate estate until the court makes the appointment.

Letters of Office/Letters Testamentary are issued by the court, granting authority to the executor to:

- Collect and secure your estate;

- Pay legitimate bills;

- Sell and reinvest assets;

- Wind up affairs;

- Distribute assets to beneficiaries; and

- Eventually close the estate.

Personal Guardianship of Minor Children

If you have minor or special-needs children, your Will names their guardian. The guardian of the person decides where your children live, where they go to school, and other lifestyle issues.

You Nominate, the Court Appoints

The personal guardian nomination you make is not an actual appointment; only the court has the authority to make that ruling, based on the best interests of the children. Your Will is the equivalent of an affidavit regarding your choice. As with other estate-planning documents, it speaks for you when you no longer have a voice. It also places a legal burden squarely on anyone who might dispute your pick and helps keep your children out of a legal tug-of-war.

A surviving parent will typically be a child's guardian. This individual will be appointed by the court even if you nominate someone else, unless there is a substantial reason to strip the person of his or her parental rights—if, for example, the surviving parent is a felon.

In seeking to prevent typical parental rights, provide as much information as possible to help the court make a ruling favorable to your way of thinking, but omit anything that could be interpreted as a defamation of character, or your estate could face a lawsuit. Be specific about known provable details, rather than make broad statements about the poor character of the person you are trying to deny guardianship. If possible, give documented facts, including court file numbers, arrests, convictions, or incarcerations.

The Best Choice

Base your selection of a personal guardian on lifestyle projections.

1. Who will impart the best value system?

2. With whom will your children feel most comfortable living?

3.   What living arrangement will be least disruptive to your children's already shaken routine?

4.   Who is best suited for the physical rigors of raising children?

Obviously, the answers to these questions are subjective, personal, and important to your estate planning and peace of mind. Like many parenting decisions, this one may be instinctual. If you are struggling, the first people who come to mind are often the right choice.

A few personal guardianship details:

*   If you are naming more than one guardian to act simultaneously, decide what happens if one of the guardians dies or, if they are now married, they split up. You can specify that you want them to act as guardians only if they are able to do so collectively, or that only one shall be permitted to act individually.

*   Direct that, depending on their ages, your children be consulted on the choice of guardian. They may have their day in court, too, especially if they are teenagers.

*   You can choose an older child who has reached a predetermined age to act as guardian over younger siblings.

*   Keep your children together and specify that a certain guardian shall be given custody only if he or she is willing to take all of them.

*   Direct that family members shall (or shall not) have generous access to your children.

*   Urge continued exposure to your desired religious or cultural influences.

Any of these and more can be in your Will.

Guardian of the Estate

You can base your choice of personal guardian on a number of factors, but if you're leaving money behind for your children's care, finances are not one of them. If the child has a financial estate, it will be administered under the jurisdiction of the court, usually requiring annual accountings. Assets left in Trust often minimize annual legal and accounting fees (see Chapters 9, 10, and 11).

The money person (the guardian of the child's estate or the trustee of a Trust for the benefit of the child) will make payments to the personal guardian as needed, so that your children are not a financial burden.

Just because the personal guardian decides where your children live doesn't mean they have to physically reside with the guardian. What if your daughter wants to finish her last year of high school surrounded by friends? If the parents of your son's best friend volunteer to provide shelter and sustenance while reporting to the personal guardian until the end of the school year, the guardian and the school can work it out.

Should you name the same individual as guardian of both the child and the finances? It may be most convenient for the personal guardian to also handle the money. If you trust the personal guardian with raising your children, you should trust him or her with the money, too, right? Alternatively, maybe you don't want to concentrate all of the authority in one person. It depends on your situation and the people involved.

If you choose two different people, then the two parties must communicate as they do their respective jobs. In that case, the guardian of the child rarely accounts for day-to-day expenses, because keeping track of such items, the cost of food and other incidentals, is extremely onerous. Hopefully, the personal guardian and the money person can agree on an allowance, with additional distributions for big-ticket items, such as private school tuition or orthodontics. For big expenses, the personal guardian usually submits a bill to the trustee, who pays the guardian directly from the child's money or Trust funds. Sooner or later, large payments must be accounted for, whether or not the same person is acting in both jobs.

When you select a personal guardian for your children, it is polite, at the very least, to obtain advance permission. Although the individual may feel honored, it may also be too much of a burden. Don't surprise someone by forcing him or her to either reluctantly accept your children or feel guilty when declining.

Funeral Wishes

Your Will is the usual forum to articulate your funeral wishes, give directions regarding burial or cremation and the disposition of remains, and choose the type of memorial, wake, or party you prefer. The executor is responsible for carrying out these wishes. Without directions, the wrong person may make these decisions for you. If you know how you want these rites and procedures observed, your Will is most often the best place to put the directions in writing. Some aspects of your immediate transition may also be addressed in your health care power of attorney (see Chapter 8).

In many instances, no directions are left. In that case, the family decides what to do with you, harmoniously or not. If everyone knows where your pre-paid funeral lot is, that may be the functional equivalent of specific directions in your Will. If your funeral plan is worthy of insertion in your Will or another written document, it is your call.

Ted Williams

Many knowledgeable fans consider Teddy Ballgame, the Splendid Splinter, the greatest hitter in Major League Baseball history. The last player to hit over .400, he has the highest batting average of anyone to hit more than five hundred homers and an amazing on-base percentage of 48 percent before anyone tracked that stat. His career was shortened by several years while he served his country as a U.S. Marine, training aviators in World War II and then in Korea, where he flew thirty-nine combat missions. Later in life, he became a Hall of Fame fisherman.

His Will specified that he be cremated and his ashes scattered in the Florida Keys. Somehow his son managed, with a scrap of paper purportedly signed by Williams, to convince a judge to deep-freeze his Dad's corpse. In the book *Frozen*, (by Larry Johnson and Scott Baldyga) the former COO of Alcor, the cryogenics facility storing William's frozen corpse, alleged grisly conditions and claimed that his severed head was batted around by an Alcor employee (an incident denied by the company and retracted by the author as part of a settlement agreement).

This farcical drama illustrates that just like life, estate planning doesn't always work perfectly. Sometimes, weird stuff happens even when you do your best.

Pearls of Wisdom

My Will must be drafted and executed in a legally recognized format. It goes into effect at my death, and I can change it anytime I desire. It directs where my probate assets go and names the person or the bank responsible for executing my wishes. Though it is important for me to select a guardian for my minor or special-needs children, the court actually makes the appointment. I can put my funeral wishes and such in my Will.

David Has No HIPAA

'bye, cuz!

¢

Chapter 8

Heath Care and Financial Powers of Attorney, HIPAA Authorization, Living Will, and Mental Health Declaration

I'm Not Dead Yet.
- Unfortunate peasant about to be carted away with a pile
of dead bodies in Monty Python and the Holy Grail -

In This Chapter...
you'll discover the gateway to estate planning. If you do only one thing suggested in this
book, complete an HIPAA authorization and a power of attorney for health care.
It's simple, and you never know when you'll need it. Learn about advance directives that
affect you while you are living but severely impaired.

Plan for Medical Information Access and Proxy Decision Making, No Matter What Your Age or Financial or Marital Status.

Estate planning is not just about money or what happens after we die. HIPAA (Health Information Portability and Accountability Act) authorizations and powers of attorney for health care (sometimes combined) are estate-planning tools that are valuable to people of all ages and means. Every competent person over the age 18 should have them.

Everyone over 18? No hyperbole. Except when it comes to alcohol consumption, your 18-year-old is no longer a child. He or she is an adult. That imperceptible change in legal capacity can make a huge difference.

Adults make their own decisions regarding health care. They don't require parental approval, nor are parents strictly responsible for their adult children's actions. As your children attain the age of majority, you may forget about some of the ramifications of this imperceptible change. For millions of young adults with limited assets, dipping their toe in the water of estate planning is an adult thing to do. The HIPAA authorization and the health-care proxy are the gateway documents to estate planning, oftentimes more essential than a Will.

You may have no immediate need for a HIPAA authorization or a health care power of attorney, but who knows what tomorrow might bring? HIPAA authorizations allow whomever you choose to access your health information.

Powers of attorney for health care appoint an agent (a proxy) to make personal medical decisions on your behalf if you become incapacitated. It is a type of "advance directive" that helps prevent a guardianship over your person, keeping your family out of court. It also provides a forum for you to articulate end-of-life philosophies and address organ donation and disposition of remains. Powers of attorney for health care can contain adequate HIPAA authorizations, but it is often appropriate for them to be separate documents.

Alternatively, powers of attorney for finances appoint an agent (a proxy) to take action regarding your financial matters, such as paying bills, if you become incapacitated.

Empower Loved Ones with a HIPAA Authorization to Access Medical Information When It Is Urgently Needed.

Among other things, HIPAA guarantees patient privacy. Think of a HIPAA authorization as your loved one's answer to the voice at the medical emergency end of the phone saying, "Sorry, I'm not authorized to discuss her condition with you—if you have a problem with this, take it up with our lawyers." The penalties for health workers (physicians, nurses, hospital administrators, and others) who violate the complex HIPAA privacy rules can include fines and jail time.

Unless you object, HIPAA does not prohibit health workers from releasing your pertinent medical information to certain immediate family members, but overly cautious health-care workers often withhold vital information from people who should have access to it. Because patient rights are paramount, a health worker uncertain about privacy responsibilities will often say "no," rather than risk trouble. Frustration and delays happen when time is scarce and nerves frayed.

> *Imagine: Your daughter is in college, a thousand miles away. You pray that she is safe in her new environment, but if she is hurt, you can find yourself in a nightmare. A call comes from a hospital: "She's here, in stable condition."*
>
> *You ask, "What happened? What's happening?"*
>
> *The worker at the other end of the phone may feel legally restricted in what information she can relay without violating HIPAA regulations, so you get no clear response or basic information. She believes that she is honoring your daughter's federal right to privacy and minimizing her potential liability, but her "take it up with our legal department" response leaves you in a lurch.*

Whether your situation involves overzealous health workers only interested in covering their butts or a conscientious person simply unsure about the patient's right to privacy, this scenario can happen regarding your spouse, your adult children, your elderly parents, or anyone suddenly taken ill.

A True Horror Story

A woman had a nervous breakdown while working for her U.S. company in Asia. Her flight home to Dallas connected in Chicago. Before she could board her connecting flight, her erratic behavior forced authorities to restrain and involuntarily commit her to a Chicago area hospital. Her husband, lacking a HIPAA authorization, was unable to get any information over the phone. He flew to Chicago, but the hospital still refused to tell him anything about his wife's condition.

The woman was refusing to authorize disclosure of her condition to her family. Luckily, the hospital's lawyers eventually agreed with the husband's lawyers that the patient lacked the capacity to block disclosure, so HIPAA privacy laws did not forbid substantive communication with the husband. In the end, the husband saw his wife, meds calmed her down, and they went home, but for a day or two the husband and the family were completely shut out.

The hospital could have refused to cooperate without a court order declaring the wife incapacitated, even though neither the husband nor the hospital was keen on incurring the significant expense of bringing or defending an emergency court petition. A simple HIPAA authorization would have prevented some of the chaos.

Do you or a loved one have a mental condition that requires medication, such as depression, bipolar disorder, or any number of other conditions? The person suffering from the condition is commonly medicated and doing fine. Then, for one reason or another, the individual goes off the meds, and Dr. Jekyll becomes Mr. Hyde. Dr. Jekyll would want certain loved ones to have the ability to monitor his condition, but Mr. Hyde is crazy-paranoid and was last seen running away from reality, potentially endangering himself and others.

A HIPAA authorization is one tool to help inform loved ones easing Mr. Hyde's return to Dr. Jekyll. It must be signed when Dr. Jekyll is sane, because Mr. Hyde would probably refuse. A HIPAA authorization can be terminated, but only if the person who signed it has the capacity to do so—and, legally, that can be a close call. (A Mental Health Treatment Preference Declaration, discussed below, if available in your state, is an even more powerful tool in this situation.)

No one should have to jump through unnecessary hoops to get essential medical information about a child, a parent, a sibling, a life partner, or a friend, whether in the hospital waiting room or thousands of miles away. HIPAA authorizations are usually drafted broadly to allow full and immediate access to medical records. Consult your lawyer and your physician if you are uncomfortable with giving broad access or concerned that a person listed on your HIPAA authorization may try to use your records for nefarious purposes.

Mental Health Treatment Preference Declaration

A Mental Health Treatment Preference Declaration ("Declaration"), available in Illinois and some other states, allows a legally competent person, as "Principal," to appoint another legally competent person as "Attorney-in-Fact," to make mental health treatment decisions for the Principal if the Principal becomes incapable of making such decisions.

Nobody can force another person to sign a Declaration, nor can signing one be a condition for admission to a mental health facility.

The Declaration goes into effect upon the determination of two doctors (at least one of whom the Principal may choose) that the Principal is incapable of understanding treatment information well enough to make an informed decision about his or her mental health care or cannot effectively communicate such wishes.

Three years after signing, if the Declaration does not go into effect, the authority of the Attorney-in-Fact lapses. If it does go into effect, it continues indefinitely and cannot be revoked or amended by the Principal, even if the Principal changes his or her mind, until the Principal is determined to be capable by a physician.

The Declaration is particularly useful for those whose symptoms come and go (often related to whether the person is on or off meds) or are expected to progressively worsen, such as people with bipolar disorder or schizophrenia.

The Declaration may give (or withhold as specified) future instructions regarding the specific symptoms for which the Principal would or would not want specific treatment, including:

- Electro-shock therapy;

- Psychotropic drugs; and

- Admittance and retention at a mental health facility for a period of up to seventeen days.

Living Will

A living Will is a statement of philosophy that you may or may not agree with. The pertinent portion of the Illinois living Will is typical:

If at any time I should have an incurable and irreversible injury, disease, or illness judged to be a terminal condition by my attending physician, who has personally examined me and determined that my death is imminent except for death-delaying procedures, I direct that such procedures which would only prolong the dying process be withheld or withdrawn, and that I be permitted to die naturally with only the administration of medication, sustenance, or the performance of any medical procedure deemed necessary by my attending physician to provide me with comfort care.

In the absence of my ability to give direction regarding the use of such death-delaying procedures, it is my intention that this declaration shall be honored by my family and physician as the final expression of my legal right to refuse medical or surgical treatment and accept the consequences from such refusal.

Joan Rivers June 8, 1933 – September 4, 2014

Acerbic comedian's living will defined "quality of life" as the ability to go on stage for an hour and be funny.

Power of Attorney for Health Care

Select someone (an "agent" or a "proxy") to make decisions relating to medical care and living arrangements when you cannot.

As you sit here reading this in the prime of life, your own incapacity may seem even more remote and improbable than death, but your world can change suddenly and unexpectedly. As a competent adult, you have the right to make your own medical decisions. You can decline medical care, including any procedure or treatment that would simply extend your life without regard to quality. A power of attorney for health care (health-care proxy/advance health-care directive) grants authority to a selected agent/proxy to make medical and other personal decisions, if and when you lack decision-making capacity.

After you sign a health-care proxy, you continue to speak for yourself for as long as you are able, so even if you give immediate authority to your agent, you will be the decision maker. Revoking a health-care proxy is very simple and can often be done verbally. Occasionally, health-care proxies are referred to as "durable" because they survive your disability, but more often, "durable" is used with financial powers of attorney, discussed later in this chapter.

Only those who are capable and aware of what they are doing can sign a health-care proxy. With luck, it will go unused, but if a sudden change occurs, this key document can save your family tremendous heartache and guide some of your crucial personal and medical decisions.

Should you become voiceless, even without a health-care proxy it is possible that your family, your physician, and the hospital staff will reach a commonsense consensus and navigate an acceptable course of action without involving a court. They might even make the same choices you would have, but why leave something so important to chance?

Unique circumstances, conflicting personalities, and differing philosophies of family members, physicians, or nurses can all factor in what are literally matters of life and death. With your fate uncertain, your family must weather a painful and expensive process that can result in a judge entrusting your care to the last person you would have chosen. A health-care proxy gives you some measure of control and peace of mind.

Avoid a Guardianship and the Courthouse

Probate courts do more than decide who gets your assets when you die. Guardianships over incapacitated adults are one of their many functions. Someone close to you may petition the court to declare you incompetent. You can be incompetent in two ways, your person and/or your estate (finances). Different criteria are used to determine each and whether or not the same or different parties handle one aspect or the other, or both.

Once declared legally incompetent, you lose many rights. Because of that, there is a legal presumption of competence—you are considered to be competent until someone has proved to a judge that you are incapable of making decisions and taking care of yourself and/or your finances. If a judge determines you to be financially incompetent and a guardianship is established over your estate, you lose control of your checkbook. Someone else pays your bills. Any contract you sign can be canceled. If you are judged incompetent to take care of your personal needs, a guardian over your person decides where you live and what type of medical treatment you get, among other things.

Before it officially declares incompetence, the court, along with assorted lawyers, physicians, and others, deeply involves itself in your life. Records and testimony from people who know you, as well as experts who may not, become matters of public record. The whole performance is staged in a public arena, and the legal fees can be exorbitant. At the heart of the spectacle is the person alleged to be incompetent. Of course, you think this can never happen to you, but it happens countless times to others, sometimes quite suddenly and unexpectedly.

A health-care proxy ensures that YOU decide who handles your personal issues, instead of the court picking someone. You can direct agents you select, conferring or limiting authority as you choose.

If you become unable to speak for yourself, then your health-care agent can decide, with your prior guidance:

- Between Treatment A or Treatment B.

- Where you live—a nursing home or your own home with a hired caregiver.

- When it is too late for heroics.

- How to follow your instructions regarding donation of your organs (immediately saving or enhancing the lives of others) or your body (contributing to scientific research, fostering knowledge, and saving or enhancing lives in the future).

Without a health-care proxy, several scenarios can lead to the wrong person making personal decisions for you:

- You have a longtime partner to whom you are not married. In most states, it is only the marriage certificate that counts.

- You are married but separated or otherwise not on good terms with your spouse.

- You have close family and friends, but they do not know your wishes or are mistaken about your beliefs and philosophies regarding life-and-death circumstances.

- Your close relations maintain vastly different world and religious views from you and/or from one another.

- You are married, but your children from a previous marriage have a poor or nonexistent relationship with your new spouse or have conflicting ideals or opinions regarding your health care.

- You do not know or are estranged from the person with whom you have the closest biological relationship.

- You have no close family.

The ideal choice for a health-care agent is a trusted loved one who (1) understands you, (2) lives nearby, (3) can decipher medical terminology, and (4) is willing and able to fight for you. Unfortunately, reality often doesn't live up to the ideal. Whether your agent is down the hall or thousands of miles away, your spouse or your son's ex-wife, the main criterion is that this person be available and dependable. In any event, as with all fiduciary designations, good drafting entails naming at least one contingent agent, in case the first cannot or does not want to act. While selecting an agent can be difficult, an imperfect choice now is better than doing nothing and leaving it completely up to chance or the courts.

Former Spouse as Health-Care Agent

In some states, if you select your spouse as your health-care agent and then get divorced, the appointment is automatically revoked unless it is renewed after the divorce. The assumption is that you do not want your ex empowered to pull your plug or direct some invasive procedure that will merely prolong your agonizing existence.

"I Want the Plug Pulled" . . . or . . . "Not So Fast!"

Ethical, moral, religious, and legal issues complicate end-of-life decision making. In addition to the living Will, the typical health-care proxy form includes end-of-life philosophies to use or modify according to your beliefs and wishes. Your directions can be general or specific.

You can tell your proxy to withhold "heroic" measures that will simply prolong your pulse, if one or more of the following are true:

- I suffer from deteriorating neurological functions that are unlikely to reverse.

- I can no longer recognize my loved ones.

- I spend most of my time with my head down or a blank look on my face, and I am incontinent.

- I am always miserable and can no longer function as the human being that I was prior to my illness or accident.

- I am being kept alive only via feeding tubes or ventilators, and my prospects for living without them are low.

- My agent believes the burdens of treatment outweigh the expected benefits, including an improved quality of life, after consulting with my personal physician.

You may instruct your agent to "treat any infections and keep me as comfortable as possible, with plenty of medication to numb the pain." Consider bolding any special language that might otherwise blend into a standard form. Give a copy of your health-care proxy to the agents you select and the physicians and the hospitals that treat you, and discuss any special provisions with them.

At the other end of the philosophical spectrum, you can request that you be kept alive as long as possible, without regard to your condition or chances for improvement. If all of your money has to be spent on medical care or nursing homes, so be it. The Illinois Right to Life Committee's Patient Self-Protection Document is an example of this philosophy, offered on its website.

A "Five Wishes" document is another organization's best effort to tackle delicate death-with-dignity issues. Essentially a health-care proxy with additional language, it may help you express your health-care wishes by incorporating medical, personal, spiritual, and emotional preferences associated with end-of-life care. If you like warm and fuzzy estate planning, check it out. It encourages discussion among family and physicians in plain English (also available in Spanish) and "can be used in the living room instead of the emergency room." Funded by the Robert Wood Johnson Foundation, the nation's largest philanthropic organization devoted to health matters, it is legally recognized by at least forty states.

A Do Not Resuscitate (DNR) order is a separate document for those in the throes of a terminal illness. A DNR must be signed by you and a physician. If you are incapable of signing, a health-care agent may sign on your behalf. If there is no health-care proxy, your closest family member or a court-appointed guardian may sign. DNRs, common in intensive-care wards and hospice settings, are the final word on cessation of life-sustaining treatment. They are usually posted in a prominent place near the patient. A physician will not sign a DNR unless you already have a serious medical condition or are elderly. They can also be revoked at any time. Some states have substituted Physicians Order for Life Sustaining Treatment (POLST) for DNRs as a new paradigm for end-of-life decision making.

Terri Schiavo

No discussion about the rights of others to make end-of-life decisions would be complete without mentioning Terri Schiavo. In 1990, Teresa Marie "Terri" Schiavo collapsed in cardiac arrest and suffered massive brain damage. Whether in a "coma" or a "persistently vegetative state," she was unable to communicate or feed herself.

In 1998, Terri's husband, Michael, petitioned a Florida court to remove the feeding tube that had kept her alive since her collapse. He argued that Terri had no quality of life and no hope of recovery. Her parents, the Schindlers, disputed that assessment. The courts went back and forth, ordering the feeding tube removed, only to later reinsert it.

The question of fact, pondered only anecdotally by millions of strangers, was whether Terri would want continued life-prolonging measures, considering her overall health.

The legal frenzy exploded when, on February 25, 2005, a judge ordered the removal of the feeding tube. State and federal appeals and intervention followed, but Terri's feeding tube was disconnected for good on March 18, 2005.

In all, the Schiavo case involved more than a dozen Florida and federal petitions, motions, and appeals, all the way to the U.S. Supreme Court. Her case directly initiated new Florida and federal legislation. President George W. Bush even cut short a Texas vacation on March 21 to sign legislation to restore Terri's feeding tube. Yet all of those efforts ultimately failed. She died on March 31.

By that time, Terri Schiavo had become more of a political symbol than a person to everyone except her closest friends and family. Multitudes of people debated whether Terri should be allowed to die or be kept alive. Lacking any advance directives, Terri had no say in the matter.

The Patient/Principal's Wishes Trump Those of the Agent

Tony was married to Shirley for seventy-one years. Shirley could no longer walk, she was in constant pain from arthritis, her hearing and vision were failing, and she was taking more than a dozen medications for various ailments. She appointed Tony as her health-care agent. A year later, he called me. Shirley had taken a bad fall and was rushed to the hospital. While alert, she signed a DNR. In no uncertain terms, she said she no longer wanted to live.

When Shirley slipped into a coma, her agent under the health-care power of attorney, Tony, wanted to resuscitate her. The hospital correctly refused his direction. Tony lacked authority because a lucid Shirley had clearly indicated her contrary wishes. Had she not done so, and despite the fact that Shirley had expressed an opposing philosophy in the health-care proxy, Tony could have exhausted a range of medical procedures. As it was, Tony was able to make sure that Shirley was as comfortable and pain-free as possible.

Proxy Decisions—More Than When to Pull the Plug

People tend to focus on the end-of-life process when discussing advanced medical directives, but a health-care proxy also extends to basic treatment and other quality-of-life issues.

What if you:

- Have a serious accident, have a stroke, or suffer some other misfortune that leaves you unable to speak? Who will direct your care and where you live, recover, and recuperate?

- Need to have an unexpected medical decision made during an operation while you are under anesthesia?

Your agent's authority can be limited in any fashion, including the prohibition of medical procedures you find abhorrent. You may insist on:

- No electrical or mechanical resuscitation of the heart when it has stopped beating.

- No tube feeding when you are paralyzed or unable to take nourishment by mouth.

- No mechanical respiration when you are unable to sustain breathing.

- No shock therapy to treat mental illness.

Brooke Astor

In her prime, New York society queen Grand Dame Brooke Astor was meticulous about grooming. Before she died in 2007 at the age of 105, civil and criminal elder abuse charges were brought against her son Anthony Marshall. The issues presented in open court, besides forgery and theft, included her sleeping in a ripped nightgown on a urine-soaked couch. Details were published in various media for the world to see. Such sad public spectacles are often presented before probate courts, at the heart of which lies a person who has become incompetent.

Availability of HIPAA Authorizations, Living Wills, and Powers of Attorney for Health Care

Doctors, dentists, and hospitals will often provide (and may insist that you sign) their HIPAA forms, usually limited to the treatment being administered by that medical provider. Health-care proxies are usually inexpensive and can be obtained from concerned organizations on the Internet.

After executing a HIPAA authorization and a health-care proxy, you should give copies of each to your physician and those associated with your personal care, such as a nursing home or another assisted living facility. Ask them to make it a permanent part of your medical file, so they know who to call in an emergency. You decide when you want to give copies to your agents, but I recommend giving a copy to the primary one as soon as you sign the document.

The Patient Self-Determination Act requires hospitals, nursing homes, and other medical institutions that receive federal funding to inform patients of their right to execute a health-care proxy and/or a living Will, but there is no law requiring patients to follow through. It is up to you to get it done.

Durable Power of Attorney for Property

Who Pays Your Bills If You Can't Write a Check?

Select an agent under a durable power of attorney for property (finances) to control your money and pay your bills should you become incapacitated. A durable power of attorney helps your family avoid the cost and aggravation of a guardianship being appointed over your estate. It is "durable" because it survives your disability or incompetence and because its purpose differs from that of a regular financial power of attorney, like one you would arrange for a house closing that you could not attend. All powers of attorney, durable or otherwise, end upon death.

Durable vs. Nondurable Powers of Attorney for Property

DURABLE POWER OF ATTORNEY	NONDURABLE POWER OF ATTORNEY
Purpose: Allows a person to act on your behalf with respect to financial transactions if you become incapacitated.	Purpose: Allows a person to act on your behalf with respect to some specific financial transaction or series of transactions, often because you are simply unavailable.
Survives your incapacity.	Ends upon your incapacity.
Relates to a wide range of transactions under any parameters you set.	Relates only to a specific transaction or series of transactions.
Effective either immediately or at some future date or (in some states) on the occurrence of a "springing" event, such as when selected parties determine you are unable to conduct business transactions.	Usually limited to a set period of time and until a specific transaction is completed, or is ongoing based on various business factors.
Ends whenever you dictate, usually when you change it, regain your ability to conduct business transactions, or die.	Ends at any time you dictate, usually when a specific transaction is completed, a business relationship changes, or you die.

All financial powers of attorney, whether durable or not, must be signed by you while you're competent. They must usually be notarized, but the requirement of having an independent witness or two varies from state to state.

Springing Powers

Durable powers of attorney for property are powerful documents. While very useful, they should not be used unless and until needed. Therefore, rather than a durable power of attorney for property conferring current authority, they are often drafted as "springing" powers that activate only upon a certain date or set of circumstances. Some states, notably Florida, do not allow for springing durable powers of attorney.

For example: springing language provides that the proxy's authority goes into effect only "when my agent, along with a physician who has personally examined me, states in writing that I am unable to properly manage my financial affairs due to a mental or physical disability."

Those springing conditions can be tightened further by inserting more barriers into the springing event, such as something like "When a majority of (name a committee of people), together with my personal physician who has examined me (and at least one other unaffiliated consulting physician, who has also personally examined me), states in writing . . ."

Springing authority can also be used with your power of attorney for health care and the HIPAA authorization, but be aware that the more onerous and complex the springing language is, the harder it may be to obtain HIPAA access and the less useful the document may be when time is of the essence. For that reason, most of the health-care powers of attorney and HIPAA authorizations that I draft go into effect immediately.

 Pearls of Wisdom

I need a power of attorney for health Care, a HIPAA authorization, and a power of attorney for property. Without these simple and easily accessible documents, my family members may find themselves part of a medical-legal maelstrom. With luck, my health-care and financial proxies will never be used, because I will always be able to speak for myself. If there is a reason why a Mental Health Declaration may apply to me or to a family member, it's good to know that such a document exists (in some states).

Chapter 9

Living Trusts – Revocable and Irrevocable

Avoid Probate with a Living Trust!
(A sales pitch in countless lawyer advertisements,
which often includes an invitation to a dinner seminar)

In This Chapter...

you'll learn that Trusts are the Swiss army knives of the estate-planning toolkit. Use them with great flexibility to transfer intergenerational wealth, reduce estate taxes, provide a consistent stream of income for your family, protect assets, ensure privacy, enhance mojo, and more. Although this chapter focuses on living Trusts, it also introduces numerous types of testamentary Trusts with various functions and potential benefits, which will be discussed more fully in later chapters.

TRUST – A legal property interest held by one person for the benefit of him- or herself or another.

GRANTOR – The person who creates a Trust and transfers assets to it.

TRUSTEE – The person or the bank responsible for administering the assets of a Trust in a fiduciary capacity for the benefit of beneficiaries.

BENEFICIARY – The person or the entity for or to whom Trust assets are being held or distributed.

Types of Trusts

Living vs. Testamentary/Revocable vs. Irrevocable

You create **living Trusts** during your lifetime.
Testamentary Trusts take effect after you die.

Living Trusts (also known as inter vivos—"between the living," in Latin) can evolve into testamentary Trusts when you die, or they may simply dissolve when their assets are distributed to beneficiaries before or after your death.

You can change **revocable living Trusts**.
The person creating an **irrevocable living Trust** cannot change it.

Revocable and irrevocable Trusts that are used for different purposes during your lifetime may align after you die.

All testamentary Trusts are Irrevocable because you can't make changes after you are dead.

All revocable Trusts start out as living Trusts because you create them during your lifetime.

Why Have a Revocable Living Trust Instead of Just a Will?

A revocable living Trust can accomplish everything a Will does, regarding the disposition of your estate. Upon your death, revocable living Trusts, like Wills, can either morph into further testamentary Trusts or distribute all of their assets outright to your beneficiaries.

Most revocable living Trusts are "self-declarations," meaning that you wear a few different hats: grantor, trustee, and beneficiary. They can be described in four words:

YOU CONTROL IT COMPLETELY

A properly functioning revocable living Trust acts as a financial alter ego. It owns your assets and keeps your family out of probate court when you die, preserving your privacy and lessening attorney fees. By avoiding probate, revocable trusts keep the details of what you do with your estate safe from the prying eyes of strangers. Wills, however, do not enable you and your family to avoid probate.

The difference between you owning your assets and your assets being owned by a revocable living Trust that you establish and control is that the Trust, unlike you, never dies or becomes incompetent. Upon your incapacity, the Trust is administered according to your best interests for the rest of your life. After you die, your revocable living Trust either becomes irrevocable under new testamentary terms, or its assets are distributed and the Trust ends. Either way, your successor trustee just needs a copy of the Trust and a death certificate to take control of your assets.

You can amend (change) the revocable living Trust's terms at any time or get rid of it altogether (revoke it). In most cases, you can use your Social Security number as a tax identification number, so no special tax accounting is required. All Trust income is reported on your regular individual or joint tax return.

Funding Your Revocable Living Trust

If you want your revocable living Trust to efficiently transfer your assets after you die, while avoiding probate, you must fund it. That means you transfer ownership of the assets to its trustee (which can be you) and/or designate the Trust as the beneficiary or the contingent beneficiary of certain assets. Instead of owning accounts as an individual or jointly, you own them as the trustee of your Trust. Think of funding your Trust simply as a name change or changing hats. Once it is funded, you may continue to spend and/or invest your Trust assets as you please, just as you did before establishing the Trust.

Funding your Trust means retitling assets or making the Trust a beneficiary. Instead of owning a bank account as "John Doe" or "John Doe and Joan Doe as joint tenants," you direct the bank to title your account "John Doe as trustee of the John Doe Revocable Trust, dated September 26, 2009." You may also fund the Trust by making it a beneficiary, payable on your death.

If you hold your assets jointly and you want your spouse or another joint tenant to continue to have independent authority to make transactions, you can accomplish that with your Trust by naming him or her the co-trustee. If worded properly, the Trust may work like a joint tenancy, as far as day-to-day transactional authority is concerned, while you and your spouse are both still living and competent.

If you do not fund the Trust, it can still carry out most of the functions of a Will, but it will not avoid probate. You do not have to title all of your assets in the name of the Trust or name it as beneficiary for it to accomplish certain goals, but only properly structured assets will be subject to its terms and at the same time avoid probate. Even after you create a Trust, some of your assets may remain in joint tenancy or payable to a named beneficiary other than the Trust via a contractual arrangement with an insurance company or some other financial institution. The existence of those assets does not invalidate the Trust, but unless they follow some path into your Trust, perhaps via a pour-over Will, as discussed later in this chapter, they will not be governed by its terms.

Skip the Chrysalis (Probate) Phase

The fact is, dead people own nothing. Like a caterpillar metamorphosing into a butterfly, your assets take a new form after you die. Assets owned by you individually without a valid beneficiary designation must survive a potentially lengthy and contentious chrysalis stage (probate) before the butterfly (your assets after your death) emerges and flutters to new owners (your beneficiaries).

A funded Trust skips the chrysalis phase. The named successor trustee can simply walk into the bank or sell your real estate, with your death certificate in hand and a copy of the Trust, although a new tax identification number may also be needed, because the Trust's use of your social security number ends upon your death.

A Mental Blackboard Exercise

To illustrate the flexibility of your revocable living Trust, visualize a blackboard. Across the top of your mental blackboard, with an imaginary brush dipped in illusory white **paint**, write the name and the date of the Trust. Most people use their own name in the name of the Trust, but some add a layer of secrecy by using numbers or some other code in the name.

Now, in mental **chalk**, write the terms of the Trust. The terms may consist of outright gifts or may subject assets to further testamentary Trusts that go into effect when you die.

After a few years, say you want to change the Trust. Mentally erase the terms you want changed and replace them with the new language you want. If you erase and replace the whole thing, that type of hyper-amendment is known as a "restatement" of the Trust.

Notice that when you erased the chalk, the name and the date, written permanently in white paint, did not change. That is because once you have funded your Trust by titling assets in its name, you do not want to have to do it again. If your life changes in myriad ways—marriage, divorce, the deaths of beneficiaries—it is usually easier to restate the Trust with all new terms, rather than start the funding process all over again.

The chalk-erase-chalk-erase cycle can continue until the day you die.

Comparison of a Revocable Living Trust and a Single-Owner Corporation

There are similarities between a revocable living Trust and a single-shareholder corporation (you own all of the equity and are the sole director, officer, and employee), but a corporation comes with additional responsibilities. The corporation must file annually with the state in which it is registered, and annual fees must be paid, or the state will dissolve the corporation.

A corporation that protects noncorporate assets from corporate liabilities must observe certain formalities, such as providing annual minutes. Corporations are usually separate tax entities with more extensive and complex filings. You must maintain separate books, to avoid mixing personal and corporate assets. If an owner is not properly adhering to these formalities, corporate creditors may be able to "pierce the corporate veil" and attack the owner personally, rendering one of the corporation's prime purposes useless.

Unlike a corporation, a revocable living Trust generally requires no annual upkeep, filings, or separate bookkeeping; it operates with minimal complications. All you have to do is fund it. Even unfunded, a Trust can still control your assets after you die (with the help of a pour-over Will and probate). After funding the Trust, you have only one other task: to update it as needed, the same as you would your Will.

Asset protection is generally not a primary purpose of revocable living Trusts. As discussed later in this chapter, irrevocable domestic asset-protection Trusts (DAPTs) are available in a few states (or in offshore jurisdictions, if you take out the word *domestic*), but a grantor with access to the assets of a revocable living Trust generally receives no lifetime protection from creditors or liability.

Incapacity Planning with a Revocable Living Trust

A designated successor trustee will take over and operate your Trust according to its terms, should you become incapacitated. In advance of your incapacity, you can define what qualifies as a springing event, with language such as:

> *"I shall be considered incapacitated when my successor trustee and a physician who has personally examined me state in writing that I am unable to conduct ordinary financial affairs due to a mental or physical disability."*

During your incapacity, you may want Trust assets to be used exclusively for your benefit. Or you may direct the trustee to support or make early gifts to future beneficiaries as a way to protect their inheritance. You may express a strong preference for staying in your home with appropriate care for as long as possible, rather than checking into a nursing home. In short, you can provide a roadmap to guide the trustee on how to use your assets during your incapacity.

Getting Married?
Revocable Trusts and Prenuptial Agreements

You can use revocable living Trusts to help protect your assets in a divorce.

Say you have a reasonably large amount of assets and are about to get married. Do you ask your spouse-to-be to sign a prenuptial agreement? You may cringe at the thought of putting the nascent relationship at risk by bringing up the issue, but you are also disturbed by the possibility of losing half of your assets. Revocable living Trusts can help ensure that your assets remain yours in the event of a divorce.

Precise bookkeeping is crucial. Before you wed, place your major financial assets into a Trust. These Trust assets, accumulated prior to marriage, must remain segregated from those you acquire during marriage. Commingling assets with those of your newly beloved puts them at risk. Once you are married, assets can be removed from your Trust, but if you move those or any other new assets back into the preexisting accounts owned by your Trust, that is "commingling." Those preexisting accounts may be endangered later, should you divorce. If your segregated Trust assets produce income that adds to your joint tax liability, perfect your paper trail and account for the extra tax when segregating premarital from post-marital assets. Add the increased tax liability from the segregated assets to the marital pool.

This method of protecting assets is not foolproof, but neither is a prenuptial agreement, which courts sometimes refuse to enforce for a variety of reasons. Purely from a legal standpoint, it is best to use both—or just don't get married. If you are writing a prenuptial agreement or have an existing one, make sure it does not conflict with your Trust. A Trust is far less inflammatory than a prenuptial agreement because:

1. It requires no signature from your future spouse. You don't even have to mention the Trust, although he or she will eventually find out anyway if any attention is paid to marital tax returns.

2. It avoids the hot-button term *prenup* and all of the accompanying baggage, which includes bringing lawyers into your marriage.

3. It can help you avoid disclosing all of your assets to your spouse, which is required of a valid prenuptial.

Advantages of Probate

Although most people think of probate as a mojo killer and something best avoided, it can serve positive functions. Four common advantages of probate:

1. Creditors' claims can be cut off within an abbreviated time period—usually six to twelve months, depending on the state—provided proper notice of death is given (actual notice

to known creditors and court-sanctioned newspaper publication to unknown creditors). In contrast, creditors' claims against a Trust are treated like claims against an individual and can remain valid for years.

You can negate this disadvantage of the funded Trust through a simple probate conducted on nominal assets. It works like this: The vast majority of your estate is non-probate, but some token amount (such as $10) is probated with the sole purpose of eliminating claims against your estate once the probate estate is closed. Even though only a small amount of money passed through probate, it may eliminate claims against your entire estate.

2. If your estate bypasses probate, but your trustee is a closet embezzler, the Trust could be wiped out before anyone has a chance to discover the crime. Although most advisors tout the privacy afforded by funded revocable living Trusts, sometimes there is an advantage to having the probate court keep an eye on things. Selecting a bank as a trustee of your Trust may also ease your mind.

3. A probate estate allows your executor to choose between calendar or fiscal year income tax election. Transferring via a Trust without an associated probate requires a calendar year. For most estates, this is not an issue, but a fiscal year election may result in a welcome extension of the filing deadline, if there are complicated tax issues.

4. Competing claims to real estate can cause a "cloud" on the title, making the property unsellable. A probate estate can "quiet title," with the court determining who owns the property, making it sellable.

"Pour-Over" Will

A minor but important ancillary document to a revocable living Trust is a pour-over Will, which is meant to pick up any probate assets not funded in the Trust and transfer (pour) them into the Trust after you die. In most cases, the pour-over Will should do as little work as possible, so that your estate avoids probate. Used correctly, the pour-over Will sweeps the probate "crumbs" of your estate into the Trust.

The probate crumbs can be substantial no matter how diligent you structure your estate to avoid probate if you are a plaintiff of a pending lawsuit at the time of your demise, or your death is the result of an accident and your family decides to sue. In that case a probate estate must be opened, because the claim (and the resulting money) is a probate asset. No amount of diligence can prevent this possibility. If you are a defendant in a lawsuit while you are living or someone wants to sue you after you die, the opposing side must open a probate to pursue or continue a claim against your estate. Even if the other side were to go through this process, that would not subject your non-probate assets to any litigation, because it occurs in a different court venue.

As with regular Wills, pour-over Wills also name a guardian for any minor or disabled children.

Irrevocable Living Trust – The ILIT

A grantor creating an irrevocable living Trust cannot change its terms. Irrevocable living Trusts are generally created to remove assets from your estate by placing them beyond your control. One of the most common uses is to own large life insurance policies whose proceeds may be subject to estate tax.

It is a common misconception that life insurance policy proceeds are never subject to tax. They usually face no income tax, but for estate tax purposes, they are countable assets of the policy owner if the policy is within his or her control. If you purchase life insurance to provide for your dependents, the last thing you want is to diminish the support the policy was meant to provide. An irrevocable life insurance Trust ("ILIT," sounds like "eye lit") removes life insurance death benefits from your estate and creates liquidity for paying estate taxes and other uses. An ILIT is especially appealing to those with mostly illiquid assets, such as real estate or a closely held business. Insufficient liquidity could force your heirs to sell assets at fire-sale prices just to pay estate taxes on time.

To ensure that the insurance proceeds are not taxed as part of your estate, the ILIT must be truly irrevocable. You cannot retain incidents of ownership, such as the right to use the cash value of the insurance policy—a drawback if you consider funding the ILIT with whole-life or universal insurance containing large cash values that you might want to tap into later. For this reason and due to its relatively low cost, term life insurance is the asset of choice for most ILITs. Second-to-die (survivorship) insurance is also usually owned by an ILIT, because its primary purpose is often to provide liquidity to pay estate taxes.

Once the ILIT is established, you will transfer into it some or all of your existing insurance policies, or the trustee can purchase new policies, then use your annual exclusion gifts of $14,000 per beneficiary (in 2017)—$28,000 if you and your spouse are making a split gift (see Chapter 21 for more on lifetime gifts)—to pay the premiums.

Any loans against existing policies transferred into an ILIT must be repaid, or the proceeds may be taxed as income. A grantor must then live at least three years beyond the transfer date for the IRS to exclude the policy's proceeds from your taxable estate. There is no three-year look-back for new life insurance policies purchased by the ILIT.

When you die, ILIT's may end and may distribute assets directly to beneficiaries or may fund further testamentary Trusts (see Chapters 10 through 15 for more on testamentary Trusts).

Because most people are hunter-gatherers of wealth, all things being equal, creating revocable Trusts tends to be more palatable than irrevocable ones. You fully control the assets in revocable Trusts while you are around to enjoy them. Irrevocable Trusts, however, get rid of assets and have a specific purpose. For many people whose assets are relatively modest, one of the prime purposes of an irrevocable Trust would be to transfer an asset that is essentially worthless during your lifetime but has great value at your death—a term insurance policy.

Irrevocable Living Trust – Escaping Creditors with DAPTs

Domestic asset protection Trusts (DAPTs) are irrevocable Trusts that shield assets from outside claims, while still allowing you to be a beneficiary (or, at least, a future beneficiary). The idea is to select a friendly trustee—never yourself—who can shift assets back to you after the creditor storm clouds pass.

Valid DAPTs require a deep connection to the state in which they are established. Having originated in Alaska, they are available in fourteen or fifteen states, with varying degrees of creditor protection. At least one of the trustees must be a resident of (or a corporation located in) the DAPT state, and some aspect of the DAPT must be administered there.

DAPTs block creditors most definitively when the DAPT jurisdiction matches the grantor's primary residency. Real estate located (or businesses operating) outside the DAPT state ordinarily makes poor DAPT-protected assets.

A grantor spending the time, effort, and fees to escape his or her creditors with a DAPT may consider combining that technique with an LLC (Chapter 22) to further confound creditor hounds.

The Reciprocal Trust Doctrine

The reciprocal Trust doctrine poses a problem when more than one party, such as a husband and a wife, create identical irrevocable Trusts. If estate tax savings is a major reason to create the irrevocable Trusts, those savings can be thrown out and the Trusts "uncrossed," if the IRS deems them reciprocal. The theory is that an "I'll scratch your back if you'll scratch mine" arrangement exists. If you and your spouse are creating more than one ILIT for estate tax savings, your attorney should differentiate between their "mirror" images to avoid invoking the doctrine.

Prince Rogers Nelson (Prince) June 7, 1958–April 21, 2016

Corvettes shine red, doves cry and they coo. Prince had no will, so his massive estate goes to who? #bonanzaforlawyers

Pearls of Wisdom

I can avoid probate by creating and funding a revocable living Trust that acts as my financial alter ego, while I retain complete control of the Trust assets during my life. I can change it any time I like. An irrevocable living Trust, often in the form of an irrevocable life insurance Trust (ILIT), removes assets from my estate, usually for estate tax reasons or to put them outside creditor reach.

Chapter 10

$$

Testamentary Trusts – Control from the Grave, Part 1

Never is the word God listens for when he needs a laugh.
- Dinky Earnshaw -

In This Chapter...
you'll discover the value of testamentary Trusts, which take effect when you die. They are irrevocable but can be flexible. Typically, they exercise control over your heirs, protect assets from claims against them, and/or avoid unnecessary estate taxes. These functions may overlap.

A testamentary Trust can spring into being from your Will or an existing Trust. It can distribute assets the way you want, creatively providing measured doses of ongoing support over time or as needed. As counterintuitive as it may seem, complete ownership of assets by a beneficiary can be a bad thing. Partial ownership via a Trust may be better.

Control from the Grave

If assets go outright to beneficiaries—with no strings attached, regardless of the circumstances—then they are not subject to a testamentary Trust. Assets to be distributed to beneficiaries in any manner other than outright need a testamentary Trust that kicks in at death.

Testamentary Trusts can direct payment to beneficiaries according to any legitimate formula. Who says you cannot exert control from the grave? Testamentary Trusts can build a protective straw, wood, or brick house around your assets and allow your cold dead hands to pull ethereal strings connected to trustees and beneficiaries.

Here are the top five examples of testamentary Trusts working to your family's advantage:

1. Your testamentary Trust directs money to be managed for, and doled out to, financially immature children. Pass control from your trustee to the children incrementally over time, or not at all.

2. Your children are fine, but events contingently redirect assets to immature grandchildren, in-laws, and others.

3. You want to leave beneficiaries assets from which they will be able to draw income but which will revert to different beneficiaries upon their demise. There are millions of nontraditional, blended, or stepfamilies in the United States begging for this treatment. These relationships may not easily fit the typical patterns offered by simple estate-planning forms found online. Improper planning can be devastating—your assets may be distributed and/or depleted in ways you never contemplated.

4. You want to shelter your money from estate taxes.

5. You want only your beneficiaries to have your assets, leaving no one else a legitimate future claim to them.

A Beneficiary's Powers of Appointment

A power of appointment is the right by a Trust beneficiary to redirect Trust assets. It determines the extent of beneficiaries' authority over Trust assets. Understanding powers of appointment is essential if you want to comprehend Chapters 11 through 14 and will also simplify and expedite conversing with your lawyer if he or she recommends a testamentary Trust.

Create a testamentary Trust, and YOU decide how much authority to give beneficiaries via powers of appointment. By carving out limits on powers of appointment, Trusts can govern the distribution of assets to accomplish medium- to long-term goals when you are no longer here to manage your affairs. If you inherit any interest in Trust, it is important to know the scope of any powers of appointment you are granted.

GENERAL POWERS

A power of appointment defines the scope of a beneficiary's right to direct where and how Trust assets flow. The beneficiary who has the authority to appoint is the "holder" of the power, which may be exercised during the lifetime of a beneficiary and/or testamentarily, upon the beneficiary's death. The holder of a general power of appointment, either lifetime or testamentary, is considered the owner of the assets subject to the power for estate tax reasons and creditor claims.

General Lifetime

A general lifetime power of appointment over a Trust asset is equivalent to owning the asset outright. If you have one, you can spend it on education or throw it all down on one spin of the roulette wheel. You can spend the money on yourself or give it away. A general lifetime power of appointment usually comes with a testamentary power that goes into effect upon your death. Any power of appointment that includes the ability to use an asset for your own "best interests" or "happiness" during your lifetime is a general one. You can leave the money fully invested to grow in value or cash it in and buy that new Ferrari you've had your eye on. It's completely up to you.

General Testamentary

A general testamentary power of appointment allows you to leave the subject assets to anyone or anything at your death. It includes the ability to distribute to at least one of the following: yourself (why you would leave assets to your dead self I will never understand), your creditors, your estate, and its creditors.

For purposes of calculating estate tax, upon your death you are deemed to have completely owned any assets subject to a general power during your life (bad, if you have a large taxable estate—as discussed in Chapter 20), but you obtain a stepped-up basis, eliminating future capital gains taxes (good). The most restrictive general testamentary power of appointment conferrable is the ability of the holder to pay only creditors of your estate.

LIMITED POWERS

Instead of a general one, a beneficiary may have a limited ("special") power of appointment. The beneficiary does not own the assets subject to the power but, depending on the terms of the Trust, can have substantial control over them.

Limited Universe

The people and the organizations to which the holder can further distribute Trust assets, during the holder's lifetime or testamentarily, can be limited. Narrow the universe of potential recipients, perhaps to descendants of the person from whom the holder has inherited the power. Or broaden it by allowing potential gifts, outright or conditional, to:

- Descendants of your grandparents, so that your parents, siblings, uncles, aunts, nephews, nieces, and cousins of any degree are included in the limited universe;

- A list of specific friends and their descendants;

- Spouses of all of the people who may be included;

- Charities;

- Anyone or anything except the beneficiary, his or her estate, or a creditor of either.

The broadest limited testamentary universe that a holder of the power of appointment can distribute to for **any** reason consists of anyone or anything, except for the holder, the holder's estate, or creditors of either. Narrowing of the potential universe of appointees at the holder's death can be key to shielding assets from the holder's creditors, excluding them from estate taxes (Chapter 12), or using generation-skipping techniques (Chapter 13). No powers of appointment, general or limited, lifetime or testamentary, can be given to the beneficiary of a disclaimer Trust (Chapter 14). The surviving spouse of a QTIP marital Trust may be given only a limited testamentary power of appointment (Chapter 12). The beneficiary of a special-needs Trust may not have any powers of appointment (Chapter 15).

Limits on Trustee Distributions Based on Need
Ascertainable Standards/HEMS

Things get tricky where the inheriting beneficiary is also the trustee. With the lifetime authority to distribute Trust assets, including to him- or herself, limiting such distributions to "ascertainable" standards avoids qualifying the power of appointment as a general one.

A trustee may (or shall) make typical ascertainable standard distributions to or for the benefit of a beneficiary's "Health, Education, Maintenance in reasonable comfort, and Support"— commonly referred to in hip estate-planning circles as "HEMS." Presumably, the IRS views HEMS as an ascertainable standard because a trustee interpreting those words, even one who is also the beneficiary, would know how much support may (or must) be provided.

A trustee/beneficiary's authority that exceeds HEMS requires careful wording for the standard to remain ascertainable. Most commonly, a broad power to distribute assets to the beneficiary beyond HEMS is for "best interests" and "happiness." Neither is ascertainable. The IRS sees permissible distributions for a beneficiary's "best interests" or "happiness" as benefiting the beneficiary in any way. A beneficiary who is also sole trustee now has a general power of appointment, rather than a limited one—a legal hair split, but an important one.

In effect, a beneficiary able to hire and fire at will trustees who are not limited by ascertainable standards can shop for the most compliant trustee. This beneficiary might as well be acting as trustee and qualifies as holding a general power of appointment.

Bottom line: <u>If</u> the beneficiary can appoint Trust assets to him- or herself (or to the estate or the creditors of either), <u>or</u> a potential beneficiary is also the trustee (or can hire and fire a trustee) not limited by ascertainable standards, <u>and</u> the trustee may distribute Trust assets to him- or herself for reasons that exceed ascertainable standards (including distributions for "best interests" or "happiness"), then a general, rather than a limited, power of appointment exists. A general power of appointment = ownership = potential exposure of Trust estate assets to the holder's taxable estate and plunder from outside parties, such as his or her creditors.

Tom Clancy. April 12, 1947 – October 1, 2013

Military thriller author makes clandestine Will change, puts $15MM tax burden on kids. When they accuse step-mom of foul play, courtroom becomes a battlefield.

"May" the Trustee or "Shall" He or She?

Seemingly endless legal interpretations can come down to a few words in any Trust. Nowhere is this exemplified more than by the incremental difference between "may" and "shall."

After you die, the trustee is obligated to follow the direction of your testamentary Trust regarding distributions to or for the benefit of the beneficiaries. Typically, the trustee either MAY or SHALL distribute for various needs of beneficiaries. Depending on such language, the trustee has more or less discretion over Trust assets.

MAY = the trustee decides

SHALL = the trustee follows the rules

A few typical testamentary Trusts, which often overlap:

CONTROL TRUSTS – For minors and other immature beneficiaries, but these are also used to ensure that the ultimate beneficiaries are the ones intended. (See Chapter 11.)

SHELTER TRUSTS – For estate tax and/or control reasons, you want assets to be used for someone's benefit, classically but not necessarily, a spouse. (See Chapter 12.)

GENERATION-SKIPPING TRANSFER (GST) TAX EXEMPT TRUSTS – These are used to keep assets away from your children's creditors or spouses and out of their taxable estate. (See Chapter 13.)

DISCLAIMER TRUSTS – When combined with the Trusts that the disclaimed assets feed into, the creative use of disclaimers can be a powerful tool for postmortem estate tax planning. (See Chapter 14.)

SPECIAL-NEEDS TRUSTS – Set aside money for the benefit of a special-needs beneficiary, without disqualifying the individual from benefits and services provided by public agencies. (See Chapter 15.)

PET TRUSTS – Provide funds and direction to the person who cares for your pet. (See Chapter 16.)

 Pearls of Wisdom

If I want to control assets after I die, as opposed to distributing them to beneficiaries outright, I need a testamentary Trust as part of my estate plan.

The terms of a testamentary Trust determine the trustee's and the beneficiary's range of authority. Testamentary Trusts may affect future estate taxes. They also determine the extent to which the assets subject to the Trusts are vulnerable to attack by those who may have claims against the beneficiary. Understanding powers of appointment is useful when creating a testamentary Trust or if I am a beneficiary of such a Trust. As holder of a testamentary power of appointment, I can direct, at least to some extent, where or how assets go to potential subsequent contingent beneficiaries.

Cheryl ✚ Ethan ✚ Rob ✚ Tammi

Cheryl was just sixteen when she came home from the hospital with baby Ethan.

He's **SO** cute!

Her folks had a pretty full house already, with four kids of their own, but baby Ethan's father "wasn't in the picture," so one more wasn't a hardship.

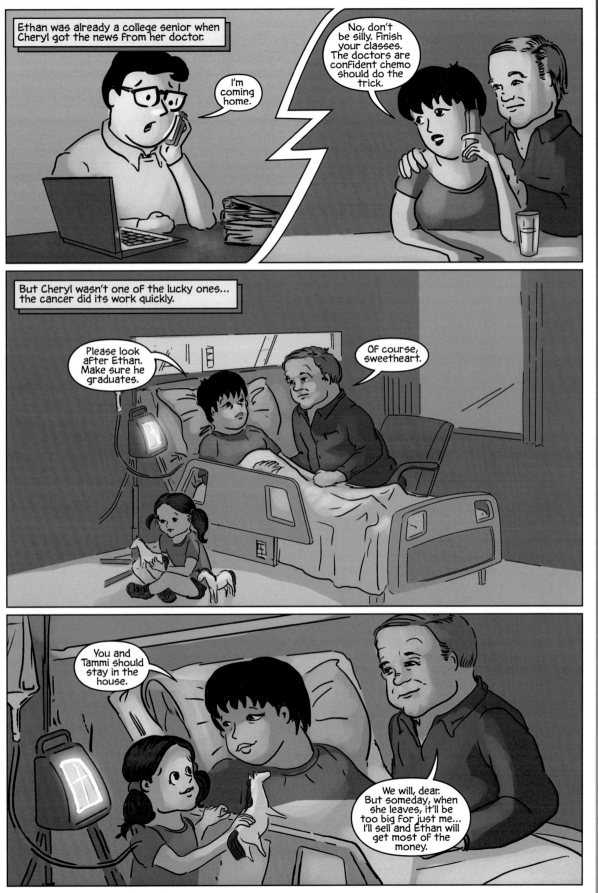

Chapter 11

$$ $$

Testamentary Trusts – Control from the Grave, Part 2

The large print giveth and the small print taketh away.
- Tom Waits -

In This Chapter...

you'll see that testamentary Trusts are all about maintaining control over assets after you die, as noted in Chapter 10. The grantor provides a road map for determining the relative authority of the trustee and the rights of the beneficiaries. For multiple reasons, including taxes, a well-drafted Trust finds balance within the continuum between flexibility and constraint. Included in that equation is the ability of third-party non-beneficiaries, such as creditors and future ex-sons-in-law, to access Trust assets.

Given the broad range of family dynamics, including incompetent or immature heirs, both young and old, testamentary Trusts can be essential to a careful distribution of assets looking forward into the future.

People sometimes unexpectedly die out of order, together, or in rapid succession. Oncoming forks in the road carry with them an abundance of reasons to control asset distributions. A tight estate plan can anticipate many otherwise unforeseen contingencies. Look beyond the initial beneficiaries and consider who is next in line.

The following are a few typical situations in which you may wish to exercise control via a Trust instead of giving an outright gift:

1. Underage Beneficiaries

Because a minor cannot inherit money directly, a guardian or a trustee must be in charge. Without a Trust, an inheriting minor's estate may be subject to onerous yearly accounting and legal fees involving the probate court.

A Trust can direct how the trustee holds, invests, and uses assets for any minor beneficiary. Often, invested Trust assets are doled out on a "may" or "shall" basis for the beneficiary's HEMS or perhaps broader, non-ascertainable standards (as discussed in Chapter 10).

Instead of creating separate Trusts for multiple very young beneficiaries, you can establish a single Trust fund, sometimes called a "spray" or "sprinkle" Trust, for them. After you die, funds will be disbursed equally or unequally, depending on circumstances, to pay for their everyday needs, including education. It can end and divide among the children when the youngest one attains a certain age. If drafted correctly, a single Trust may spare the trustee a certain amount of accounting work, while remaining fair to all of the beneficiaries.

Beyond the everyday costs of a young beneficiary transitioning from childhood to adulthood, the trustee of a single-fund Trust may have the authority to distribute funds for certain big-ticket items, such as buying a house or a car, paying for a wedding, investing in a business, and the like. Those types of disbursements are often considered advancements and are reconciled when the single-fund Trust is divided among the beneficiaries.

You can provide for a caveat within that caveat: Say, you bought cars for your two younger children on their 18th birthdays. At your death, a single Trust fund is created that benefits all three children. Even big-ticket items paid out of the single Trust fund, such as a car, do not have to be considered advancements if you have made similar distributions to other children in the past. Give the trustee the flexibility to determine what is fair.

In situations of potential minor or disabled beneficiaries, you may wish to provide income to the guardian so that your children are never a financial burden to the person good enough to take responsibility for them. Specify that the guardian may live in your home while raising your children, build onto his or her own house, or cover the cost of a nanny, or maybe permit the guardian to reduce outside work hours and receive a stipend to compensate for the loss of revenue.

2. Financially Inexperienced Young Adult Beneficiaries

When a beneficiary attains the legal age of majority, usually 18 or 21, receiving an outright inheritance can warp his or her perspective. The future may be bleak for a kid whose profligate spending or reckless investment choices squander a major inheritance ("major" being relative). The beneficiary can spend the rest of his or her life deeply regretful, having blown a lifetime opportunity for financial stability.

Even more insidious, a large unearned outright gift can ruin the beneficiary's character. Inheriting a fortune and never having to work for material comforts can distort reality. The result is a selfish personality, characterized by an absence of empathy for those less fortunate. Which is worse, a "Trust fund baby" or a "blew-my-inheritance loser"?

A typical Trust pattern mandates income distribution to the beneficiary beginning at a certain age, coupled with future increased access to principal, usually granting the trustee the flexibility to make further distributions as needed. The beneficiary can then gain increasing control when specified via a right of withdrawal or by becoming trustee over portions of his or her Trust share. Couple this with discretionary principal distributions and either a HEMS ascertainable limited power of appointment or a best interests/happiness general one.

3. Other Adult Children Who Have Shown Lapses in Judgment

She has bad habits and must never completely control the inheritance. You fear that his spouse will hijack the money, or that she will gamble it away, go on a shopping spree, be an easy target for scammers, or simply quit working and cease to be a productive member of society. A Trust can ensure the essentials, including a roof over the beneficiary's head.

You can grant control to the beneficiary incrementally or not at all. Trusts commonly allow fractional withdrawals of Trust principal: "one-third at age 25, one-half the balance at age 30, and the full balance at age 35." Or you can ignore age and specify increasing control by the number of years since your death. You can also come up with your own creative formula. Another tactic allows the beneficiary to act as sole trustee over his or her inheritance at those milestones, removing the incentive to withdraw and mix money with other assets, potentially making them accessible by a future ex-spouse.

Robin Williams. July 21, 1951 – August 11, 2014

Mork's 3rd wife never quite Hooked his 3 kids, who hate her. I Doubtfire-ing the lawyers would even help. Vague will = fight over Good Will Hunting Oscar

4. Provide Incentives

Trust provisions can entice a beneficiary to:

- Go to college.

- Attain a certain grade point average.

- Become gainfully employed. Add distributions by mathematical formula to employment earnings. Higher earnings mean larger Trust distributions.

- Attain a certain net worth through his or her own efforts.

- Get married.

- Invite his or her siblings to marriages, christenings, bar/bat mitzvahs, or other life-cycle occasions.

You can also persuade a beneficiary not to:

- Fail a drug test.

- Have children outside of marriage.

- Pierce his or her body or cover it with tattoos (but are you going to insist—and will the inheritor allow—a full body search for proof?).

You may cringe at such provisions that tell other people how to live. Yet if you have done that your whole life anyway, why stop at death?

Make sure any incentives or any other controls are flexible, because what you think makes sense today may not in the future. A child who must obtain a college degree or earn a certain salary to receive any assets may become disabled and, for this or some other valid reason, be unable to comply. In addition, any incentive (or disincentive) provisions should be readily verifiable by a trustee. Children outside of marriage may be verifiable, but investigating a prohibition on extramarital affairs might involve more than a trustee can stomach.

Provisions containing incentives are usually enforceable, but the court could dismiss those contrary to public policy. A provision that your child not marry someone of a different race or religion may be invalid.

Commingling v. Segregation

Generally, an inheritance is separate property, rather than a community or marital asset. Commingling assets changes that equation. Even after your beneficiary acquires full control over assets via a right of withdrawal or a general power of appointment, the individual should keep them segregated from his or her spouse's or their joint assets. The same goes for Trust income. Proper segregation requires that money only come out—new money is never added. Extra taxes owed in the marital estate caused by the inheritance must be paid from the segregated funds. Strict segregation makes it difficult for a beneficiary's future ex-spouse to get hold of an inheritance.

5. Blended Family

In a second marriage with children from your first, you are the glue that holds certain relations together. When you are gone, will step-relations drift apart or even become completely estranged? Whether it is your house or any other asset, legal ownership includes the right not to share. The kids could kick a spouse with no legal interest out of your house immediately after your death. However, a joint tenant on the house at the time of your death can sell it, pocket the money, and give the proceeds to his or her beneficiaries, excluding yours. The joint tenant can do this even if your children are the sole beneficiaries of your Will and/or revocable Trust. A testamentary Trust and correctly titled assets can take care of both your kids and your mate.

The Trust can permit your spouse to live in the house for the rest of his or her life, for a set period of time, or until some event occurs. What happens when the yoga instructor from down the block brings your husband a vegan casserole a week after you die, then moves in with him a month later? Or when your wife gets with her personal trainer who happens to be the same age as your middle child? Your Trust can prevent them from living in your house.

This reasoning extends to the rest of your assets. Set aside a pool of money for your spouse's care that reverts to your children upon your spouse's death, or give your spouse a portion of your assets outright, so that your children are not waiting for him or her to die to get their inheritance. Yet you should never leave assets outright to your children or your most recent love interest and expect them to share. They may get along great now, but relationships change, especially when money is involved and emotions are running rampant. One misunderstood comment or glance may strain the relationship beyond the breaking point.

Spouses or life partners who lack a commonality of interests, such as children together are similar to blended families. They may want to use testamentary Trusts to ensure the ultimate destination of what is left of their assets upon the second person's death. Selecting an independent trustee and/or giving that trustee limited (or no) powers of appointment confers only the desired amount of authority, if any, over the assets.

Keep Your Eye on What Is Important

Think about the future flow of your assets, and consider potential contingencies. However, as with everything, avoid unnecessary complexity whenever possible, and concentrate on your most important goals. Overcomplicated Rube Goldberg estate-planning mazes that attempt to satisfy your every wish can ultimately prove to be unworkable.

 Pearls of Wisdom

There are numerous non-tax situations where I may wish to control assets via a testamentary Trust.

125

Chapter 12

$$\$\$\$$

Planning for Couples –
Shelter Trusts and Marital Trusts

The reports of my death are greatly exaggerated.
- Mark Twain -

In This Chapter...

you'll find out how you can establish shelter Trusts if you want to limit a beneficiary's control of the Trust assets. Its classic use is for married couples to reduce or eliminate estate taxes upon the survivor's death. Much of the reasoning discussed in this chapter, including capital gains tax issues, applies to any Trust that does not include a general power of appointment. Shelter Trusts are an essential tool in the kit of those fortunate couples to whom estate taxes apply. Marital Trusts guide the distribution of assets for various reasons, including postponement of estate taxes.

Understanding Powers of Appointment (in Chapter 10)
is Key to Understanding This Chapter 12

APPLICABLE EXCLUSION AMOUNT – The amount that you can leave to your designated heirs (other than your spouse, who in most cases can be left unlimited amounts outright if he or she is a U.S. citizen) without incurring any estate or gift tax.

The applicable exclusion amount for 2017 is $5,490,000 and may change annually, according to inflation adjustments. This number, $5,490,000, will be used in most of the following references.

UNLIMITED MARITAL DEDUCTION – Spouses who are U.S. citizens may transfer an unlimited amount of assets to each other, while alive or after death, without any gift, income, or estate tax implications.

Eliminate Estate Taxes

If the combined federal estate of you and your spouse (or life partner) exceeds or may someday exceed $5 million, seriously consider shelter Trusts. If you are completely single and plan to remain so, or you and your mate have no hope of attaining a combined $5 million estate, you have no estate tax "problem," although if you and your spouse live in a state with its own estate tax, a shelter Trust may serve to eliminate that tax.

Formally known as an applicable exclusion amount shelter Trust, or the "B" Trust of an "AB" Trust (think Below ground, as opposed to Above ground) or "bypass" Trust (because its assets bypass the estate of the surviving spouse), shelter Trusts take a long view of wealth. They have been a historical staple of estate planning for affluent couples whose combined wealth approaches or exceeds the applicable exclusion amount.

Thanks to the unlimited marital deduction, an estate left outright to a surviving spouse at the time of the first spouse's death is untaxed. If the combined estate of the spouses exceeds the applicable exclusion amount, it is taxed in the survivor's estate, subject to "portability" (discussed later in this chapter). A properly maintained shelter Trust separates the taxable estate of the first-to-die from the survivor's, reducing or eliminating estate tax upon the survivor's demise.

The need to shelter was more prevalent when the threshold for taxes was only $600,000, during the 1980s and the 1990s. From 2001 through 2012, the president and Congress were unable to settle on a threshold number, resulting in more than a decade of uncertainty. Through 2012, many believed that the threshold for taxes would revert to $1 million per person. The year 2013 put the issue to bed for a while, fixing the applicable exclusion amount at $5 million plus inflation adjusters. Few couples, estimated to be about .2 percent of estates (about two of every one thousand), would pay an estate tax according to the U.S. Congress Joint (Senate and House) Committee on Taxation in 2015 (when the applicable exclusion amount was $5.34 million.)

Though far fewer couples now need shelter Trusts because of the increased threshold for federal estate taxes, the shelter Trust strategy is still worth examining if you have or aspire to have a net worth exceeding that amount. To understand shelter Trusts, view a couple as a single unit, rather than as individuals. Working at its maximum efficiency, a shelter Trust preserves each individual's entire $5.49 million applicable exclusion amount. Collectively, $10.98 million may be exempt from federal estate taxes, effectively doubling the individual exclusion amount, assuming:

• Your collective total net worth is at least $10.98 million.

• You and your spouse want to leave your combined estate to each other, no matter who dies first, for his or her lifetime use, following the first death.

- You divide your estate into equal shares of $5.49 million.

- The applicable exclusion amount is $5.49 million at the time of the first death.

- Upon the death of the first spouse, his or her $5.49 million is left to a shelter Trust.

- The surviving spouse subsequently dies, with his or her own estate worth $5.49 million.

- The applicable exclusion amount remains $5.49 million at the time of the survivor's death.

Assuming no asset growth during the survivor's life, a shelter Trust (or maximum use of the exemption portability, discussed below) will eliminate taxes on the evenly divided $10.98 million estate referred to above, potentially saving in excess of $2 million.

Balancing Estates

In order to fully use shelter Trust strategies, couples must often balance their estate. If a spouse dies first with an estate below the applicable exclusion amount, and the surviving spouse is worth more than the applicable exclusion amount, then they are underusing the shelter strategy and paying avoidable estate taxes, assuming no use of portability for reasons discussed below. If the spouse receiving assets is a U.S. citizen, the unlimited marital deduction simplifies estate balancing by eliminating gift tax and the reporting requirement.

Since the Supreme Court ruled that DOMA (Defense of Marriage Act) was unconstitutional, federal law treats same-sex marriages the same as traditional marriages. Civil unions, domestic partnerships, and common-law marriages receive no such treatment and do not benefit from the unlimited marital deduction.

Gifts to non-spouse individuals (discussed more fully in Chapter 21) in excess of the annual exclusion amount (currently $14,000 per year per person) are limited to a lifetime total before they are taxed, and anything greater than $14,000 per year per person must be reported to the IRS. All reportable gifts in excess of the annual exclusion amount deplete the $5.49 million applicable exclusion of the person making the gift upon that person's death, dollar-for-dollar. For example: If you give $1,000,000 one-time to one lucky person in one calendar year, then after filing a gift tax return to report the gift, you will have reduced your estate's remaining applicable exclusion amount to $4,504,000 (or $5,490,000 minus $986,000—the amount of the gift minus the $14,000 annual exclusion).

Gifts to non-citizen spouses in excess of $149,000 per year per person are limited to $5.49 million before they are taxed, and anything greater than $149,000 per year per person must be reported to the IRS. The excess of a gift of over $149,000 also depletes the applicable exclusion amount of the person making the gift.

While the unlimited marital deduction is an important tool for balancing large estates of married couples, its overuse can be counterproductive in cases where a shelter Trust would help eliminate eventual estate taxes. Married couples who know that if one spouse dies, everything goes to the survivor tax-free may become complacent in their planning. Properly used, a shelter Trust can eliminate estate taxes, rather than just defer them until the surviving spouse's death.

BASIS – Acquisition cost of an asset, used to calculate gains and losses.

CAPITAL GAIN – The profit on the sale of an asset that has grown in value. It is the difference between the basis of an asset and the net proceeds from sale of the asset. An asset sold for a lower price than its acquisition cost may be reported as a capital loss.

CAPITAL GAINS TAX – The tax paid on realization of a capital gain.

STEPPED-UP BASIS – An IRS principle that makes an heir's cost basis equal to the value of the asset at the date of the giver's death—or, alternatively, six months later—rather than its original value. If a gift of an appreciated asset is made during the giver's lifetime, the person who receives it takes the original (carryover) basis, and there is no step-up. The stepped-up basis eliminates capital gains on the appreciation that occurred during the lifetime of the person who originally acquired the asset.

Portability

A remediation technique for large estates, portability partly eliminates the need to balance spousal estates. Similar to disclaimers (Chapter 14), the use of portability is postmortem work, typically done when the estate of the deceased spouse is well below the applicable exclusion amount, while the surviving spouse's well exceeds it.

In essence, portability permits legally married couples to forgo dividing their estates during their lifetime, because any unused estate tax and lifetime gift exclusions of the first-to-die spouse are added to those of the surviving spouse. These amounts are known as the deceased spouse's unused exclusion amount (DSUEA).

Though portability may make the division of some married couple's assets for estate tax planning unnecessary, it spawns a few considerations:

- It requires the filing of a purely informational estate tax return upon the first spouse's death to preserve the DSUEA. The value of the first spouse's estate is left open on the estate tax return until the second spouse dies. Upon the survivor's death, if his or her estate exceeds the applicable exclusion amount, then before the survivor's estate is taxed, any excess is used to fill the first-to-die spouse's remaining applicable exclusion amount as it existed at the time of that first death.

- If it turns out that the survivor's estate is below the applicable exclusion amount, then the legal/accounting fees spent doing a purely informational tax return on the first death may have been a waste of time and money.

- It applies only to the most recent spouse's unused credit, so a survivor who remarries renders the informational tax return a waste because the DSUEA disappears and may subject the survivor's estate to taxes if it exceeds the applicable exclusion amount.

- It does not allow for the growth that a shelter Trust may provide. For instance, a shelter Trust funded with $5.49 million invested wisely could grow to $10 million by the time it is paid to contingent beneficiaries, but portability would allow only for the shift of the DSUEA, sans any growth, out of the estate of the surviving spouse.

- It does not adjust for inflation.

- It works only for legally married couples.

- The generation-skipping tax exemption (see Chapter 13) is not portable.

- State estate taxes are not portable.

- It is decidedly convoluted (like much of estate planning) but useful for some wealthy married couples.

J. Howard Marshall. January 24, 1905 – August 4, 1995

Billionaire industrialist spends last 14 years of life married to Anna Nicole Smith, stripper in a club where they met. 20 years of litigation between estates.

Pros and Cons of Shelter Trusts

If you are married, the decision to use a shelter Trust may require weighing the effects of three different taxes:

1. Federal estate tax;

2. State estate tax (if your state has one); and

3. Capital gains tax (if your assets grow in value after your death).

However, taxes are not the only consideration.

Shelter Trust Advantages

- By granting a surviving spouse limited or no powers of appointment, you can ensure that assets eventually go where you want them to.

- You may protect assets from creditors of the surviving spouse.

- In estates much larger than the applicable exclusion amount, the surviving spouse does not have to jump through portability's hoops to obtain estate tax savings for your children.

- If distributions of assets are subject to ascertainable standards, shelter Trusts have the flexibility to either preserve principal for the eventual contingent remainder beneficiaries or favor lifetime use by the surviving spouse.

- A truly independent trustee or co-trustee may also distribute Trust assets to the surviving spouse for non-ascertainable reasons, including his or her "best interests" and "happiness."

- The right of a surviving spouse to deplete shelter Trust principal, if given, does not require him or her to do so. If shelter Trust assets accumulate or grow during the surviving spouse's life, any increase in value is passed to the ultimate beneficiaries with no estate tax, which can be twice as steep as capital gains tax.

Shelter Trust Disadvantages

- As a couple, you may have to divide your assets during your joint lifetime for the strategy to work most effectively.

- The surviving spouse inherits additional bookkeeping chores, because the shelter Trust is a tax entity separate from the surviving spouse's own estate.

- Appreciating assets do not receive a second step-up in basis following the death of the surviving spouse. If a moderately sized combined estate—let's say, $5 million—remains below the applicable exclusion amount, it may result in unnecessary capital gains taxes upon the surviving spouse's death, without saving any estate tax.

- Even if the combined marital estate exceeds the applicable exclusion amount, portability can avoid both estate and capital gains taxes when the surviving spouse's estate minus the DSUEA is below the applicable exclusion amount. This may be the preferred method in a combined estate that will not exceed $10.98 million.

Marital Trust and the Unlimited Marital Deduction

Whether or not a shelter Trust is first funded with the applicable exclusion amount, the unlimited marital deduction allows the balance of the first-to-die spouse's estate to go to a surviving spouse a few different ways, while still deferring or eliminating taxes:

- Assets may distribute outright to the survivor, without any marital Trust. If the combined amount of the survivor's estate and the outright inheritance puts the surviving spouse's estate over the applicable exclusion amount at the time of the survivor's death, estate tax will be assessed on the survivor's estate at that time. If the survivor's estate does not exceed the applicable exclusion amount, there will be no federal estate tax and all non–retirement plan assets step up in basis, eliminating potential capital gains taxes for beneficiaries.

- Assets may distribute to a marital Trust with a general power of appointment. Using this arrangement, the surviving spouse must receive all income, can take principal out during his or her lifetime, and may leave the marital Trust to whomever he or she wishes upon death. The tax consequences of a general power of appointment marital Trust are the same as an outright gift, but it is often preferred because it provides a Trust framework to handle the assets, especially in the event of an incompetent survivor.

A Shelter Trust for Your BFF?

Some shelter Trust strategies work for non-spouses, especially when you want to give someone a lifetime gift but still direct ultimate disposition of the asset. Let's say you have a "Best Friend Forever" who may need the income, but when the BFF dies, you want whatever is left to go to charity.

In this case, a shelter Trust works but lacks three facilitating tools:

1. *No unlimited marital deduction*

2. *No portability*

3. *No marital Trust*

The lesson is that if you "only" have $5 million, you can leave it all to your BFF and still control the situation from the grave, but it may come with some logistical difficulty.

QTIP Marital Trusts

Upon the death of the first-to-die spouse, assets may also distribute to a qualified terminable interest in property (QTIP) Trust, a type of marital Trust created by federal statute that qualifies for the unlimited marital deduction, but limits the surviving spouse's powers of appointment so that the assets are preserved for remainder beneficiaries chosen by the first-to-die spouse. As with any marital Trust, a QTIP Trust requires the surviving spouse to receive *unconditionally* all of the Trust's income during his or her lifetime. The trustee can, if specified in the Trust, pay principal to or for the lifetime benefit of the surviving spouse, but no one else may receive distributions from the QTIP Trust during the lifetime of the surviving spouse.

The surviving spouse benefiting from a QTIP Trust may also be given a limited testamentary power of appointment to direct distributions, usually to descendants or other family of the deceased spouse. QTIP Trusts are often used in blended families, enabling the grantor to protect children from a previous marriage or other relatives, while benefiting the surviving spouse during his or her lifetime.

QTIP Trust assets are included in the estate of the surviving spouse, subjecting them to estate taxes if both spouses' combined estate exceeds the applicable exclusion amount. On the other hand, its use allows for a step-up in basis upon the survivor's death, thereby potentially eliminating capital gains.

Though the QTIP Trust is subject to federal estate taxes if the combined estate exceeds the applicable exclusion amount, the trustee can elect to port the deceased spouse's unused exclusion amount (DSUEA) on a filed estate tax return, thereby receiving the federal estate tax benefits of a shelter Trust, while also enjoying potential capital gains advantages absent from the appreciation of shelter Trusts. Combining a QTIP Trust with portability does not protect against state estate taxes the way a traditional shelter Trust often does, nor is the growth on the ported assets protected from estate taxes as it is with a shelter Trust.

A "reverse" QTIP Trust is an election made on an estate tax return modifying the QTIP Trust so that it converts the first-to-die spouse's QTIP Trust into a generation-skipping transfer (GST) tax exempt Trust for the benefit of contingent beneficiaries.

Do not confuse this QTIP with the trademarked product that people stick in their ears, even though the package tells you not to!

Qualified Domestic Trust (QDOT) for an Inheriting Non-Citizen Spouse

If you or your spouse is not a U.S. citizen, and you wish to defer estate taxes until after the survivor's death, any bequest in excess of the federal applicable exclusion amount that benefits the survivor must be made to a qualified domestic Trust (QDOT).

Without a QDOT, the excess of a spousal gift over the applicable exclusion amount is taxed upon the first spouse's death.

Requirements for a QDOT to "Qualify":

- The executor must make an irrevocable QDOT election on the federal estate tax return.

- At least one trustee must be a U.S. citizen or a U.S. bank. The non-citizen spouse may be a co-trustee and can even appoint as the co-trustee a U.S. citizen/bank.

- If the value of the QDOT exceeds $2 million, either a U.S. bank must be co-trustee or the individual U.S. citizen co-trustee must furnish a bond or its equivalent to the U.S. government.

- If the value of the QDOT is less than $2 million, no more than 35 percent of its value can be invested in real estate outside the United States, unless a U.S. bank is co-trustee or the individual U.S. citizen co-trustee furnishes a bond or an irrevocable letter of credit to the U.S. government.

- As with any marital Trust, the QDOT must pay income to the surviving non-citizen spouse, usually taxed as ordinary income.

Principal distributions for generally ascertainable standards (i.e., HEMS) may be made to the surviving spouse and descendants with no estate tax consequence. However, if principal distributions are made for reasons that exceed ascertainable standards, the trustee must withhold an appropriate amount to pay any resulting future estate taxes. Excess distributions of the principal not based on need are taxed as part of the estate of the first spouse to die, along with the amount remaining in the QDOT upon the surviving spouse's death.

If the deceased spouse did not establish a QDOT, but one is required to defer estate taxes, the surviving non-citizen spouse may do so within nine months of the first spouse's death. A QDOT is unnecessary if the surviving spouse becomes a citizen within nine months after the death, but it ordinarily takes longer than nine months to process citizenship.

If you or your spouse is not a citizen and your combined estate may be subject to federal estate tax, then a QDOT should be on your estate-planning agenda.

Pearls of Wisdom

If my spouse and I take a long view of our assets, we can mitigate or even eliminate estate taxes. Even if taxes are not an issue, we can control our separate assets so that the surviving spouse benefits from the first-to-die spouse's assets, but upon the survivor's death, those assets revert to the beneficiaries as directed by the spouse who died first.

They enjoyed Libby's wedding...

...but time ran out for Sam not long after, and Linda joined him a few years later.

PARKER

SAM   LINDA

Then...

This lawsuit... unbelievable.

My insurance won't cover the entire judgment. The 40lk is safe, but.... Know any good lawyer jokes?

I should've gone with them to the lawyer's office. First we had to pay all those taxes, and now the sharks are gonna take a huge bite out of my inheritance.

Chapter 13

$$$

Generation-Skipping Transfer (GST) Tax Exempt Trusts

If you want to make God laugh, tell Him your plans.
- Old proverb -

In This Chapter...
if you want your wealth to benefit more than the generation immediately behind you, or if you want to add a layer of protection to the assets you bequeath to the next generation, then generation-skipping planning may be worthwhile.

Reasons for Skipping a Generation Include:

• Estrangement from your child.

• The child has a taxable estate of his or her own and does not need your assets.

• Your child is a big spender who cannot be trusted to preserve an inheritance for his or her own well-being and/or your grandchildren's education.

• You have plenty of money and want to spread it broadly throughout the family.

• You want the money to go to your child, but you and/or the child fear outsiders trying to get a piece of the inheritance. For instance, you fear the child's spouse may weasel his or her way in. Perhaps the child is in the type of business or profession where there is an ever-present danger of a major lawsuit.

You can leave money directly to a grandchild, outright or in Trust. If giving outright, consider carefully the grandchild's potential for acquiring a warped perception of reality by receiving more than he or she can handle. A large unrestricted gift may also usurp your own child's parental role. If your affluent child makes it a point not to spoil his or her children, should you? The skip directly to the grandchild can also be made subject to Trust provisions that give the grandchild as little or as much authority as directed.

GST Taxes

Large estates require additional tax considerations. Transfers to grandchildren or more remote descendants can be subject to a generation-skipping transfer (GST) tax, assessed at the highest transfer rate, on top of any other estate or gift tax. The GST tax is imposed on transfers to any non-descendant beneficiary who is more than 37½ years younger than you. The 37½-year rule excludes spouses, so when oil tycoon J. Howard Marshall left everything to his wife, Anna Nicole Smith (63 years his junior), it was not a generation skip. GST taxes are also not imposed on money left to a grandchild of yours who inherits by virtue of the parent's death.

Though the GST tax generally enables the IRS to tax large estates at every generation, there is a GST tax exemption equal to the applicable exclusion amount. Leaving the full exempt amount to a grandchild incurs no tax, but that gift has used up your entire applicable exclusion amount. Anything beyond the applicable exclusion amount left to anyone other than a spouse or a charity is federally taxed at 40 percent. If that excess goes to a grandchild/ youngster, it may be taxed again: 40 percent once and then 40 percent a second time. Ouch!

GST Tax Exempt Trusts

Understanding Powers of Appointment (Chapter 10) is Key to Understanding GST Tax Exempt Trusts

Most people want their children, rather than their grandchildren, to receive the bulk of their estate. Even then, a generation-skipping transfer (GST) tax exempt Trust brings peace of mind that assets will be protected after death. Spray provisions allow Trust assets to benefit your descendants or an expanded class of beneficiaries at any generation, so the trustee typically "may" or "shall" help any child, grandchild, or great-grandchild, according to need. A spray provision in a GST tax exempt Trust, controlled by skipped children as trustees of their own separate GST tax exempt Trusts, may allow each child, as primary beneficiary of such trust, to use the assets exclusively for his or her own benefit during that child's own lifetime, restricted only by ascertainable standards (usually HEMS—Health, Education, Maintenance, and Support). A skipped child can also hold limited powers of appointment, lifetime or testamentary, to distribute among the universe of people or charities specified in your Trust document.

From a tax standpoint, a GST tax exempt Trust saves you no estate taxes but gives your children an additional exemption if they need it. A segregated GST tax exempt Trust, including any growth during the skipped children's lifetimes, never becomes part of your children's taxable estates.

Even if you say, "I just want my kids to get everything," a GST tax exempt Trust may do them a favor. The "skipped" child or children can both be trustee and enjoy the Trust as primary beneficiary, even though not technically the "owner." The Trust directs the extent of their authority. Limited powers of appointment can come with tons of discretion, but as long as the powers are not general, the GST tax exempt Trust protects its assets from potential financial enemies.

Further down the control spectrum is a structure that names someone other than the skipped child as trustee. Conservatively, you can give a non-beneficiary trustee complete discretion over distributions to the skipped generation, using the word "may" instead of "shall," and preserve more money for the later generations. Or, more liberally, you can allow a trustee to make distributions for non-ascertainable "best interests" or "happiness." Techniques such as naming a co-trustee will provide intermediate levels of control, so skipped children cannot act alone—though you must always keep in mind the "may" versus "shall" verbiage. You can also treat children differently, using GST tax exempt Trusts for some and not others.

The assets of the GST tax exempt Trust are protected from skipped children's creditors (even if those children are both the trustee and the primary beneficiary) because they wear two distinct hats. Absent commingling, sloppy bookkeeping, or a failure to observe the provisions of a GST tax exempt Trust, the two roles are clearly defined and the assets are protected.

Trustees can make distributions to beneficiaries, including themselves, only for HEMS ascertainable standards. Trust assets are protected from the creditors of a beneficiary with only limited powers of appointment. However, a general power of appointment, lifetime or testamentary, will destroy the protective generation skip as it does with any shelter Trust, potentially allowing access to creditors who may pierce the Trust shield and plunder its assets.

If you restrict a skipped child/primary beneficiary/trustee's authority to make distributions based on ascertainable standards/HEMS and ensure that the beneficiary's powers of appointment are limited, he or she may be afforded tremendous authority while still erecting a wall of protection around Trust assets. Just as with any shelter Trust, the most important prohibition is commingling, because it would be a breach of his or her fiduciary obligations as trustee, and the wall around the assets would crumble. Creditors and the contingent default beneficiaries, the ultimate beneficiaries receiving your child's share upon his or her death, assuming no limited power of appointment is exercised (usually your child's own children or nephews and nieces), might successfully sue the primary beneficiary.

Complex facts, laws, and equities all come into play, but a solidly drafted and strictly adhered-to GST tax exempt Trust is a significant barrier to creditors. Even if your children are young, with no children of their own, generation skipping can be an effective strategy to protect assets, whether via a third-party trustee or by allowing your children to incrementally become trustees and gain broad limited powers of appointment at certain ages.

When you consider a GST tax exempt Trust, factors to weigh include your skipped children's need for creditor protection, potential tax savings to their estate, and whether the inheritance amount is worth the additional bookkeeping and income tax reporting. Also, as with any shelter Trust, appreciating assets may incur additional capital gains upon the beneficiary's death.

If the skipped child is also a trustee, consider the child's potential liability to the default contingent beneficiaries—the grandchildren/skip people—if the child commingles or otherwise bungles his or her fiduciary obligations. Rule of thumb: Never let the skipped child who is also the primary beneficiary act as sole trustee over his or her GST tax exempt Trust (or any other Trust, for that matter) if the skipped child is likely to bollix the works.

Dynasty Trusts: A Financial Forever?

The ancient common law Rule against Perpetuities ("Rule") prevents any contingent interest in a Trust, no matter how remote the possibility, from vesting more than "lives in being plus 21 years" after the time the document was created. This short but ridiculously complex doctrine prevents Trusts from lasting forever, so that the king can collect his tax when the lord of the manor dies.

Any clause in a Will or a Trust that violates the Rule invalidates the entire document. "Lives in being" may include any gestating but unborn children. Preposterous possibilities, such as the "fertile octogenarian" and the "precocious toddler," and questions about exactly what a "life in being" is have been the bane of law school students for generations.

Twentieth-century lawyers would often treat the Rule by including a "savings" clause in the Trust: Any violation of the rule results in the offending bequest being excised and the beneficiaries are paid their share of the Trust assets outright, instead of subject to the Trust terms.

In more recent years, some states have abolished it, while others now allow grantors of Trusts to "opt out" of the rule. This trend has paved the way for dynasty or perpetual Trusts to last forever ("perpetual" and "forever" as defined only within our limited human time frame).

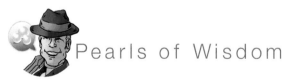

Pearls of Wisdom

I might consider a GST tax exempt Trust, even if I have no grandchildren, to protect my heirs' inheritance.

Chapter 14

$ $ $

Trusts Funded by Disclaimers

Just Say "No!"
- Nancy Reagan -

In This Chapter...

you'll learn that a disclaimer is a form of postmortem estate-planning action that people take to avoid inheriting. Refusing a gift of value is contrary to the human hunter-gatherer nature, but a creative use of disclaimers can confer familial benefits in the long run.

Why Disclaim?

Disclaiming—in effect, saying "no" to a gift—can help accomplish a number of planning goals, which include reducing a combined taxable estate or shielding assets from an inheritor's creditors. Disclaimed assets must flow as if the person disclaiming had predeceased the person from whom he or she is inheriting.

How Disclaimers Work

An effective disclaimer must adhere to certain technicalities, both state and federal, to avoid being treated as a taxable gift. The disclaimer must be made in writing within nine months of the death that triggers the inheritance. During the nine-month period, the person disclaiming must not take any benefit or exercise any control over the assets disclaimed; this includes not cashing dividend or interest checks or reinvesting lapsed certificates of deposit. The person disclaiming cannot direct the asset flow in any direction other than where the assets would have gone had he or she not survived.

An example of a basic disclaimer, without any Trusts: Mom dies without a Will, unmarried, and survived by her two adult children, a son (Child One) and a daughter (Child Two). The children are 50/50 intestate beneficiaries in most states. Child One has three children of his own, while Child Two has no children. If Child One disclaims, his interest in the inheritance passes to his children outright in equal shares. Even if he has historically favored one child over the others, the intestate formula directs the asset flow as if he had not survived Mom. If married Child Two disclaims, no interest passes to her husband, because he is not an intestate heir of Mom. Instead, her share is distributed to Child One, who can further disclaim and allow his sister's assets to flow to his children.

Estate plan documents that anticipate disclaimers work like a pachinko machine: remove a barrier or two, and let the ball fall where it may. Regular shelter Trusts are more like a pinball machine: when triggered, flippers can redirect the ball via limited powers of appointment (Chapter 10).

The disclaimer strategy works only if the disclaiming inheritor shares a commonality of interests with the person from whom he or she is inheriting, because an inheritor who wants to see the money go in a different direction will not disclaim. Disclaiming is therefore typically not a strategy relied on in blended families.

Disclaiming allows assets to flow through a first-level beneficiary to contingent beneficiaries below, but it can also be done surgically by breaking down the ownership of an asset into current and future interests. Documents drafted with disclaiming in mind allow a disclaiming inheritor, even if that person is also the trustee in control, to retain the lifetime benefit of income and principal from Trust assets for HEMS (Chapter 10). Splitting hairs? Maybe, but splitting ownership into its various components can accomplish certain goals with 20/20 hindsight.

Married couples can ease future estate tax uncertainty by weaving disclaimer planning into their Trusts. Picture a combined spousal estate below the approximate $5.5 million threshold for taxes on a single individual. Absent estate tax or control concerns, the survivor should inherit outright or in Trust with general powers of appointment so that he or she does not have to segregate shelter Trust assets and there can be a second basis step-up upon the survivor's death, eliminating potential capital gains taxes. If it turns out that the combined estate exceeds the tax threshold, this can be accomplished through use of a disclaimer. Married couples can employ it in tandem with portability over DSUEA (Chapter 12) to reduce the survivor's taxable estate.

Disclaimer planning between spouses who share a commonality of interests leaves the decision regarding estate tax sheltering to the surviving spouse, by giving him or her an outright gift subject to the potential disclaimer. After the first death, upon examination of the combined estate, the survivor determines whether to make a disclaimer. It can be partial, applying to some but not necessarily all of the estate, to the extent that the survivor believes assets may need to be sheltered from future tax.

Even if you prefer fewer controls being placed on the survivor, consider a shelter Trust, rather than the outright gift/disclaimer method described above, if the combined estate definitely exceeds the approximate $5.5 million applicable exclusion amount.

On one hand, assets left outright and subject only to disclaimer give the survivor total freedom. Without disclaiming, the survivor can invest, spend, and bequeath the inheritance in any manner he or she desires. However, it may lead to an eventual estate tax.

On the other hand, a shelter Trust created by a disclaimer is more restrictive than a regular shelter Trust, because the disclaiming beneficiary can never exercise a power of appointment over the disclaimed assets, restricting the ability to redirect those assets further down the line.

Imagine that your spouse survives you, along with three children. After your death, he or she becomes the trustee of any continuing Trust. Your spouse will receive Trust income and can still take from the principal for his or her HEMS or the HEMS of your descendants.

However, a child who develops special circumstances after one spouse dies can only be properly dealt with by the survivor via the limited powers of appointment of a regular shelter Trust, increasing or decreasing the child's contingent share or subjecting it to new conditions. The surviving spouse can also make lifetime gifts to children or grandchildren, equally or not, from a regular shelter Trust. Meanwhile, the shelter Trust created via disclaimer is not as adaptable.

Consider the following side-by-side comparison of Trust features:

REGULAR SHELTER TRUST	SHELTER TRUST CREATED BY DISCLAIMER
Automatically created upon death and funded pursuant to the structure of the assets. Surviving spouse must live with its terms.	Created only if the surviving spouse decides to create it and follows the rules of disclaiming, within nine months of the first spouse's death. If the Trust is created, assets must flow as if the disclaiming inheritor had predeceased the person from whom he or she is inheriting.
Surviving spouse may be the trustee.	Surviving spouse may be the trustee.
Trustee/spouse may distribute income and principal while still living to him- or herself and/or to other contingent beneficiaries, based on HEMS.	Trustee/spouse may distribute income and principal while still living only to him- or herself, based on HEMS.
Spouse may make lifetime or testamentary gifts equally or unequally to a defined class of people (usually, descendants) or charities during the surviving spouse's lifetime.	No appointment (gifts) can be made to anyone during the surviving spouse's lifetime.
Spouse may change testamentary distribution and add new Trust conditions governing the ultimate beneficiaries' shares following his or her death.	Whatever is left in Trust upon the surviving spouse's death is distributed to the contingent beneficiaries named, and that distribution cannot be changed by the surviving spouse.

In addition to the considerations regarding disclaimers vis-à-vis a surviving spouse, disclaimer language can give your children who are Trust beneficiaries the option to create and fund a GST tax exempt Trust going forward (Chapter 13).

Timeshare Treatment

If you happily own vacation timeshares, particularly those that are deeded, you may wish to transfer ownership of those interests to a Trust so that your heirs can inherit them and avoid probate in the states where the timeshare deeds are recorded.

If, however, when you are given a choice between using your timeshares and paying the yearly maintenance fees, you (and by extension your heirs) would walk away from them, advise your executor and trustee to disclaim the undesirable inherited timeshare assets so that the maintenance fee obligations definitely end when you die. Provide that the contingent beneficiary of the timeshares is the company to whom you write your yearly maintenance check.

 Pearls of Wisdom

I learned that disclaimers can be used as a postmortem estate tax-planning maneuver (along with portability, as discussed in Chapter 12) to lessen estate taxes.

Chapter 15

$ $

Special-Needs Trusts

A society may be judged by how it treats its weakest members.
(Said by various people with different twists, dating back at least as far as Aristotle)

In This Chapter...
you'll see why planning your estate is crucial if you are responsible for a family member unable to care for him- or herself. Even if you are not the person's primary caretaker, consider that a direct gift, made during your lifetime or upon your death, can wreak havoc on his or her life.

Third-Party Special-Needs Trust for Disabled Family Members

The issues of a beneficiary with legally recognized special needs extend beyond his or her ability to handle money. Government-sponsored group housing provides food and shelter. A meaningful life may require enrollment in work, educational, rehabilitative, and social programs, while government stipends may provide any additional bare support. However, all of this government assistance is available only to those with essentially no assets of their own.

A traditional method of keeping a special-needs beneficiary "poor" is to disinherit that person, while creating an informal understanding with another beneficiary who can step in to provide extra funds. Unfortunately, such moral obligations often go dishonored. You may be lucky enough to have a stellar beneficiary with a perfect moral compass, but that script can flip abruptly and unexpectedly, sending money to someone else. Would your son-in-law honor the moral obligations of your daughter/his wife or simply ignore them?

In many cases, buying your way into programs reserved for indigent special-needs people is impossible. Yet a special-needs beneficiary does not have to be at the mercy of the system, especially if a little extra money can make a big difference. He or she simply cannot control the assets.

A third-party special-needs Trust is funded with assets owned by someone other than the primary beneficiary with special needs. Also known as a third-party supplemental-needs Trust, it ensures the fulfillment of the primary beneficiary's future needs without bequeathing the money outright. An outright distribution can disqualify the special-needs beneficiary from government financial aid or programs. A special-needs Trust allows a trustee to supplement the primary beneficiary's needs that are not covered by Medicaid or other government sources. The Trust is not intended to be used to provide basic food, clothing, and shelter or to be available to the primary beneficiary for such until all local, state, and federal benefits for which he or she qualifies have first been exhausted.

The trustee may have the discretion to pay for enhanced quality of life, including:

- The additional cost of a private room, rather than shared.

- The cost of vacations, especially to visit family.

- The cost of a companion or an attendant necessary for travel and other activities.

- Reimbursement for attendance or participation in recreational or cultural events, conferences, seminars, and training sessions.

- Elective medical, dental, or other health services not otherwise provided.

- Exercise equipment.

- Electronics, including cell phones, computer hardware and software, and audio and video equipment.

- Newspaper and magazine subscriptions.

- Additional food, clothing, and whatever else brings the beneficiary dignity, purpose, optimism, and joy.

These expenditures must be paid directly to providers, rather than to the primary beneficiary, to avoid disqualification from or interference with government assistance.

For additional peace of mind, instruct the trustee (or someone the trustee designates) to visit the special-needs beneficiary on a regular basis, inspect his or her living conditions, and evaluate things like:

- The need for physical and dental examinations by independent doctors.

- The primary beneficiary's grooming and overall appearance.

- Education and training programs.

- Work opportunities and earnings.

- Recreation, leisure time, and social needs.

- Appropriateness of existing residential and program services.

- Legal rights to which the primary beneficiary may be entitled, including free public education, rehabilitation, and programs that meet constitutionally mandated standards.

Establish and fund a third-party special-needs Trust for a family beneficiary during your lifetime or upon your death. Most often, the largest amount of funding occurs upon your death, but anyone can make a gift to the Trust once it is established. The special-needs beneficiary can never be the trustee or control the assets of a special-needs Trust.

Any funds remaining upon the death of the special-needs beneficiary are distributed to the designated contingent beneficiaries and are not subject to claims from government agencies.

And us? Can we pay for him to stay here?

Well, there is a process, but you'll need a lawyer to petition the court for an OBRA Trust.

A what?

You'll need a lawyer to explain it. But even if you go that route, I'm not sure Jeff would be able to stay.

I should also tell you...Edward and Susan had been subsidizing Ruben's lifestyle for the past few years. Even if an OBRA trust allows Jeff to stay, none of that money can go to Ruben.

Ed never was a wizard with money or planning, but this is unreal!

First-Party Payback Special-Needs Trusts (OBRA '93)

A person with substantial non-exempt assets, who is otherwise ineligible to receive Medicaid, may still qualify for government benefits through the use of a "payback" Trust, also known as a "first-party," "self-settled," or "OBRA '93 (d)(4)(A)" special-needs Trust. "OBRA '93" is shorthand for Omnibus Budget Reconciliation Act of 1993.

The payback Trust, a type of living Trust, is funded with the primary beneficiary's own assets during his or her lifetime and must reimburse government agencies from remaining Trust funds when the primary beneficiary dies. Payback Trusts are often funded by either a direct inheritance (because no third-party special-needs Trust was established) or money received in settlement of or from a successful lawsuit brought on behalf of the special-needs beneficiary, stemming from the cause of the disability, such as a car accident or medical malpractice. The payback Trust can also prevent child support or alimony from disqualifying a beneficiary.

Unlike a third-party special-needs Trust, only the primary beneficiary's parent, grandparent, or guardian may create a payback special-needs Trust without court approval and only for a primary beneficiary under the age of 65.

OBRA '93 Trusts ensure that special-needs individuals with excess assets remain qualified for Medicaid. Qualification is immediate, and unlike some other programs that confer Medicaid eligibility only following a five-year look-back period (see Chapter 17, "Elder Law/Medicaid" discussion), asset transfers to an OBRA '93 Trust require no look-back period for validity.

A "pooled" Trust may be created for a special-needs person older than age 65, but a bank or a similar institution, rather than a family member, must control all pooled assets. Pooled assets are, however, countable and thus disqualifying, with regard to Medicaid's five-year look-back period.

Compare an OBRA '93 Trust
to a
Third-Party Discretionary Special-Needs Trust.

OBRA '93 TRUST	THIRD-PARTY TRUST
Established with the special-needs person's own assets, often his or her own savings, a direct inheritance, or money from a tort lawsuit brought because of negligence resulting in the disability.	Funded with assets from anyone other than the primary beneficiary, usually via lifetime or testamentary gifts made to the Trust.
Created by the special-needs individual's parent, grandparent, or a guardian appointed by a court with proper jurisdiction. A concerned sibling cannot create an OBRA '93 Trust without court sanction.	Created by anyone other than the primary beneficiary.
Trust assets remaining after the death of the primary beneficiary must first reimburse Medicaid for payments made to or on behalf of the primary beneficiary during that person's lifetime. After Medicaid is fully paid, any remaining balance can go to designated beneficiaries, such as family members or charity.	Upon the death of the primary beneficiary, remaining assets can be distributed to any specified contingent beneficiaries designated by the grantor of the Trust, such as family and charities. There is no Medicaid payback from the third-party Trust.

Decanting

Some states allow for the "decanting" of Trusts. Decanting, similar to disclaimer and portability, is postmortem estate planning. Like fine wine being poured from a bottle into a glass, it allows for an existing "problem" Trust to pour into a new Trust that better serves the needs of the beneficiaries. The trustee, the beneficiary, and the remainder beneficiaries must remain the same, but new terms can account for changed circumstances that constricted a beneficial interest.

Decanting can save a Trust beneficiary who inherits a regular Trust but would have been much better off inheriting via a third-party special-needs Trust. Where provided for by statute, it is a court-free alternative to the OBRA '93 payback Trust. The original Trust can decant into a third-party special-needs Trust to confer all of its benefits to the special-needs beneficiary (as discussed in this chapter) without causing a disqualification or requiring an eventual payback to the government.

Pearls of Wisdom

If I want to leave assets to a special-needs beneficiary, a third-party special-needs Trust will allow my money to be used for the beneficiary's best interests without causing a disqualification from benefits.

If I or some other benefactor do not follow this advice and instead leave assets outright to a special-needs beneficiary, all is not lost. If the beneficiary is under age 65, then an OBRA '93 payback Trust can allow a continuation of benefits, but the assets cannot be preserved for contingent beneficiaries. Plus, the OBRA Trust's involvement with probate court will often result in additional legal fees. In some states, a "bad" Trust can be decanted into one with terms that will not result in the dreaded disqualification from government benefits.

Chapter 16

$$\$\$$

Pet Trusts

A house is not a home without a pet.
- Unknown -

In This Chapter...
you will learn some of the ways to include your non-human
friends and family in your planning.

Love Your Pet?

Are you a pet owner, a pet parent, or an animal companion? Do you own your dog or cat—or does your dog or cat own you? Have you ever bought a birthday present for your pet? Does your pet sleep on your bed? Do you schedule pet play dates? Have you ever decided where to live or vacation based in great measure on whether pets are allowed or whether the place is suitable for your pets?

If you answered yes to any of these questions, your pet is more likely a cherished family member than a possession. According to an American Pet Product Manufacturers Association National Pet Owners Survey, in 2012 Americans spent an estimated $53 billion on their approximately 86 million cats, 78 million dogs, and countless other critters—more than the gross domestic product of more than half of the countries in the world.

Billions are spent yearly on such consumer items and services as:

* Premium dog walking, luxury doggy daycare and spas, top-shelf foods, and boutique clothing and jewelry.

* Pet psychotherapy and chiropractic and acupuncture treatment.

* Animal cosmetic procedures, including canine braces to fix crooked teeth and Neuticles, a testicular implant to make neutered pets look anatomically correct (and, no doubt, improve macho self-esteem).

- Medical procedures, including cancer surgery and expensive drugs. Operations costing $5,000 to $15,000 and more are not unusual.

Stay United with Your Pets

You can place a provision in your revocable living Trust to ensure that you and your pet remain together if you become incapacitated and relocate to a skilled-care facility, if possible.

Pet Trusts

Pets sometimes present difficult end-of-life decisions. Will a treatment or an operation improve quality of life or merely extend suffering? When you are gone, will anyone care enough to spend the money for your pet's cancer surgery or expensive drugs the way you would? Don't you want to know that your pet is provided for?

Historically, pets were considered personal property, but the law has evolved to honor pets as beneficiaries. Be careful not to just bark out instructions, though. Be sure to give them some bite by complying with your state's requirements for a valid and enforceable pet Trust. More than three-quarters of all states have statutes providing for pet Trusts.

Typical pet Trusts, whether established under statute or not:

- Identify pets as lifetime beneficiaries after you die or become incapacitated. The right language can cover current and future pets, so even those not named in your Trust will benefit. Identifying pet beneficiaries also means ensuring that the right animals benefit from your planning. Photos or microchip implanting can prevent misidentification or outright fraud.

- Set aside a suitable amount, anywhere from $5,000 to $50,000 or more. The amount required to properly fund a pet Trust varies, depending on the age and the number of the animal beneficiaries, the type of care you specify, and the compensation level, if any, of both the trustee and the caretaker. A court may reduce an amount that it determines substantially exceeds the high range of expected need. According to a 2008 Lawyers Weekly USA poll, an average pet Trust is funded with $25,000.

- Select a human or a corporate trustee to invest the pet Trust money during your pet's lifetime and dole it out to the caretaker for the pet's care. As with all Trusts, always name contingent trustees, in the event that your initial selection is unable or unwilling to act. No, your pet cannot act as trustee.

- Select a caretaker. If you select an individual, also name contingents, in case the first cannot or will not act. Preferably, you should first discuss with the caretaker his or her willingness to take your pets. For pets without a suitable caretaker, you or your future trustee can pick a nice pet retirement resort.

- Whether people or charities, name a contingent beneficiary to receive any remaining pet Trust assets after the pet dies. Unfortunately, pet Trusts are part of your taxable estate and not regarded as a charitable gift, even if a charity is the contingent beneficiary.

- Consider the conflict of interest faced by a caretaker who is also a contingent beneficiary, because he or she stands to inherit any remainder when the pet dies.

- Specify compensation or a fixed gift for both the trustee and the caretaker, whose gift may be conditioned on properly caring for the pet.

- Consider income tax issues. The Trust will pay income taxes on retained investment earnings. Income paid out in the form of compensation to the trustee or the caregiver is ordinary income to the recipient.

- Leave a detailed plan of care, including such elements as a preferred veterinarian, any preexisting medical conditions, feeding (brands, amounts, and supplements) and grooming needs, plus other important items.

- Direct the ultimate disposition of the pet's remains. Cremation? What to do with the ashes?

- Terminate the pet Trust when it no longer covers any living animal.

First-Class Furry Care

For an endowment fee, programs associated with the veterinary departments of some universities will match your pet's needs, locate the best foster care, and monitor that care for the rest of the pet's life.

Various private companies offer long-term premium boarding services with 24/7 individualized attention, located on acreage that is rural, hilly, and wooded. Some offer the choice between shared suites for social pets or private rooms for the loners, specially prepared meals or their predetermined favorites as you instruct, swimming areas and game-playing, heated beds, massage therapy, and a vet on call 24/7.

Horses, and their enormous costs, typically result in the most difficult pet Trust planning. The average lifespan of a horse is 25 to 30 years. Some live 40 years or more. Is your estate large enough to support the proper provisions?

Not everyone with a beloved family animal needs a pet Trust. My chocolate lab, Chloe, needs no Trust. My only dilemma is deciding how to establish rotating custody of her with fair visitation rights to her many devotees.

Leona, Part II

As the Beatles say, "Money can't buy love." Leona Helmsley left $12 million (reduced by a judge to $2 million) in Trust for her beloved Maltese, Trouble.

None of the people she selected wanted the trouble of caring for the appropriately named ill-tempered beast. The trustees eventually found someone willing to take Trouble . . . for $5,000 a month. Additional annual costs were estimated to be $100,000 for security, $8,000 for grooming, $12,000 for food, and veterinary care of up to $18,000.

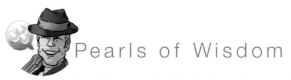

Pearls of Wisdom

A pet Trust may be the best way to ensure that a portion of my bounty will be used for the care of my pets who survive me.

Chapter 17

$ $

Estate-Planning Potpourri

Misers aren't fun to live with, but they make wonderful ancestors.
- David Brenner -

In This Chapter...
you'll learn random nuts and bolts of estate planning,
plus a few typical questions and answers.

How to Hire a Lawyer

It's possible to draft your own estate-planning documents that distribute assets, minimize taxes, and ameliorate or avoid death probate. Templates are available on the Internet or in bookstores. Or, you can hire a lawyer.

Most lawyers rely on formbooks written by banks and legal software companies, perhaps the same forms found online. The problem with basic forms is that they usually require circumstantial tweaks; a change to Article IV may crosswire Section 7.4 or Section 9.1, and so forth, and so on.

A good lawyer must understand estate planning, the forms he or she is using, and the effect of changing them. Find a lawyer who understands both the nuances of estate planning and your priorities, someone who concentrates a significant portion of his or her practice on estate planning. Avoid lawyers who fill in the blanks of a basic template they don't truly comprehend.

If you don't know an estate-planning lawyer, ask around. Check with friends, a knowledgeable acquaintance, your financial advisors, or your CPA. Search the Internet. Many offer a free or flat-fee initial consultation. Be prepared for the meeting, but you shouldn't have to do too much. Chapter 6 discusses the organizational process. If interviewing a lawyer, ask what you should bring.

When meeting a prospective client for the first time, I like to first obtain contact information. Then I want the names (and the contact information, if important to the estate plan) of the players: all living ancestors, descendants, siblings, and siblings' descendants. This gives me a picture of the overall family. I may also need the names and the contact information of trusted friends or anyone else who might appear anywhere in your documents. From these people, you will select your primary and contingent beneficiaries, guardians for your minor or special-needs children, and trusted agents to make health-care decisions and handle your finances upon your incapacity or death.

An initial consultation with the lawyer generally lasts an hour or two. Good communication is essential, because the initial consultation is an opportunity to assess the attorney's personality, competence, and skills. Don't underestimate the importance of personality. Find someone with whom you can work efficiently and feel comfortable discussing the potentially intimate details of your family and finances. You both must come to a shared understanding of the pertinent issues in your life as they relate to your planning. If you don't click with a particular attorney, that's enough reason to continue to search.

After your first meeting, ask yourself three questions:

1. Did he or she listen to what you had to say and ask the right questions to flesh out your wishes?

2. Did the attorney communicate his or her own thoughts in a manner you understood?

3. Is he or she experienced in estate planning? If you don't feel as if you can judge the attorney's professional competency, ask someone else to speak with him or her.

The next obvious question is cost. The lawyer should be able to give you a price or at least a fee range. Find out what is or is not included in the representation.

If the lawyer offers an engagement letter, sign it if you are comfortable with his or her competence, you feel that your personalities mesh, and you have a meeting of the minds regarding the scope of the work. If you are not immediately certain whether you wish to proceed with the lawyer, bring the engagement letter home and cogitate about it. Discuss it with others, perhaps another lawyer.

Once you begin, the lawyer should continue to provide the same level of attention that you received initially. Does he or she return your telephone calls or emails promptly? The number-one reason for client dissatisfaction with lawyers and other service professionals is failure to return communications. If you feel your lawyer is not diligently working on your estate plan, voice your dissatisfaction. If necessary, find another lawyer.

Prior to signing your estate plan, review draft documents with your lawyer. If you don't understand something that looks important, speak up. A lawyer who understands your goals should be adept at patiently explaining how the provisions of your documents apply to your life. If you feel you have attained a meeting of the minds, you will enjoy some degree of estate-planning bliss.

Where to Keep Your Documents

Some attorneys keep all original signed documents and give clients electronic versions, photocopies, or "conformed" copies. Conformed copies of Wills usually have no signatures, but the names and the addresses of the witnesses are typed in. Others give their clients all of the originals and keep only electronic versions or photocopies on file. If your attorney keeps the originals, inquire as to their location and safety. If the lawyer is a sole practitioner or has a small office, ask about the lawyer's own succession plan and who will handle the documents in the event of his or her own death.

If the lawyer who drafted your documents holds them in safekeeping, your family is not obliged to hire him or her to modify or carry out the plan.

For many documents, photocopies will suffice, but an original Will lost by a client is generally presumed to have been revoked, even if a photocopy can be produced. That presumption probably does not apply to an original lost by the attorney in whose care it was placed. If the original documents are in your possession, it is vital to store them in a safe, yet accessible, place, such as a bank safe-deposit box or a fireproof safe in your home.

Keep a photocopy or an electronic version of any originals in a readily available safe-deposit box, to avoid a trip to the bank or a call to your lawyer whenever you need to check a provision or show it to a financial institution or a medical provider. I sometimes send clients .pdfs of their signed documents as an email attachment. There are also online estate-plan storage vaults that allow worldwide access.

The rules governing access to your safe-deposit box when you die vary by state and by bank. Most banks will seal a box on learning of the death of its sole lessor; some will do so even if there is a surviving authorized signer. Be certain to understand the bank's rules before storing your original estate plan documents there.

If you keep documents in a solely owned safe-deposit box, be sure to name an authorized signer or a joint lessee. Without one, the bank may require your heirs to open a probate estate just to gain access. You don't have to give away the key, but tell someone where it is or put it in a place where it will be found. When beneficiaries do not trust one another, require the beneficiaries to open it together upon your death, to avoid a perception that the box was looted. For suspicious children, it may be worthwhile to give one child the safe deposit box key and another signing authority, forcing them to accompany each other to rummage through its contents.

If you use a home safe for your documents, give the combination or an extra key to someone you trust. Security experts recommend bolting smaller safes to the frame of the house to prevent burglars from simply walking away with them.

Financial information should also be accessible. Uncertain beneficiaries who may have missed insurance policies in your records can request, for a modest fee, a policy locator search from Medical Information Bureau (MIB) Solutions (mibpolicylocator.com). MIB claims access to more than 180 million insurance records that may provide an executor with the information necessary to file a claim on behalf of the estate.

Ernie Banks. January 31, 1931 – January 23, 2015

Mr. Cub signed a Will 3 months before death. His caretaker/manager got everything. The jilted family stepped up to bat, but may strike out in court.

Reviewing Your Plan

Review your documents periodically to account for changing needs and circumstances. Structure your assets to efficiently use existing planning.

Top 6 Changes That May Trigger the Need for a Review:

1. Have your children attained legal adulthood since you signed your Will? Are they now capable of making decisions on their own? Can they be trusted with larger sums of money? When a child matures to where you would be comfortable giving him or her full control over an inheritance, consider eliminating existing restrictions.

2. Have there been deaths, marriages, births, or divorces in your family? How has your family evolved? Documents often provide for future children, but new kids should make you think again about your plan. In some states, a divorce will nullify a spousal bequest in a Will unless the gift is renewed, but various joint tenancy assets and retirement plans and life insurance policies with beneficiary designations may still go to a former spouse. Review asset structure and consider changing your Trust upon divorce, even if its terms automatically cancel any bequest to an ex-spouse.

3. Do additional family members have special needs? If an heir is no longer able to care for him- or herself or make financial decisions, bequests to that person must be reviewed.

4. Have any of your fiduciaries died, become disabled, moved, or otherwise changed, so that they are no longer able to serve your estate plan?

5.   Have your financial circumstances changed? Have you inherited assets? If your employment status or the size of your estate is substantially different, it is time for a review.

6.   Have you moved? Residency in a new state can have consequences for estate plans.

Even if nothing has changed (other than everyone aging), examine your plan every three to five years. After five to seven years, financial powers of attorney may go stale. Laws that continually change, mostly incrementally but sometimes drastically, may majorly impact your plan.

If your lawyer retires or your confidence in him or her falters, find a new one to do the review. At an initial consultation, either free or for a modest fee, most lawyers will examine your current plan and comment on how they would update it.

Can you update your own plan, or do you need your lawyer for even the smallest alteration? Though you should defer to the understanding you have with your lawyer, making certain changes is possible on your own. Here are the top three:

1.   *Address changes.* If a fiduciary or a beneficiary moves away from a listed address, you might be able to write the new address into the plan yourself without a problem. Advise your lawyer to update his or her records as well. Your lawyer may feel more comfortable making those changes formally.

2.   *Specific tangible personal property distributions, if initially handled properly.* Your Trust can reference a separate list of assets, so if you acquire new tangible personal property ("stuff") or change to whom it goes, it may be easy to make those changes yourself. This less formal method, while efficient, is not as ironclad as listing items directly in a Will or a Trust itself. Most states do not formally permit separate lists used in conjunction with a Will, unless executed with the same formality as the Will, but many people do this informally anyway, and their wishes are often honored.

3.   *New children or grandchildren are born or adopted.* An estate plan written to account for the possibility of new additions to the family may not require lawyer updates every time there is a birth. When you first draw up the plan, discuss this with your lawyer. Also discuss whether future adopted descendants should be beneficiaries. You can draw an age line ("if adopted before the age of 12") or distinguish between those whom your child adopts together with a spouse, as opposed to those already born to a spouse of your child; this is akin to changing the status of step-descendants to actual descendants.

Many other changes require the deft drafting skill of a lawyer. Crossing off or writing in heirs and changing bequests or fiduciaries is not something that you should get in the habit of doing. Such informal alterations may not withstand attack from someone who feels slighted or may not be honored by financial service companies or health-care professionals.

When you meet with a lawyer to review your estate plan, examine the structure of your assets, too. Ownership and beneficiary designations can be just as important as the EP documents.

Moving to Another State

Estate planning and administration law is uniform in many respects throughout the United States, but there are differences among states. In an attempt to unify various state laws, many states have adopted a statute known as the Uniform Probate Code.

The U.S. Constitution requires that "full faith and credit shall be given in each state to the public acts, records and judicial proceedings of every other state." Generally, this means that a legal document valid in the state where it was signed is valid anywhere in the country. So a Will, a Trust, or a power of attorney that's valid in a certain state should be valid nationwide and may be valid in other countries. However, if you move to another state, it is prudent to review your estate plan with an attorney there.

Income tax issues make this particularly true if you are married and move to a community property (CP) state. CP states include Arizona, California, Idaho, Louisiana, Nevada, New Mexico, Texas, Washington, and Wisconsin (plus Alaska, if the couple agree to characterize certain assets as community property ones). CP states classify marital assets as owned equally between spouses.

In non-CP states, two Trusts are often preferable to divide assets between spouses for estate tax reasons, although the increased estate tax exemption (see Chapter 20) and the potential use of portability (see Chapter 12) are making single Trusts more popular. In a CP state, a married couple with equally valuable assets will usually share a single Trust to take advantage of favorable capital gains treatment.

Powers of attorney (proxies), for both health care and finances, are also state-specific, so it is prudent to use your state's form. Financial institutions and health-care workers are quicker to honor the statutory document they are used to seeing. An initial refusal to honor a relatively strange document can cause delays and hassles while other people or committees are consulted on its efficacy.

No lawyer understands the legal nuances of every state. If you move to another state, have your estate plan reviewed by a lawyer in the new jurisdiction—especially if you intend to stay there.

Selecting a Trustee: Banks Versus Individuals

As trustee of your revocable living Trust, you can name either an individual or a bank as a successor trustee.

Selecting a person as successor trustee requires contingency planning. Your first choice may die, become incapacitated, move to the other side of the globe, or just drop off the face of the planet. Select one or more backups, in case your original choice cannot act.

Pick people for the right reasons. If choosing among your children, do not designate your eldest based solely on age. He or she is not necessarily the wisest, fairest, or most detail oriented. Your eldest child's feelings may be hurt, but so be it. Favoritism based on solid reasoning is not a bad thing.

You may also select individual co-trustees who work well together. While a single trustee can conceivably become drunk with power, two can create gridlock. Selecting three has the advantage of the co-trustees making decisions by deferring to the majority. Any more than three, and your co-trustee structure might become unwieldy. While still living and competent, you can change your choice of trustee, present or future, just as you can any of the revocable living Trust's other terms.

I'm not generally a big fan of naming estate planning attorneys as trustees by virtue of simply being your estate planning attorneys. Appropriateness may depend on your relationship. A longtime family lawyer, intimately familiar with your family's dynamics, may make a great trustee or co-trustee. If your relationship is new, however, this individual may not be the best choice. Consider the limited resources of a sole practitioner or a relatively small firm and (as with the lawyer retaining your original documents) whether the lawyer has his or her own detailed business succession plan.

When selecting an individual trustee (and the same reasoning applies when selecting an agent for property or an executor), look for certain qualities:

- Exemplary ethics and sound judgment;

- Trustworthiness; and

- A sense of responsibility, enough not to put the unopened bank and brokerage statements in a drawer and forget about them.

If you are concerned that an individual might be overwhelmed by the complexity of the Trust—an argument often used by bank Trust departments to encourage the use of their services—simply grant the person the authority to appoint a co-trustee, such as a bank. If he or she is honest and capable of making informed decisions without being unduly influenced by a bad player, then even a person who lacks financial acumen may be the right choice as trustee, especially since he or she can always hire an attorney, CPA or other professional advisor to assist in managing the Trust, if necessary.

Banks offer impartiality, emotional detachment, continuity, and investment expertise. They don't get sick, die, or move away. They don't share family grudges or rivalries. They will understand the documents and transparently account for asset distributions. For all of these reasons and more, banks are often by far the best choice as trustee for larger estates. It is what they are paid to do every day.

You may give your beneficiaries the authority to select or replace any corporate trustee with another corporate trustee. An untouchable bank may act arrogantly toward your beneficiaries, whereas beneficiaries who can fire the bank may get better treatment.

The drawback of choosing a bank as trustee is cost, typically 1 to 2 percent annually. Of course, the net cost of not using a professional trustee could be much higher if the selected individual does poorly. Handling an estate can present a daunting task for even the most intelligent trustee. Another option is to pair the individual trustee/beneficiary (say, your adult child) with the bank, so he or she can rely on the bank's expertise, while maintaining a measure of control. Banks generally do not discount fees, however, just because there is an individual co-trustee.

The minimum fees charged by banks often make them inappropriate for small Trust estates. Generally, unless your estate is worth more than $250,000, the fees charged by large financial institutions may be prohibitive. Some have minimum fees that justify a $100,000 account, but $1 million is more typical. If the value of your estate does not approach $1 million and you want to use a bank, look carefully at the fee/service continuum. A community bank may be best, particularly for an estate on the smaller side.

You Are Named as Trustee! Congratulations or Condolences?

While you may consider the appointment an honor, it can also be disorienting and painful. Battling beneficiaries, ambiguous Trust language, and weird circumstances are recipes for a volatile cocktail, one with ensuing personal liability if not mixed correctly. If you are not sole beneficiary or have no general power of appointment, drink carefully. You may have to account to remainder beneficiaries for your actions.

Before you become a trustee, do an honest self-assessment. Are you focused? Can you sweat the details? Be prudent with money? Are your own personal financial affairs in order? Are you organized? If you are able to make discretionary distributions to a beneficiary, are you able to say "no" to unreasonable demands?

Nine suggestions:

1. Follow all Trust terms. If assets are distributed outright, that job is easier than one where the trustee has continuing discretion and must balance the needs of current and future beneficiaries.

2. *Keep good records.*

3. *Communicate with the beneficiaries (and do not communicate confidential Trust information with non-beneficiaries, except as required). How might handling their money affect your existing relationship with the beneficiaries? Would any of them benefit from anger-management therapy to curb their bullying? Would you stand up to bad behavior, or would you hide?*

4. *Do not favor one beneficiary over another.*

5. *Obtain professional help, especially if you don't completely understand your role or if you need help with special assets, such as a business or real estate. Hire an attorney to represent you as trustee. Accounting, legal, and appraisal fees are ordinarily paid by the Trust.*

6. *If there are sufficient assets, consider appointing a corporate co-trustee to do the heavy lifting.*

7. *Know where the exits are. If you feel in over your head, exit stage left with a predetermined strategy.*

8. *Keep track of your time, even if you don't think that you will need or want compensation.*

9. *Do not self-deal (steal, borrow, charge unreasonably high trustee fees, and invest in business transactions where you profit) or fall into conflict-of-interest situations.*

Investment Policy Statements

As a protective roadmap for a successor trustee, consider creating a written investment policy statement (IPS) to articulate objectives, such as investment guidelines, risk tolerance, performance goals, diversification requirements, communication expectations, and review parameters.

An IPS provides guidance to the future trustee. Whether written by you or the successor trustee, it offers protection from disgruntled beneficiaries unsatisfied with the Trust's performance, compared to the overall market, and also gives the beneficiaries ammunition against a trustee who skirts the boundaries of the statement without adequate justification.

Investment policy statements should be flexible. An IPS set in stone may not serve the best interests of the beneficiaries, if circumstances change considerably. Do not create a Trust or an IPS that sets up roadblocks, rather than providing safe and effective routes.

Guidance, Not Handcuffs

I've had clients who take the idea of an investment policy too far. You can pass on an investment philosophy with spectacular details if you wish, but your own successful history of investing does not mean you should tie the hands of future trustees, forcing them to retain particular securities or keep a real estate portfolio intact.

Discussing Your Estate Plan with Future Beneficiaries

The decision to discuss your estate plan with future beneficiaries depends on your family and the possible issues that your plan presents. Sharing a plan that treats everyone equally can facilitate a smooth transition.

Yet what if certain issues are bound to stoke controversy? If a beneficiary who receives less than his or her siblings learns of your intent, it may be more difficult later on for this beneficiary to contest your wishes. Alternatively, it might be foolish to exacerbate an existing familial conflict and cultivate discord earlier than necessary. Some issues are best left for later. You understand your family's dynamics best, so only you can decide when the time is right.

Consulting with Your Fiduciaries

It is usually best to advise fiduciaries—that is, trustees, executors, guardians, and agents for property and health care—of their future roles. This is especially true for guardians.

Are you certain that the person you name as guardian will not see caring for your children as a major imposition? It's better to know early if someone does not want to or cannot act. If you select a guardian without consulting that person first, then when your children are dropped at his or her doorstep, the individual may resent you, possibly taking it out on the children. Or the person may feel overwhelming guilt for declining to act as guardian.

Try not to concern yourself with the hurt feelings created by your fiduciary selections. Making these choices can be difficult and may stir bad feelings and jealousies, but you must not let those fears dictate your selection.

The Importance of Record Keeping

Record keeping, especially regarding cost basis, can be tedious, but you may need it later. Many investors fail to keep track of an asset's basis, the price you paid for purchases. When inheriting assets other than cash, record the value of the asset at the time of the owner's death as your stepped-up basis. Use it later to measure gains and the resulting tax on sale.

For stock gifted during the lifetime of the person giving it, determining basis may be more difficult because you must know its value at the time it was purchased. It's better to ascertain the basis of a lifetime gift when the donor is alive, so ask questions sooner, rather than later.

When a financial professional cannot help establish basis, contact the corporation whose stock it is or the transfer agent listed on the share certificate. They might help you determine the stock's basis, but a stock purchased fifty years ago may have split ten times and changed names, or it may have been acquired at various times through a dividend reinvestment plan (DRIP), leading to a basis labyrinth.

Consult a real estate appraiser if you receive a lifetime gift of real estate that you wish to sell. If you have no information on the property, the appraiser can access historical data and prepare something for you that may be acceptable to the IRS. The basis of real estate may also be elevated by the value of subsequent capital improvements.

Elder Law and Medicaid

Elder law is a hybrid of various legal issues facing older Americans. Historically, estate planning addressed many of them before elder law became a specialty area of law. Demand for disability planning (particularly, powers of attorney), guardianships (most commonly needed for those who become disabled and lack valid powers of attorney), Medicaid eligibility, and elder abuse (including exploitation and neglect by family members, caretakers, and nursing home staff), together with an aging population, combine to make this a growing legal field.

Where abuse allegations are made, social service agencies and professionals may work alongside police and lawyers, leading to civil actions brought by families to recover stolen money and criminal prosecutions that may result in years of incarceration for those who prey on the elderly and other vulnerable individuals.

Myriad segments of the U.S. economy are geared toward aging, including health care, evolving housing needs, and home assistance, whether by skilled-care professionals or simply competent companions.

Many elderly people wish to stay in their own homes. With sufficient resources, you may direct in your durable power of attorney for property (Chapter 8) and revocable living Trust (Chapter 9) that, if necessary, you receive 24/7 home care while you can afford it, rather than reside in a facility.

Three Questions for When You Turn 50:

1. Are you ready to welcome your silver years and join AARP?

2. Will you follow your physician's advice and get a colonoscopy?

3. Should you invest in long-term care insurance?

Some people have physical limitations that prevent them from living at home, and they are left with only the option of an assisted living facility or a nursing home and a swollen annual price tag of $100,000 or more. Medicare may cover only one hundred days per year of nursing home rehabilitation, provided that you show improvement from treatment. After that, you must pay (and pay and pay) until you have substantially exhausted all of your assets. Few things destroy an estate faster than a long stay in an assisted living or nursing home.

Planning for those places may involve buying long-term care insurance (which includes the home care preferred by so many), but many people put off buying it until it is cost-prohibitive, due to their age and/or poor health. Long-term care insurance bought in your mid-40s to mid-60s may make economic sense. The industry trend is to package it with a universal life insurance policy.

Naturally, some older people (and their future presumptive inheritors) are eager to shelter assets so that Medicaid, a needs-based federal program administered by each state, will pay for the residential facility. However, keep in mind that Medicaid cares for indigent people. To qualify, your assets may total no more than about $2,000, plus enough life insurance to pay for your burial and a few possibly exempt assets.

Though not meant for wealthy people who purposefully impoverish themselves, Medicaid will sometimes pay for those who give away all of their assets to their children or others. "Spending down" to qualify for Medicaid by transferring assets to others can work, but when the government determines your Medicaid eligibility, it typically counts as assets gifts made to people or Trusts within a five-year "look-back" period prior to the Medicaid application.

Any asset transferred for less than full consideration is viewed as a gift of the value of the difference, so selling your house to your daughter for a dollar is not a legitimate impoverishment strategy. In general, qualifying for Medicaid without giving up the bulk of your assets requires planning long in advance and finding a way to support yourself during any look-back period.

Bad news for married people: the assets of the community spouse (the healthy one) must also be minimal. Most states allow the healthy spouse no more than about $110,000, plus certain exempt assets. Some states permit the community spouse to seek a court order to increase that amount if he or she has a solid reason for doing so.

What qualifies as exempt assets varies from state to state and may include things such as a principal residence, an automobile, and burial insurance. Medicaid will not force the sale of a principal residence while you, your spouse, or a dependent child are living there, but it can put a lien on the residence so that the state is reimbursed on an eventual sale.

While transfer of a primary residence to a non-dependent child during the look-back period would normally disqualify the parent from receiving Medicaid, there is a prominent exception. If the child in question has resided in the property for at least two years prior to the parent entering nursing care, and during that time provided care that, until that point, was essential in allowing the parent to remain at home, then the transfer may be disregarded, allowing the parent to qualify for Medicaid. To ensure this result, the child should keep detailed records of his or her time living with the parent and the caregiving efforts made to keep the parent at home.

Unfortunately, some people find that divorce is the only way to preserve the bulk of their estate when a spouse is incapacitated over a long period of time, and even that tactic does not always provide a clear path, especially if one spouse lacks capacity. The potential drainage of another person's assets to pay for long-term care is one of the few advantages non-traditional relationships have over married couples in the world of estate planning, especially when the marriage occurs late in life.

In the past, people have sought to simultaneously protect their assets and qualify for Medicaid through the use of irrevocable Trusts or certain annuities, but federal and state laws have frustrated many of these maneuvers, and the investment choices are extremely limited. Another strategy involves the community spouse refusing to disclose assets, but this tactic can result in a loss of the community spouse's social security and other benefits. This particular strategy may also slow down system benefits with miles of bureaucratic red tape, agitating the intended nursing home recipient.

Who Is the Client?

Some lawyers dread meeting with adult children who want their parents to qualify for Medicaid. On top of government agencies trying to put an end to the spend-down strategy as being just plain wrong, attorneys face an additional ethical problem, namely: Who is the client, the parent or the child?

Typically, adult children claim they need advice on the best way to "protect" Mom's money, but they are really trying to protect or accelerate their inheritance.

Usually, the client is the person whose assets are being spent down, and without his or her cooperation and full understanding, efforts to do so are problematic for all concerned. Mom or Dad must clearly be competent and understand fully what she or he is doing. A lawyer could help adult children transfer Mom's or Dad's assets to her or his descendants in good faith, thinking this is what the individual wants, then might wind up in court against Mom or Dad, who is shouting, "They stole my money," while pointing at the children and the attorney perceived as complicit.

Estate Planning ≠ Financial Planning

Estate planning does not replace financial planning. Financial planners make specific investment recommendations, determine your present and future financial needs and goals, and strategize to get you there within your risk parameters.

The two professions do intertwine. A financial planner will provide investment assistance to preserve/grow principal or provide income. An estate-planning attorney provides the documentation to structure your investments and other wealth. A financial planner who is not an attorney is prohibited from drafting estate plan documents, but a financial plan often highlights estate-planning needs. If you employ both a financial planner and an estate-planning attorney, these professionals should cooperate to give you and your family a comprehensive plan.

Pearls of Wisdom

I obtained answers to some of the most common real-world questions that may occur to me as I navigate the estate-planning road.

Mara & Britta—What's For Charity?

Chapter 18

$$

What's for Charity?
Part 1

No one has ever become poor by giving.
- Anne Frank -

In This Chapter...
you'll learn why charitable giving is central to many estate plans.
Enhance your legacy and elevate the lives of others.

Giving Spirit

Being dead is free. There is no need for money. No more eating or going on vacation. No tuition bills. No property taxes or rent. No need to buy this or that. No keeping a nest egg for peace of mind. All of the money, equity, and things that you depended on to support your lifestyle and well-being is distributed to others. Accumulation is no longer important—only distribution and disposal remains.

Giving comes naturally to people who have a genuinely charitable spirit toward those outside their immediate loved ones. Their philanthropic activities and good deeds can continue from beyond the great divide. If you have been materially successful but too distracted, selfish, lazy, or fearful of depleting your nest egg to pay sufficient attention to charitable endeavors, then your estate plan is the final opportunity to conquer those shortcomings and contribute to the greater good.

Charity begins at home, but it does not end there. Charitable acts can skip along for years after death. Ponder the causes you can support, the people you can help, and the beauty you can enhance and preserve. The countless possibilities can be ramped up to help great numbers of people or scaled back for a single family in need. If your riches are plentiful and your intended beneficiaries financially secure, use this unique opportunity to help others and soothe your soul.

Give creatively or simply, quietly or loudly, with or without tax benefit. No matter how it's done, charity is invariably a legacy enhancer. Of course, even the most generous thoughts accomplish nothing without action.

Do Unto Others - Planned Giving

Tikkun olam ("repairing the world") is central to Judaism, comprised in part by *mitzvot* (good deeds) that include tzedakah, a righteous duty of justice and obligation. While charity as a spontaneous act of generosity to the poor or needy or to a worthy cause is a *mitzvah* (good deed), tzedakah goes further, approaching the estate planning concept of planned giving, which is thoughtful and systematic giving that requires special effort.

Twelfth-century philosopher Maimonides defined eight rungs of the tzedakah ladder, each greater in virtue than the previous, bringing the giver closer to heaven.

In descending order, they are:

1. Giving a poor person work (or lending him or her money to start a business) so that the individual will not have to continue to depend on charity. The giver has then helped the recipient both short term and for the rest of his or her life. "Give a man a fish, you have fed him for today. Teach a man to fish, and you have fed him for a lifetime." Also, once the master has taught the pupil how to fish, he can sell him fishing equipment.

2. Giving anonymously to an unknown recipient.

3. Giving anonymously to a known recipient.

4. Giving publicly to an unknown recipient.

5. Giving before being asked.

6. Giving adequately after being asked.

7. Giving willingly, but inadequately.

8. Giving unwillingly.

Virtuous and regular giving builds strong communities and supports those members who may have otherwise become destitute as the victims of catastrophic loss from disaster or illness. Though given different names, every major religion instills some version of charitable giving.

Christian almsgiving is an expression of love towards those less fortunate. Common to most denominations is the collection of tithes (meaning "tenth" in old English, for the suggested portion of earnings to give) to support the church's mission and the community. Private acts of charity, done out of love and not for acclaim or admiration, are most encouraged.

One of the five pillars of Islam is *zakat*, an obligatory practice governed by a strict set of rules requiring all Muslims to give 2.5% of their earnings and saving and a greater percentage of their harvest to the poor. Islam teaches that all wealth and things belong to the Almighty, we simply hold it in trust.

Hindu, Buddhist, Jain and Sikh teachings all include *dāna*, which is, in part, an act of relinquishing one's ownership and investing in another with no expectation of return. Dāna is a form of good karma and makes the giver wealthier.

Tzedakah, tithing, zakat and dāna are only a sample of religious/cultural concepts that have evolved to become universal guides for giving. Whatever your belief, consider setting aside a meaningful portion of your estate for others because it is the right thing to do. If you decide you have the money and the inclination to make a difference, large or small, quietly or publicly, put it in writing.

Charitable Charger

Empower your children with your giving. Set aside a percentage of your estate for each of them to direct to a charity or charities of their choice.

Consider:

- The mojo boost of supporting a dear cause, enhancing the world's beauty, or helping those in need.

- The lesson of selflessness that your beneficiaries learn from your charitable example.

- The honor or praise recognizing your gift: a plaque at your club, a brick at the park, a bench at the neighborhood garden, or a scholarship fund named for you or your family.

- The estate tax advantages of eliminating the value of any gifts from your taxable estate.

- Lifetime or testamentary gifts, made by using planned giving techniques with varying degrees of flexibility and lifetime control; income streams for charities, the donor, or other individuals; elimination of capital gains taxes; potential income tax deductions; an active role for your beneficiaries within the charitable structure of your gift; and ultimate disposition of the assets.

In 2006, Warren Buffet announced that he planned to donate $44 billion to charity, including $30 billion to the Bill & Melinda Gates Foundation. Few people can identify with those numbers, but he obviously sees more important applications for his wealth than simply free-riding his family. He notably described the perfect inheritance as ". . . enough money so that they (family members) feel they could do anything, but not so much that they could do nothing."

A Lyrical Message

Sue began her Will: "You can't always get what you want . . . ," using the Rolling Stones to teach her adult children a lesson. They may be disappointed that her generosity cost them their inheritance, but the money was hers to give as she pleased. She hopes they hear her final message about giving.

Finding the Right Charities

U.S. domestic charities must meet the requirements of IRS code section 501(c)(3), exempting charitable organizations from paying income taxes and granting tax deductions to those who give to them. Because religious organizations generally also have 501(c)(3) status, donations to your church, synagogue, mosque, or temple are probably deductible.

Where should you give? All of the need, suffering, and extreme poverty in our otherwise beautiful world make it easy to find a favorite cause. Locally, your house of worship and alma mater are obvious choices. Beyond that, well-known institutions such as the United Way, the American Red Cross, the Salvation Army, and the ASPCA do great work. There are thousands of worthy organizations, whether working in tiny niches or benefiting humanity on a massive scale.

A few charitable causes to consider:

- Feed the hungry.
- Educate those who cannot afford books, let alone tuition.
- Clothe the needy.
- Help a family avoid the choice between eating or staying warm.
- Fund research and treatment of a disease or a medical condition.
- Help someone afford to get or stay healthy.
- Protect vulnerable children.
- Give to veterans who have defended our way of life.
- Benefit those in active military service who currently defend our way of life.
- Subsidize a high school arts or athletic program that fell victim to budget cuts.
- Repair or enhance the environment.
- Plant a neighborhood garden.
- Help aid abandoned or abused animals.
- Endow the arts.
- Subsidize bus rides to the store or a medical clinic for the elderly.

Visit www.charitynavigator.org, a 501(c)(3) organization that evaluates charities and helps givers locate trustworthy organizations in areas of interest. Since its inception, the company has examined more than 10,000 charities and currently rates more than 5,000 as one to four stars. It categorizes charities by the type of work performed (animals, environment, arts, health, education, religious, etc.) and shines a light on both well-run (where most of the money goes to its mission) and poorly run organizations (where too much lines the pockets of operators or goes into annual fundraisers). The website can filter charities by star rating or rate a specific organization by request, also comparing it with other similar charities.

Put Airline Miles to Good Use

Specifically bequeath unused airline miles to an organization that could use them to move relief personnel to disaster areas, transport those who need medical care to distant hospitals, or grant wishes to children and others. Certain airlines allow testamentary transfers to specific organizations whose missions are substantially tied to the need for airline transport and have strategic alliances in place. As with other "virtual" assets, be sure to leave the necessary password information!

BASIS – Acquisition cost of an asset, used to calculate gains and losses.

CAPITAL GAIN – The profit on the sale of an asset that has grown in value, the difference between the basis and the net proceeds.

CAPITAL GAINS TAX – The tax paid on realization of a capital gain.

Tax Breaks

The IRS has long supported the noble tradition of American community spirit by rewarding charitable gifts with tax breaks. Though a charitable urge is the prime motivation to give, substantial tax advantages may follow, including deductions that can offset income and the elimination of capital gains tax that is paid when selling an appreciated asset during your lifetime.

Assets gifted during your lifetime or transferred at death to charities and other 501(c)(3) organizations are also disregarded when computing estate and gift taxes.

Michael Jackson. August 29, 1958 – June 25, 2009

Between 2010 & 2013 K of P's estate grosses > any living artist. Will leaves 20% to charity, balance to mom & kids. Nothing to dad, who challenges & loses.

The Sebastian Kresge Story

In 1899, Sebastian S. Kresge opened a modest store in downtown Detroit. Eventually, Kresge's evolved into the giant retailer Kmart, land of the blue light special, with more than 1,800 stores and 220,000 employees. In January 2002, Kmart filed for Chapter 11 bankruptcy protection, but thereafter merged with Sears to try to remain a viable retail entity.

Meanwhile, back in 1924, Mr. Kresge, with a personal gift of $1.3 million, had established the Kresge Foundation to "promote the well-being of mankind." Today, the Kresge Foundation grants support to a broad range of organizations, reflecting almost the entire array of the nonprofit sector, a $3 billion foundation that distributed more than $120 million in 2013. This illustrates how a charitable legacy can outlast all of the other good and great things we do during our lives.

Picking the Best Assets to Donate

A portfolio may include a low-basis appreciated asset that is best sold for diversification purposes. Selling it means paying capital gains tax. That asset makes a great lifetime gift to charity because it means a tax deduction of its full value (up to a certain percentage of your income), and the capital gains disappear.

The same asset, held until death, goes to the beneficiary with a stepped-up basis (computed using a date of death value), eliminating all accrued capital gains taxes. This low-basis item, gifted during your lifetime to an individual beneficiary, is fully taxed, using a carryover basis when it is subsequently sold.

Assets under the umbrella of an IRA or another retirement plan require further analysis. As pre-tax investments, they generally have a $0 basis, meaning that every dollar withdrawn during your life or after your death by a beneficiary is fully taxed in the income tax bracket of the person making the withdrawal.

The only IRA beneficiaries exempt from fully taxed required minimum distributions (RMDs) are charities, making them spectacular IRA beneficiaries. Benefit a great cause with completely tax-free assets. Unfortunately, there are limits placed on lifetime gifts of IRAs to charities. See below and Chapter 19 for more about testamentary gifts of IRAs to charity, including the care that's necessary when you designate charitable organizations as beneficiaries.

How to Make a Testamentary Charitable Gift

The simplest form of testamentary charitable donation is an outright gift upon death via a Will or a Trust, with or without strings attached. The asset gifted is not part of the taxable estate. Naming a charity as a beneficiary of insurance, annuities, and other financial holdings is one way to make the transfer. A charity is also a great IRA beneficiary, provided you do not name individuals and charitable beneficiaries in the same account.

Specify a use (i.e., a gift to your church's "building fund" or your alma mater "to fund scholarships for needy students in my family's name"), and give the trustee authority to ensure that your directions are followed. The gift can be withdrawn and can go to an alternate charity if your direction as to its use is not carried out to the trustee's satisfaction.

Besides outright gifts, with or without strings, there are other ways to donate that involve the giver receiving something in return. Charitable Trusts and foundations sometimes benefit both charity and individual beneficiaries, such as you, your family members, or your friends, with outright or split-interest planned giving tailored to suit your goals. See Chapter 23 for more on charitable Trusts and foundations.

Chapter 18: What's for Charity? Part 1

$ $

John D. MacArthur

When he died in 1978 at the age 80, John
D. MacArthur, who owned Bankers Life and
Casualty, was America's second wealthiest
person. By many accounts, he was a stingy
man, the type who instructed employees to
bring rubber bands from home after snagging
them from home-delivered newspapers.

For most of his life, MacArthur reportedly
refused to plan his estate, avoiding his
lawyer's attempts to discuss his mortality. For
years, his simple Will left half of his fortune
to his second wife, Catherine, and a quarter
to each of his two children. Already in his 70s, after years of needling from his lawyer
to properly plan his estate, he finally took action. Though a miser, he realized that
without planning, his insurance and real estate empire would be eviscerated by taxes.

The John D. and Catherine T. MacArthur Foundation was established for essentially the
most generic charitable purposes. In fact, Mr. MacArthur was probably motivated more
by tax savings than by philanthropy. By all accounts, he wanted nothing to do with the
foundation and directed his advisors to "figure out what to do with it" after he died. It
is now one of the largest philanthropic organizations in the country, distributing more
than $250 million in grants annually for work done in more than sixty countries. NPR
listeners hear its name numerous times every day, working for "a more just, verdant,
and peaceful world."

The foundation is perhaps most widely known for the MacArthur Fellows Program, aka
the "Genius Award," which provides twenty to thirty unrestricted fellowships every year
to individual American "writers, scientists, artists, social scientists, humanists, teachers,
entrepreneurs, or those in other fields" who have demonstrated "originality, insight, and
potential." Each Fellow receives $500,000, distributed in quarterly installments over five
years.

Genius gifts enable the Fellows to "advance their expertise, engage in bold new work,
or, if they wish, to change fields or alter the direction of their careers" and "exercise
their own creative instincts for the benefit of human society." As a "no-strings-attached"

award in support of people, rather than projects, the grant requires no specific production or reports from recipients, nor is any evaluation made of their creative work. Because nominations are anonymous and selections made secretively, most recipients are unaware of their consideration until notified that they won the award.

John D. MacArthur would have been a historical footnote, but he spectacularly enhanced his legacy via a creative estate plan, albeit one well-funded and administered by people with vision and imagination.

 Pearls of Wisdom

Estate planning presents a unique opportunity to contribute to my favorite causes. On top of the tax advantages, testamentary gifts to charity always enhance my legacy.

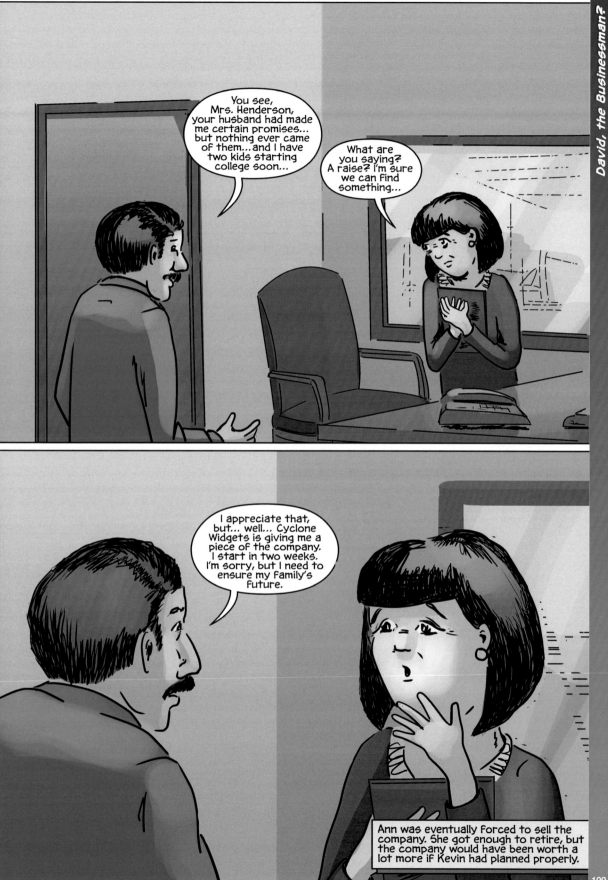

Chapter 19

$$$

Special Asset-Planning Challenges – Life Insurance, Real Estate, Family Businesses, and Retirement Plans

"It's not that I'm afraid to die. I just don't want to be there when it happens."
- Woody Allen -

In This Chapter...
you'll do a more detailed analysis of your assets, as well as learn about the value of life insurance, special issues of family businesses and real estate, and the importance of retirement plan beneficiary designations.

Life Insurance

Upon your death, will liquidity be needed to pay off a mortgage? Fund your children's college education? Keep your business afloat? Supplement your family's inheritance? Help a charity?

People usually buy life insurance to insure against a specific risk, although some do after crossing paths with a great salesperson or because a family member sells it. Regardless of the reason you purchase life insurance, it's helpful to know how much of a payout to reasonably expect and when, as well as who will benefit from the premium payments.

Beneficiary Designations

Policy beneficiaries determine the ultimate flow of money. Without a beneficiary, insurance proceeds pay to the decedent's estate. See Chapter 3 on why a policy is usually best not paid to an estate.

Most people realize the importance of designating a primary beneficiary, but many gloss over contingency planning as a thoughtless notation on the insurance application.

People, companies, charities, estates, and Trusts can all be primary and contingent beneficiaries. Trusts are often the best choice, for the reasons discussed in Chapters 10 through 15.

Types of Insurance

The myriad types of life insurance policies feature different price points, benefits, drawbacks, and estate- and financial-planning consequences.

Term

Term life policies are in effect for a period of time, commonly ten to thirty years but sometimes as brief as one year, and are relatively inexpensive. When purchased, the policy dictates how long the premium stays level, ensuring costs do not increase during its coverage period. The longer the term policy premium stays level, the higher its cost.

If you die during the term, your beneficiary gets the death benefit. If you outlive the term, either the coverage stops or premiums increase dramatically, making it unlikely the policy will be extended. While term policies require a relatively low outlay of money, the end of the term brings mixed news: You are still living (good news) but are left with a worthless policy, and the insurance company keeps the money (bad news). At the end of the term, your ability to buy a new policy will depend on your age and health. By then, you may be uninsurable (more bad news).

Permanent

Permanent insurance policies include "whole life," "universal," and others, each with a dizzying array of options. Permanent insurance is intended to last for life, and it builds equity in the policy. The distinguishing feature of most permanent life insurance policies is that as long as the premiums are paid, either with new money or with the policy's own built-up cash value, coverage cannot be dropped. The policy can be customized to emphasize either the investment aspect of the cash value or the value of the death benefit.

Whole Life

Whole life insurance policies provide the most certainty. Accordingly, the initial premiums are generally the highest, but they neither increase nor decrease if paid. Death benefits also remain constant.

Whole life policies often pay dividends based on the company's investment portfolio and financial health. Those dividends can be credited toward annual premiums or, if approved by the company, to purchase more death benefits. You can withdraw the cash value, usually as a loan that must be paid back with interest. Withdrawals also decrease the death benefit. Qualifying for a larger death benefit usually requires additional coverage and a health exam.

Universal

As is the case with whole life insurance, a universal insurance policy may accumulate an equity cash value but can be more flexible. In contrast to whole life, you typically control the timing and amount of the premium payments, sometimes skipping them entirely.

In a standard universal policy, cash value beyond the amount required to pay the death benefit grows at a variable interest rate with a guaranteed minimum. Withdrawals may decrease the death benefit. By changing the yearly premium, universal policy owners may increase the death benefit while the policy is in force, although, as with whole life, this may require a health exam.

Universal policies are not guaranteed, so premium payments, cash values, and death benefits can vary in the future. The insurance industry created them with the goal of putting the consumer in control. If insufficient premiums leave your universal policy under-funded, however, the policy could lapse without an infusion of new cash payments.

Variable universal policies are not tied to interest rates. As with standard universal policies, the premiums and the death benefits do not fluctuate with interest rates. Instead, you choose from one or more pooled funds, similar to mutual funds, whose values change. If the selected funds perform poorly, the premium payments will rise to cover the death benefit cost.

Hybrids

Some hybrid insurance policies combine aspects of those above. A term policy may have a rider allowing conversion to whole life, or whole life may have a term "kicker" with a higher death payout sooner in the policy. A guaranteed universal rider can be added to a universal policy, specifying the annual premium that keeps it in force.

Some insurance companies offer an interesting hybrid universal policy that resembles term insurance without a true term. It insures to 120 years old, longer than the life span of any person in modern history, but lacks cash value, making the premiums more affordable than a permanent policy but more expensive than a term. As long as you pay the level premium, it does not end, ensuring a death benefit, but avoiding payment of a premium for investment cash value.

Estate Tax on Life Insurance

Life insurance proceeds are generally not subject to income tax, so the beneficiaries will receive the entire amount of the policy. However, death benefits are part of the decedent's taxable estate. If insurance proceeds create a potential estate tax problem (Chapter 20), an irrevocable life insurance Trust (Chapter 9) may lessen or eliminate its impact.

Survivorship

Married couples whose heirs could face the cash crunch of estate taxes or who just want to add a big bang to their estate may consider a survivorship life insurance policy (also known as second-to-die insurance, death-tax insurance, or legacy insurance), which insures two lives and pays on the survivor's death. Compared to insuring two lives separately, these policies are relatively inexpensive. To avoid estate tax upon the survivor's death, usually a second-to-die policy is owned by an ILIT (Chapter 9) or members of the next generation, instead of the insured.

Real Estate

For beneficiaries, a number of factors may make selling investment properties a better option than retaining them. A savvy real estate owner's beneficiaries do not always inherit those skills. For them, a passive portfolio may work better.

Emotional factors may complicate the issue of personal residences. A good estate plan may address the possibility that children will want to live in the family residence, especially those who were raised there and have indicated an interest.

The same thinking applies to a vacation home. Suppose an ancestral cottage should stay in the family, but two children live relatively nearby, while another lives thousands of miles away. A proper estate plan could treat the situation a number of different ways. Maybe it leaves the cottage to those who will actually use it, giving a bequest of similar value to the distant child. Or perhaps it is left to a Trust for the benefit of a group of descendants, allowing expenses and maintenance costs to be charged in proportion to whoever uses it most often. The Trust can include a maintenance fund to cover expenses.

Blended families can complicate residential real estate. Consider the mother of grown children who has remarried. She dies, leaving behind a house. Should her husband get the house outright, depriving her children? If not, then under what terms can her husband continue to live there while her kids are awaiting their inheritance? If he has the right to live in the house until his death, should his new girlfriend/wife as well? Testamentary Trusts can resolve these types of issues, as discussed in Chapters 10 and 11.

Rental real estate must be actively managed, maintained, and repaired. Beneficiaries will have to collect rent and pay property taxes, insurance, and utilities. Property that sits empty or neglected can be an enormous cash drain. Consider whether your intended beneficiaries are willing and able to handle these challenges, or if it might be kinder to order the property sold and the proceeds distributed, even if value is lost doing so. Of course, rental property that generates a regular stream of income may be worth the effort.

Family Business

Value

If a business is based entirely on the owner's talents or production, then when the owner dies, its value may consist solely of accounts receivable (minus payables), inventory, equipment, and cash on hand. This does not present much of an estate-planning challenge, because the business is virtually worthless without the owner.

If the business will be sold when the owner dies, then it is worth only what someone will pay for it. A trustee and other advisors should work to maximize its value for beneficiaries following the owner's advance planning.

Claudia Cohen. December 16, 1950 – June 15, 2007

Gossip columnist, heiress, billionaire Ron Perelman ex, gives Ron control of estate for daughter Sam. Legal fees: $60MM and counting. Will contest or corp takeover?

Succession Planning within the Family

Owning a business that will continue under the control of beneficiaries comes with complex considerations. For it to succeed through multiple generations, effective succession planning depends on many factors, including these five important issues:

1. *The beneficiary's ability to manage the company.* Be realistic. If the beneficiary is ill equipped, set up a training program or have the business sold upon your death. A business left to an overmatched beneficiary is a disservice to the business (and to its non-family employees), the beneficiary, and to any other beneficiaries who may benefit more by a third-party sale.

2. *The importance of treating beneficiaries as fairly as possible.* If your business goes solely to certain beneficiaries, are there other assets that can equalize the interests among all of the other beneficiaries?

3. *If you have more than one child, ensure clear lines between ownership interests and management functions.* For instance, perhaps you can stipulate that two children get an equal ownership share of the business, but one is in control and the other has none. This creates other sub-issues:

    • Shall the heir without control have access to the company's books?

    • Keeping the non-controlling heir out of the management loop, with no access to the books, may foster resentment. Does the non-controlling heir simply take the controlling child's word about profitability, which may affect income flow for both of them, or should the non-controlling heir have the means to audit the books?

    • How will the non-controlling heir be fairly compensated in the future? A job with a salary and health insurance? Dividends? Jobs for his or her own children?

    • If the non-controlling heir dies after inheriting, will there be safeguards that his or her heirs are treated fairly?

4. *Timing.* If more than one beneficiary is part of the business continuation picture, consider initiating an early dialogue with them regarding operations and visions of the future.

5. *Effective succession documents that foster a smooth transition of the business from one generation to the next.* Without proper planning, your business could end up in probate, with the wrong people making decisions. You certainly don't want your death to spark a family feud between people who work in the business and those outside it.

Life Insurance Can Help Accomplish Business-Transfer Goals:

- Provide income to a family if the breadwinner is no longer around to operate the business.

- Infuse the business with a cash bridge when the owner, the key person with the knowledge and skill to run the company, is gone.

- Fund a buy-sell agreement to provide cash in exchange for business equity.

- Equalize the interests of various beneficiaries so that if one receives a valuable business, another gets a comparable cash gift.

Buy-Sell Agreements

Buy-sell agreements, often funded by life insurance, transfer the stock of a business upon a specified event, such as death, disability, or retirement. At an owner's death, beneficiaries sell his or her shares of the business back to the company, keeping surviving partners or children involved with the business in control of the company.

A buy-sell agreement can achieve four goals:

1. Set the value of stock.

2. Provide a mechanism or a formula for valuation.

3. Provide a ready market for the sale of shares.

4. Offer stability to the business by preventing unnecessary friction brought on by new shareholders.

There are two broad types of buy-sell agreements.

1. A cross-purchase agreement: the other shareholders agree to purchase your shares.

2. A stock redemption agreement: the corporation agrees to buy your shares.

Advantages of both forms depend on the circumstances, which include the number of shareholders, their age differences, discrepancies in insurability, and valuation/basis issues.

Retirement Plans

Required Minimum Distributions—RMD/MRD

On or before April 1 (April Fool's Day!) of the year after they turn 70½ (the required beginning date, RBD), IRA participants—that is, individuals who contribute to an IRA or whose employers contribute to one for their benefit—must start withdrawing funds and paying income taxes on those funds. The tax paid is based on the participant's income tax bracket, which the extra IRA income can bump up. A required minimum distribution (RMD) or minimum required distribution (MRD)—RMD and MRD are the same thing—table dictates the amount that must be withdrawn annually, based on life expectancy. The penalty for not taking the RMD by the end of the year can be as high as 50 percent of the RMD not withdrawn.

If any IRA funds remain when the participant dies, beneficiaries may be able to defer taxes for a considerable period of time. Depending on how beneficiaries are designated with the custodial financial institutions, the inheritors can, more or less, take all funds out at once and pay the taxes or withdraw only the amount dictated by RMD life expectancy tables and defer taking the rest. The beneficiary designation determines the beneficiaries' RMD and extent of control over their IRA shares, making it a potentially crucial planning component.

Unless the beneficiary is the participant's spouse and is under age 70½, the beneficiary must withdraw the RMD and pay tax. Otherwise, IRS penalties run the gamut from 50 percent of the RMD not withdrawn to an acceleration of future RMD. If you are inheriting an IRA, be aware of relevant deadlines to make elections and withdraw the RMD.

RMD table calculations are based on actuarial tables. Longer life expectancy = smaller RMD = better potential tax deferral. At the same time, consider that this is only one side of the planning equation for an IRA inheritance. The other is the beneficiary's right to withdraw more than the RMD and pay taxes sooner than he or she would if only the RMD were withdrawn, leaving the balance in the IRA.

Notwithstanding a low RMD, individual beneficiaries could act contrary to their interests by taking out everything at once, spending it all, and being on the hook for major taxes. IRA planning may therefore involve walking a beneficiary designation tightrope: on one side, a favorable RMD; on the other, control over beneficiaries and possible contingent beneficiaries who may be poor decision makers.

Beneficiary Options—Competing Considerations

Anyone who inherits the IRA of a non-spouse must take the RMD beginning on or before December 31 (New Year's Eve!) of the year following the participant's death. Spouses can "rollover" an inherited IRA and not be subject to an RMD until they themselves have attained age 70½. A spousal rollover allows a surviving husband or wife to treat an inherited IRA as if he or she were the original participant, name new beneficiaries, defer taxes based on the surviving spouse's RMD, if any, or spend it all and pay the tax.

A "designated beneficiary" (DB) is an individual (or a qualifying Trust) who may "stretch" the IRA, reducing RMD so that it is based on his or her life expectancy (or the participant's life expectancy, if the participant was younger than the beneficiary). There are two ways to ensure that a DB is able to stretch an IRA: either by naming the individual directly or by naming a qualifying Trust.

Although individually named designated beneficiaries may stretch an inherited IRA, and a spouse can roll it over, the results of a participant granting such outright control may not work out as expected, if:

- *You and your spouse do not share a commonality of interest in contingent beneficiaries.* Typically, this is an issue for blended families or spouses with different immediate family ties. A lifetime interest left to a beneficiary—including a spouse with whom you do not share all children—that should go to your children, rather than to your spouse's, needs a Trust beneficiary. This is especially true when the lifetime beneficiary's own future beneficiaries may differ from the participant's, because any individual inheriting an IRA outright can name new beneficiaries.

- *An IRA is a large portion of your estate, estate taxes are an issue, and sheltering the IRA is necessary to eliminate estate taxes.* A Trust can ensure that your spouse gets the RMD and any additional IRA money from the shelter Trust, as needed, at the trustee's discretion (see Chapter 12 for shelter Trusts). If you and your spouse share a commonality of interest in contingent beneficiaries, this strategy is sometimes implemented through the use of postmortem disclaimers ("Just say no," discussed in Chapter 14), so that even if your spouse is named as a beneficiary and wants to benefit from it, he or she can disclaim all or part of the IRA to a contingently named Trust with sheltering provisions to protect it from future estate tax.

- *If your spouse does not need the IRA assets and is near 70½ or older.* In that case, from a tax standpoint, you'd be better off choosing a younger beneficiary—a child, a grandchild, a nephew, or another family member or friend—who can better defer taxes by using a stretch.

- *A beneficiary is a minor.* Control may be subject to costly annual oversight by the probate court until the beneficiary reaches majority (usually 18 or 21, depending on his or her state), at which point the beneficiary gets full control and can spend it all immediately.

- *An immature adult beneficiary should not have unlimited immediate access to the entire IRA.* Most inherited IRAs are withdrawn well ahead of their maximum stretch schedules, and an astounding number are withdrawn more or less immediately. In some instances, the beneficiary spends the money and is left unable to pay taxes.

- *Contingencies kick in.* Even if the primary beneficiary is appropriate, what if he or she predeceases the participant? The answer depends on the contingent beneficiary designation with the financial institution. Usually, the dead beneficiary's share either lapses in favor of the remaining beneficiaries (per capita) or is further distributed to his or her descendants (per stirpes), who may be very young. If no contingent beneficiary is named, then any undistributed amount passes to the probate estate and is distributed according to the participant's Will (if there is a Will) or the state's intestacy laws (if there is no Will). A probate estate, with or without a Will, cannot be a DB, because it lacks a life expectancy.

Contingency planning, in this and other areas of estate planning, requires a new perspective and weighing the possibility, though not the probability, of money going to the wrong person at the wrong time. This could also happen if a beneficiary who takes control of the IRA dies and redirects the money into the wrong hands. Although planning for every scenario is impossible, most can be anticipated to some degree.

Charities as IRA Beneficiaries

IRA assets make ideal charitable gifts for three tax reasons:

1. Charities never have to pay income tax on the assets once the gift is made.

2. RMD is not a factor.

3. IRAs left to charity are excluded from taxable estate calculations.

To allow individuals the best stretch treatment, it is not advisable to name a charity as beneficiary of the same IRA, primarily or possibly even contingently. Because charities are not DBs, mixing the two can trigger an accelerated five-year payout requirement for the individuals, forcing them to pay taxes in that relatively brief time frame. Set up separate IRA accounts for individual and charitable beneficiaries.

Trusts as IRA Beneficiaries

Naming a Trust as beneficiary allows you to maintain some postmortem control over the direction of IRA assets. If your Trust does not qualify as a DB, naming it may result in the relatively harsh tax consequences of a five-year RMD, denying the individual beneficiaries of the Trust the ability to stretch the IRA according to their life expectancies.

Even with the unfavorable tax consequences of naming a non-DB Trust, circumstances may favor the additional control of a Trust over an immature or disabled beneficiary, rather than the potential maximum tax deferral gained by designating that individual as a direct beneficiary. Better still, if the Trust is one of the "qualifying" stretch varieties discussed below, then it may qualify as a DB and may give you some of the desired control and ability to better defer income tax.

If you name a Trust as an IRA beneficiary, it must meet four or five requirements to qualify for DB stretch treatment:

* The Trust must be valid under state law.

* The Trust must be irrevocable at the time of the IRA participant's death.

* The Trust beneficiaries must be identifiable from the Trust document.

* The IRA custodian must receive certain documentation by October 31 (Halloween!) of the year following the death of the IRA participant.

* If there are multiple beneficiaries and depending on the type of Trust, postmortem RMD issues must be resolved by either September 30 or December 31 of the year following the death of the IRA participant, depending on the nature of the issues.

Qualified inherited stretch IRA Trusts ("stretch" or "qualified," for short) can either stand alone or be a part of your revocable Trust. The future trustee of your stretch IRA Trust controls and invests your IRA assets, according to your directions. Stretch IRA Trusts cannot mix gifts among DBs and non-DBs.

There are two types of qualified Trusts that allow for DB status and stretch treatment:

Conduit Trust

Conduit Trusts allow the IRS to metaphorically "see through" the document in order to calculate RMD, based on the age of the oldest individual beneficiary, just as if only that beneficiary had inherited the IRA. The IRS requires that all RMD must be distributed outright to the beneficiary immediately. In other words, the trustee of a conduit Trust is not permitted to accumulate RMD.

If there is more than one beneficiary of a conduit Trust, RMD is determined by the age of the eldest beneficiary. Wide age discrepancies among the primary and contingent beneficiaries can result in the negative tax consequence of the youngest beneficiary (who has a longer life expectancy) being treated the same as the oldest beneficiary (who has the shortest life expectancy).

Accumulation Trust

An accumulation Trust is any Trust named as beneficiary of an IRA that is not a conduit Trust. Accumulation trusts, unlike conduit Trusts, do not require immediate outright distribution of IRA withdrawals to the Trust's beneficiaries. Some accumulation Trusts qualify for stretch treatment but have to have certain terms to do so.

The rules are complex and require careful consideration by the drafting attorney. An accumulation Trust may divide among multiple DBs, but to do so and still receive favorable desired stretch treatment for the individual beneficiaries, it must navigate quirky pitfalls to avoid a shortened RMD, including, but not limited to:

- Individual and charitable IRA gifts cannot be made from the same Trust, primarily or possibly even contingently, because charities cannot be DBs. Any mixed charitable portion would still be tax-advantaged, but the individual beneficiaries could lose their ability to stretch beyond five years.

- Specific money bequests cannot be made from the IRA.

- The IRA may not pay debts of the Trust estate.

- Beneficiaries may not have powers of appointment over the IRA assets that can direct assets to charities. And if the power allows for distributions to older beneficiaries, the life expectancy of the oldest potential beneficiary may determine the stretch.

- If the IRA pays to a common fund Trust with more than one beneficiary, the age of the eldest determines RMD.

- If the Trust postpones any payments to a beneficiary until he or she reaches a certain age and provides that failure to reach that age directs the Trust to a contingent beneficiary who is older or not a DB (such as a charity), that may also destroy or warp the stretch.

As a consequence of the complex rules associated with naming Trusts as IRA beneficiaries, many financial advisors and CPAs counsel against doing so. Also, drafting attorneys drop age restrictions and omit contingent beneficiaries who may have inferior DB status for the same reason. The drawback to this approach is that it may result in a lack of control where control is needed to prevent a beneficiary from just blowing through the IRA.

Postmortem Patches

If your Trust has provisions that endanger optimal stretch ability, all is not lost, provided that certain actions are taken by September 30th of the year following death. For example, charities can be paid and specific bequests distributed, leaving only the individual beneficiaries who will qualify for DB status for purposes of calculating RMD. If charitable bequests are payable entirely from IRA funds, it may result in even better tax treatment, because charities pay no taxes.

Prior to the September 30th deadline, a Trust can often be divided among different individual beneficiaries, allowing each to stretch the RMD, based on his or her life expectancy, rather than on that of the eldest individual. Sometimes the financial institution holding the IRA might not be cooperative in dividing the IRA to allow the longer stretch. One option is to move the IRA postmortem to a financial institution willing to cooperate with the strategy by means of a direct IRA-to-IRA transfer, ensuring that it remains in the name of the Trust. Only after the transfer has been made can the IRA divide among beneficiaries, allowing each to use his or her own life expectancy to obtain individualized stretch treatment.

Like disclaimers, decanting, and the use of portability, these postmortem maneuvers have a pitfall: To be effective, all of the parties, including the trustee, the beneficiaries, and possibly contingent beneficiaries, need to reach a written agreement by the deadline. Contingent beneficiaries lacking legal capacity further compound the problem.

Trusteed IRAs

Some financial institutions provide services based on their own Trust templates, in which they act as trustees, in addition to their more traditional service as passive IRA custodians.

As trustee, the institution controls IRA distributions, doling out the assets to the inheriting beneficiaries according to the institution's Trust template. Trusteed IRAs are similar in many respects to regular conduit Trusts, as discussed earlier.

The trustee of either a regular qualifying Trust or a trusteed IRA can be given discretion to make distributions exceeding the RMD for a beneficiary's health, education, maintenance, and support (HEMS) needs or, even broader, for the beneficiary's "best interests" or "happiness."

Features of Trusteed IRAs:

- *Safe tax deferral and control.* IRS regulations determine the DB status of Trusts. The documents prepared by the financial institution trustee will follow these rules, minimizing the need to continually amend a regular qualifying Trust as laws change or the likelihood that the IRS will challenge the optimal stretch ability of the individual beneficiary.

- *Only for large IRAs.* The cost structure of trusteed IRAs makes sense only for large IRAs, the definition of "large" varying among various banks, brokerages and trust companies.

- *Limited control.* Financial institutions offering trusteed IRAs may resist customized Trust provisions if they vary from their usual format. Yet in today's competitive financial services industry, some may be willing to accommodate custom terms.

When compared to regular qualifying trusts, trusteed IRAs have their perks and their drawbacks. The following are a few of the most prominent pros and cons:

- **Pro**—*More certain stretch ability and less danger of unintended results.* Drafted correctly by your lawyer, a regular qualifying Trust will qualify as a DB and allow for the desired stretch treatment or rollovers, but you must keep a closer eye on it than on a trusteed IRA. As IRA laws change, you may have to amend a regular qualifying Trust to ensure the least RMD to beneficiaries.

- **Con**—*Large IRAs only.* Some banks, brokerages and trust companies won't take a trusteed IRA worth less than a certain amount. Yet you can create a regular qualifying Trust regardless of the size of the IRA.

- **Pro and Con**—*Decreased control.* Seemingly simple controls over a beneficiary may inadvertently jeopardize a regular qualifying Trust's DB status. A trusteed IRA can't direct disbursements to precisely fit your desires, but you won't have to worry about possibly subjecting a beneficiary to an accelerated RMD.

Hybrid Beneficiary Designations

Some financial service companies allow the naming of individuals subject to the provisions of a Trust. For example:

> *To my children (names) in equal shares, provided that if a child shall not survive me, his or her share shall be distributed, per stirpes, to his or her then living descendants, and if any descendant of mine who shall be a beneficiary is younger than age 25, such share shall be subject to Article XY (governing that descendant's retirement plan distributions) of the Joey Doe Retirement Benefits Trust dated July 4, 1976, as amended.*

This can be an ideal beneficiary designation for participants who are comfortable making an outright gift of an IRA to their adult children but would prefer certain protections for any of the IRA that ultimately falls to a grandchild. As with trusteed IRAs, financial institutions are often reluctant to embrace customized designations but may accommodate them, due to marketplace competition.

The hybrid approach allows each person inheriting to stretch using his or her life expectancy, a big advantage if there is a wide age discrepancy between the youngest and the oldest potential beneficiary.

Qualified Retirement Plans

Although SEPs, 401Ks, 403Bs, and other qualified retirement plans share financial- and estate-planning attributes with IRAs, they are not identical. When you leave employment, it may be possible to use a participant rollover to create a regular self-directed IRA. The amount of flexibility depends on the plan agreement. Generally, if the retirement plan allows a participant rollover, all of the IRA strategies discussed above are in play.

The employer or the plan provider should be able to explain the rollover conditions, in the event of retirement or job change. Usually, plans that allow a participant rollover also grant a beneficiary rollover at death, but some then require a five- or even a one-year payout.

Final Thoughts on the Complex World of IRA Beneficiary Designations

IRA beneficiary considerations can be extremely convoluted, but proper planning may bring considerable rewards and are often as important as the investment mix. Careful planning using Trusts may be the best solution, but applicable rules are relatively untested. In the end, it may be best to weigh optimal tax deferral versus desired control.

Now is always a good time to review your beneficiary designations on file with the IRA custodian or the qualified plan administrator. Keep the confirmation with other important papers. Be certain that IRA assets will flow to loved ones as truly intended. While you are at it, do the same for any insurance policies and annuities.

The Long Arm of Creditor Claims

IRAs and qualified retirement plan assets (most notably, 401Ks) are generally protected from creditors and shielded from most claims, in the event of bankruptcy. These retirement plans enjoy the same protected status when inherited by a spouse. However, inherited IRAs and qualified retirement plan assets are subject to valid creditor claims against a non-spouse. If an IRA is instead payable to a Trust, various provisions can prevent the Trust beneficiary's creditors from targeting that asset. If there are concerns about an heir's creditors, shielding an IRA inheritance by making a restrictive Trust the beneficiary may be best, though it may cost some of its stretch potential.

 Pearls of Wisdom

If I own insurance, I should know what type it is and whether my beneficiary designations are in line with my goals.

Real estate is a special asset, and its sale or retention after my death is worth consideration.

If I own a business, I should give serious thought to what will become of it without me. Smooth business transition is an art. My family, like all families, is unique. I may want to discuss succession issues with my lawyer and other advisors, my partners/shareholders, and possibly my beneficiaries.

My retirement plan's beneficiary designation is a crucial component of its value.

Chapter 20

$$\$\ \$\ \$$$

Estate, Gift, and
Generation-Skipping Taxes

Taxes are the price we pay for living in a civilized society.
- Oliver Wendell Holmes, U.S. Supreme Court Justice -

In This Chapter...
you'll discover the levels at which estate, gift, and generation-skipping taxes kick in.

Estate Tax on Gifts at Death

At death, up to $5.49 million (in 2017), minus any reportable gifts made during your lifetime, passes to beneficiaries free from federal estate tax. Most people have no federal estate-tax problem, if having five and a half million dollars can be considered a problem. The threshold for federal transfer tax of $5.49 million per person is known as the "applicable exclusion amount." About .2 percent (one of every 500) estates qualify.

Tax on Lifetime Gifts

Lifetime gifts to charity and between U.S. citizen spouses are uncapped and untaxable. Other lifetime gifts of up to $5.49 million (in 2017) can be made without incurring transfer tax. The $5.49 million limit is in addition to the $14,000 that one person can gift another every year—annual gifts to any non-spouse (or non-citizen spouse) greater than $14,000 must be reported to the IRS. Gifts reported on an informational gift tax return are subtracted from the individual's remaining applicable exclusion amount at death.

Generation-Skipping Transfer (GST) Tax

Those taking a long view of wealth may consider generation skipping. The government wants to collect transfer taxes at every generation. Both lifetime and testamentary gifts greater than $5.49 million to family members two or more generations younger or unrelated individuals more than 37½ years younger face the punitive generation-skipping transfer (GST) tax. The GST tax is assessed at the highest rate, 40 percent, after any regular transfer tax has been assessed. As discussed in Chapter 13, generation-skipping Trusts can give lasting protection to Trust assets, saving taxes in the estates of your descendants.

Unified System

The transfer tax for estates, gifts, and generation skips is unified. At various times throughout their history, lifetime, testamentary, and generation-skipping gifts all had different thresholds, but they currently align at $5.49 million. Lifetime gifts deplete the amount of each remaining at death (see Chapter 21 for more about lifetime gifting to anyone other than a spouse or a charity). For estate tax or gifts that require payment of gift tax, the highest federal rate is 40 percent.

Gifting to a Spouse during Life or at Death: The Unlimited Marital Deduction

The unlimited marital deduction allows gifts of any size, whether during life or upon death, to a U.S. citizen spouse, with no tax or reporting requirement. Gifts to a life partner who is not a legal spouse do not qualify.

If a spousal gift is made via a testamentary or other irrevocable Trust, rather than outright, the recipient must receive unconditionally all income generated for life to avoid gift and estate tax (yes, even if he or she remarries!).

As pointed out in Chapter 12, overuse of the unlimited marital deduction may result in unnecessary estate tax upon the surviving spouse's death. In those instances, a shelter Trust, automatically created or generated postmortem via disclaimer (Chapter 14), may save taxes in the long run.

A Brief History of Federal Transfer Tax and Its Political Background

In 1906, when proposing a federal tax on inheritances, Theodore Roosevelt said that a "man of great wealth owes a particular obligation to the State, because he derives special advantages from the mere existence of government." A decade later, in 1916, Congress implemented an estate tax to help pay the cost of what was then known as the Great War. After an exclusion of $50,000 (about $1 million today), the top rate was 10 percent.

The tax became permanent in 1926 and topped out at 20 percent. In 1987, the exclusion was $600,000 and had grown to only $675,000 by 2001. The top rate shot as high as 77 percent during World War II but declined in the 1970s, finally settling at 55 percent in 1984 (plus an additional 5 percent surtax on estates between $10 million and $17.184 million), which also lasted until 2001.

President George W. Bush's 2001 Tax Act struck a blow to the federal estate tax, sending the rate tumbling and resulting in no tax on any estate in 2010. Embedded in the act was a Sunset Provision, a compromise thoroughly ridiculed by both sides of the aisle and commentators of all stripes. The estate tax was set to come roaring back on January 1, 2011 (later bumped back to January 1, 2013), with a $1 million exclusion and a 55 percent top rate (plus the 5 percent surtax).

Congress passed the 2012 American Taxpayer Relief Act (ATRA), signed by President Obama just after the stroke of midnight on December 31, 2012. Providing some degree of certainty, ATRA "permanently" set the unified federal applicable exclusion amount, the generation-skipping tax exempt amount, and the lifetime gift amount, all at $5 million per person, to be annually adjusted for inflation after 2010.

Republicans generally favor a higher exclusion amount or even elimination of the estate tax altogether. The 1990s saw opponents of the tax revive the fifty-year-old term death tax, riding the political wave of visceral disgust evoked by the notion of taxing the dead. In the opening session of the 114th Congress, held on January 6, 2015, Republicans introduced the Death Tax Repeal Act to permanently repeal all estate, gift, and generation-skipping taxes.

Democrats, alternatively, tend to favor an estate tax (or a death tax, if it better suits you).

George Steinbrenner. July 4, 1930 – July 13, 2010

Yankees win 7 World Series during his 37 year reign. Times death perfectly.
He dies a billionaire in 2010, the one year when there was no federal estate tax.

State Estate Taxes

On top of federal transfer taxes, certain states levy their own transfer tax of as much as 20 percent on estates that can be smaller—in some instances, much smaller—than the $5.45 million federal threshold for estate taxes.

When your state's estate tax exclusion threshold is less than the federal one, a fully funded shelter Trust intended to reduce federal estate taxes may result in hundreds of thousands of dollars in state estate taxes upon the death of the first spouse. This problem is usually solved by a shelter Trust that is "Q-Tippable," essentially requiring that the surviving spouse receive all trust income with discretionary principal payments based on need.

Although a single asset may not be taxed by multiple states, your estate may owe tax in every state in which you own property, perhaps reason enough to sell that rarely used vacation home.

Elimination of the current federal deduction for state estate taxes has been proposed and remains a possibility. Besides the potential migration of Americans for climate and other reasons, state estate taxes are an additional reason for wealthy people to choose the proper state as a principal residence in anticipation of death.

Estate Tax on Non-Resident Non-Citizens

Subject to various exceptions, exemptions and treaties with other countries, the estate assets of non-resident non-citizens "situated" in the United States are generally taxed to the extent their value exceeds $60,000. A non-resident non-citizen spouse in receipt of such an estate may benefit from a qualified domestic trust (QDOT), as discussed in Chapter 12. Non-resident non-citizens may also benefit from annual gifting, as discussed in this chapter and in Chapter 21, which, to a spouse, may be up to $147,000 per year.

 Pearls of Wisdom

The value of my assets and the potential federal and state estate taxes must be considered in my planning. Also, certain gifts must be reported to the IRS.

233

Let me guess? vampire?

Yes. Those that would suck any life or goodness from whatever victim they can latch onto.

Okay, zombies and vampires. Get a grip, Don, you're dreaming. Or on a bad basic cable show.
Let me guess, this is some metaphorical journey. I said I wanted to stop all the bad things I saw from happening to my family.
So, if the lesson is that I have to do what is necessary to achieve my goal, I've got to put one foot in front of the other, no matter how long and tedious the process, until I reach the top of the tower.

Chapter 21

$$\$\$\$$$

Lifetime Gifting and Other Ways to Reduce Your Taxable Estate

*Anyone may so arrange his affairs that his taxes shall be as low as possible;
he is not bound to choose that pattern which will best pay the Treasury . . .*
- Learned Hand, U.S. Supreme Court Justice -

In This Chapter...
you'll overcome your hunter-gatherer instincts by gifting assets to people during your lifetime.

Annual Gifting as an Estate-Depletion Technique

To reduce future estate taxes, many people make tax-free gifts of their annual exclusion amount ($14,000 In 2017) each calendar year to as many people as they like. Annual exclusion gifts can be made to friends, family members, or even complete strangers. These gifts can also accomplish estate planning or personal goals and do not require filing an IRS return. The annual exclusion amount increases based on inflation.

Dollar for dollar, yearly gifts exceeding the annual exclusion amount deplete the exclusion amount available to your estate upon death. Every dollar of value transferred is one that will not be taxed in your estate. Once a calendar year passes, the opportunity to make annual exclusion gifts for that year is gone. You cannot go back in time to make gifts for missed years.

As a coherent estate-planning strategy, annual gifting makes sense if the money is definitely not needed. It also comes with advantages. You can see your beneficiaries enjoy the money while you are alive. If invested, the gifted money's growth also takes place outside your estate. For extra bang:

- Spouses can each make a gift to the same person or make a joint gift of $28,000 (a "split gift"). A split gift requires a simple IRS filing, but there is no tax or depletion of the applicable exclusion amount.

- If the person receiving a gift is also married, you can make a similar gift totaling $56,000 to the couple each year. In this way, a married couple gifting to their three married children can reduce their estate by more than $1.5 million during the course of a decade without filing gift tax returns.

There is a hitch to annual gifting, especially when the recipient is young. The gift must be a "present interest," meaning that the donee, the person receiving the gift, must be immediately able to use or spend it as desired. This requirement may undermine the purpose of a gift, perhaps one that was meant to be used for college education.

There are ways to withhold immediate and total access. Would you like to set up a college fund for your grandchild? Rather than just hand $14,000 to the grandchild every year for ten years and hope that he or she respects your wishes, consider asking a financial advisor about the following four common tools:

1. Uniform Transfer to Minors Act (UTMA) account

2. 2503(c) minor's Trust

3. Crummey Trust

4. 529 plan

James Gandolfini. September 18, 1961 – June 19, 2013

Tony Soprano's dead? Fuhgeddaboudit! No living trust, so everything is public record, $40MM tax bill, baby daughter rollin' in cash when she gets her share at 21.

Uniform Transfer to Minors Act (UTMA) Account

The principal advantage of an UTMA is simplicity. It does not require a lawyer, just the child's date of birth and Social Security number to set up an account with a bank, a broker, or a mutual-fund company, titled "[Custodian's name] as custodian for [minor's name] under the [name of your state] Uniform Transfer to Minors Act."

The custodian, selected by the donor, administers the account until the child reaches a certain age, usually between 18 and 25, depending on the state. As donor, you can name yourself custodian, but if you die before the UTMA assets are distributed, they may become part of your probate estate. To avoid this, name a secondary custodian.

The first $1,000 in UTMA earnings is income tax free for children under 14, and the next $1,000 is taxed at the child's rate. Income or dividends greater than $2,000 will be taxed at the minors' parents' top marginal tax rate, regardless of who the donor is. For children older than 14, earnings are taxed at their own rate, usually the lowest tax bracket, because few children have much income.

UTMA accounts come with two disadvantages:

1. When the child reaches the statutory age of payout (usually 18 or 21), he or she gets complete control. The child can spend money intended for college on a car or at a casino instead. He or she has that right.

2. The UTMA may mess up the child's ability to receive college financial assistance. Federal financial-aid formulas require children to contribute a certain percentage of their savings toward college each year. Any dollars in their name count heavily against them when applying for aid packages.

Minor's Trusts—2503(c)

A second option for annual gifting is a 2503(c) Trust, named after the applicable section of the Internal Revenue Code. The IRS considers gifts to a 2503(c) Trust gifts of a present interest, even though the beneficiary has no right to withdraw income or principal until his or her 21st birthday—or sooner, if the donor so provides.

Four other requirements of a 2503(c) Trust:

1. The trustee must have unfettered discretion to use funds for the beneficiary. For example, funds cannot be restricted to paying educational expenses.

2. A trustee who is also the beneficiary's parent cannot use the assets to discharge parental obligations of support, such as providing food and shelter.

3. A beneficiary who has attained the age of 21 must be given a testamentary power of appointment to decide who gets trust assets upon the beneficiary's death.

4. On turning age 21, the beneficiary can do whatever he or she wants with Trust assets, even in the face of evidence that the individual cannot be trusted.

A method of retaining some control is to continue the 2503(c) Trust beyond age 21. To satisfy the IRS's present interest requirement, the child must have a window of opportunity of at least thirty days to withdraw the assets, starting on his or her 21st birthday. If the beneficiary waives that withdrawal right in writing, he or she gives up access, and the trustee continues to control the assets, usually with staged rights of withdrawal at certain ages.

Less common is the 2503(b) Trust. While similar to the 2503(c) Trust, it is different, in that (1) all investment income must be paid out as it is generated, (2) the beneficiary's income interest from the Trust also does not qualify for the federal gift-tax annual exclusion, and (3) payment of the principal to the beneficiary is not required, nor is it necessarily subject to withdrawal at the age of 21.

Crummey Trust

Another option for annual gifts is a Crummey Trust. Crummey Trusts may benefit multiple individuals but do not qualify for a GST tax exemption (discussed in Chapters 13 and 20).

Unlike a 2503(c) Trust, a Crummey Trust can be restrictive and creative regarding the use of assets. It still requires notice to the beneficiary of a withdrawal right, but instead of the money being given when the beneficiary attains majority age, the Crummey Trust must notify each beneficiary of every gift made.

Named for a California family that had its gifts to an irrevocable Trust subject to a limited withdrawal right unsuccessfully challenged by the IRS, the mountains of paperwork that historically came with Crummey Trusts left trustees and beneficiaries feeling quite crummy. Yet recent legal developments have drastically cut down on the burden of the annual notice requirement.

The most common Crummey Trusts are irrevocable Trusts that own life insurance ("ILIT," as discussed in Chapter 9). The insured grantor makes gifts to a Trust account, from which the trustee pays the insurance policy premiums. The trustee must notify each beneficiary of the gift to the Trust account and of his or her right to withdraw a portion of the gifted funds for a specified period, usually 30 to 90 days. The grantor assumes the beneficiary does not exercise the Crummey rights and withdraw the money (because then there would be no money to pay the insurance premium). Most Crummey Trust beneficiaries will waive the right to withdraw a few hundred or thousand dollars for the promise of hundreds of thousands or millions of dollars in death benefits, free from estate tax.

In some cases, if the trustee desires a record, beneficiaries sign a receipt acknowledging having been made aware of the gift but declining to exercise the withdrawal right. The whole process satisfies the IRS that a completed gift was made. Without it, the payment is still part of the insured's taxable estate. Properly sent and kept Crummey letters can be a pain, but if done correctly, all payments made to the Crummey Trust are removed from the donor's taxable estate.

Sometimes a trustee forgets to send out Crummey letters. While a perfect paper trail is ideal, missing Crummey letters do not doom the Trust. At worst, only the gifts/insurance premium payments are includable in the donor's taxable estate, not the death benefit. Backdating Crummey letters is frowned upon by the IRS.

Crummey powers in a Trust and the Crummey letters that are sent must be drafted properly for Trusts with more than one beneficiary. Absent the correct language, a beneficiary's failure to withdraw the gift can become a gift from that person to other beneficiaries of the same Trust, subject to tax.

Fly on the Wall

The IRS generally frowns on prearranged or sham transactions, but the use of 2503(c) Trust notifications (at majority age) and Crummey letters (each year when a contribution is made) are charitably described as convoluted. The beneficiaries are told of their right to take a portion or all of a contribution to a Trust, but they decline to do so. The letters/notifications draw a fine line between the IRS requirement for a completed gift to be a full present interest and the desire to postpone a beneficiary's actual use and control of Trust assets.

Most often, the beneficiary follows the plan (though some may call it a ruse), but what if he or she refuses? There may be subtle ways of coercing a person not to exercise a withdrawal right. Listen in on this imaginary exchange between a gifting father and a 21-year-old beneficiary of a 2503(c) or Crummey Trust that delays beneficiary control until he attains age 30

> *Dad: "This notice says you have a right to take money from this Trust account, but I prefer you wait."*
>
> *Son: "Actually, Dad, I think I'll just take the money now."*
>
> *Dad: "No problem. If you do, I guarantee you will never get another dime from me."*
>
> *Son: "Where's the pen?"*

529 Plans

A 529 education plan is an account operated by a state or an educational institution that accepts gifts made to the account beneficiary for educational purposes. The plans vary by state, but there are no income restrictions. A donor can make cash contributions of five years' worth of annual exclusion gifts (currently totaling $70,000) for any one beneficiary in a single year. Any additional gifts to that person for the next five years will require a gift tax return and will deplete the donor's $5.49 million lifetime gift exemption and applicable exclusion amount.

The 529 donations come with no federal income tax deduction, but some states allow for it on their return. Plan growth and income used for qualified educational purposes will never be taxed. A donor can control the 529 account and even change the beneficiary designation, if the original beneficiary does not use it for education. There are generally no age restrictions, so 529 money can also fund adult education. At death, any unused 529 assets are includable in the donor's taxable estate and also the donor's probate estate if there is no successor or contingent owner.

The reason 529 plans are unique is that donors retain a great degree of control over the assets—the timing of distributions and the ability to change beneficiaries—while still potentially removing these from their taxable estate.

The Big Lifetime Gift

Gifts greater than the annual exclusion amount deplete your applicable exclusion amount, potentially leading to a gift tax of 40 percent once both exclusion amounts are exhausted. If you are very wealthy and you expect significant future growth in the gifted assets, you may be willing to pay it. Sometimes, it is better to pay a tax early and remove future appreciation from a large estate.

Basis Issues—Choosing the Right Assets for Lifetime Gifting

When lifetime gifts of appreciated assets are sold for fair market value, the IRS uses a different basis to calculate capital gains than it does for assets passing to beneficiaries at death. Though preferable to regular income taxes, taxpayers would just as soon forgo capital gains taxes, if possible.

An asset's basis is its initial cost. Growth in the asset's value is capital gain. The capital gains tax on a lifetime gift is calculated by sale price minus the original cost of the asset (its carryover basis). The same reasoning behind keeping an appreciated asset even if you would prefer to sell it—avoiding capital gains tax—also applies to making lifetime gifts of those assets: you do not want the beneficiary to have to pay the tax when the asset is sold.

Beneficiaries who inherit appreciated assets when you die get a special tax break in the form of a "stepped-up" basis. When they sell the inherited asset, they pay tax only on the difference between its sale price and its value on the date of your death—the stepped-up basis—rather than on its original acquisition cost (the carryover basis): a spectacular tax break for your beneficiaries. They pay capital gains taxes only on the increase in value between the time of your death and the sale. Capital gains accrued during your lifetime disappear.

Unless you expect greater appreciation in the future, it's often wise to make lifetime gifts of assets that have appreciated little or not at all since purchase. Leave highly appreciated assets in your estate until death or put them to good use during your lifetime by giving them to charities. Lifetime charitable gifts often come with an income tax deduction of the asset's full value, rendering basis irrelevant.

The Education and Health-Care Exception

Payments of tuition and medical bills can be used to augment the annual gift exclusion. You can pay anyone's tuition or medical bills, no matter the cost, without triggering gift tax. With annual university expenses continuing to climb, this is a great way for grandparents to help grandchildren with education expenses, while simultaneously draining large sums from their taxable estates.

For payments to be exempt beyond the annual gift exclusion, the institutions must be paid directly. Money given with the intent that the donee use it for tuition or health-care costs will not qualify and will instead deplete the annual exclusion and, if larger than the annual exclusion amount, will also deplete the applicable exclusion amount.

 Pearls of Wisdom

I discovered some of the methods for depleting my estate during my lifetime, while preserving it for my family.

"A-pock-a-lips"

Ooooo... Scrooge always wound up back on his bed!

OOF!

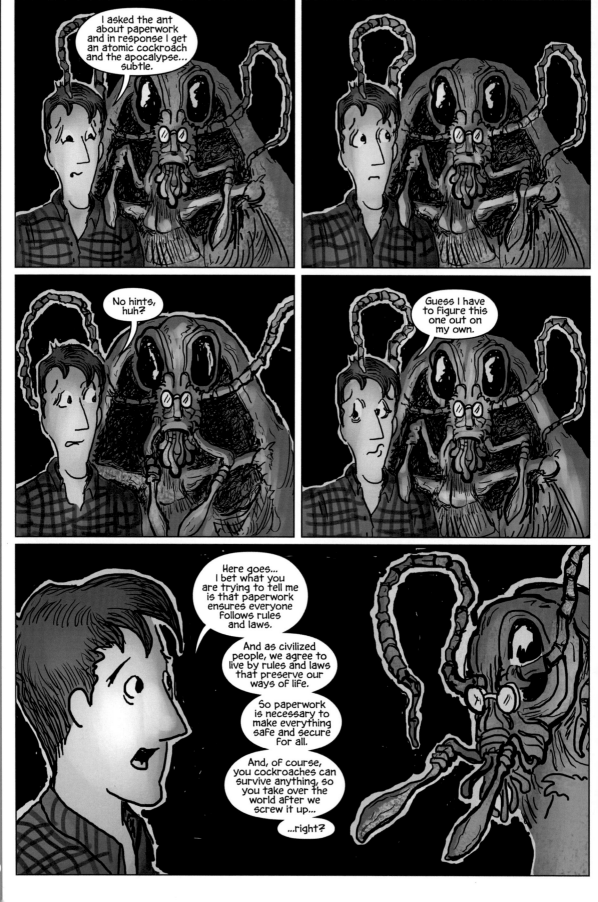

Chapter 22

$$\$\$\$\$$$

More Aggressive Estate Tax Reductions and Freezes (Brrrr)

There may be liberty and justice for all, but there are tax breaks only for some.
- Martin A. Sullivan -

In This Chapter...
you'll learn about some of the acronymic trusts and techniques used by the very wealthy to gift assets out of their estates, often while retaining some measure of control or benefit.

Split-Interest Gifts

If you are blessed with an estate large enough to face estate taxes even after more mundane gifting and sheltering techniques have been exhausted, some sophisticated reduction and freeze techniques may be worth considering. Specialized Trusts and other entities and tactics, if they work as planned, are often tailored to minimize the taxable value of a large gift and ensure that any appreciation occurs outside your taxable estate.

The best assets for estate reduction and freezes are those expected to appreciate greatly. Business owners sometimes use freeze techniques to both minimize estate taxes and incrementally transfer control of their businesses.

The everlasting chess match between the designers of aggressive freeze strategies and the IRS is a perennial part of the high-level estate-planning landscape. Certain strategies that were popular decades ago have been banned by Congress. Although some high-end estate-planning firms continue to design their own hybrid techniques, a few of which were successfully patented, the more common remaining legal acronymic entities include:

- Intra-family installment sales to transfer a family business, sometimes involving self-canceling notes ("SCINs"), coupled with the oxymoronic (irrevocable) intentionally defective grantor Trust (IDGT).

- GRATs: (Irrevocable) grantor-retained annuity Trusts pay a fixed annual income to the grantor, and at the end of the term, provided the grantor still lives, the assets belong to the heirs, free of estate or gift tax. If the grantor dies during the term, the assets, including appreciation, are included in the grantor's estate. Many point to aggressive GRATs, such as the highly effective "zeroed-out GRAT" and short-term GRATs (between two and ten years), as unfair loopholes of the super wealthy.

- GRUTs: (Irrevocable) grantor-retained Unitrusts pay interest income to the grantor, recalculated annually based on the changing value of the assets.

- GRITs: (Irrevocable) grantor-retained income Trusts are the estate plan equivalent of having your cake and eating it, too, and are mostly banned for family beneficiaries (except for QPRTs, discussed below).

- FLPs and FLLCs: Family limited partnerships and family limited liability companies to transfer assets that may capitalize on hefty discounts, due to:

    o Lack of marketability to third parties; and/or

    o Diminishment of control by the person transferring.

These sophisticated estate reduction and freeze techniques require considerable bookkeeping, along with a significant or total surrender of control over the funding assets. They are appropriate only for large estates with major estate tax issues.

Aggressive use of these more exotic entities increases the likelihood of an IRS audit, but if your estate is large enough, the benefit to your family may be worth the time, effort, and cost. The necessary legal and accounting fees make them appropriate only for the very wealthy. Even a million-dollar legal bill is a bargain if the savings amount to a hundred million or more.

 Linda McCartney. September 24, 1941 – April 17, 1998

Non-citizen Sir Paul sole lifetime beneficiary of QDOT, so tax man can Let It Be til after Beatle's death. But no Revocable Trust for privacy? No trusts for kids? Help!

QPRTs

A qualified personal residence Trust ("QPRT," sounds like cue pert) removes a personal residence and up to one vacation home from the owner's estate and leaves them to beneficiaries, minimizing estate taxes. QPRTs are relatively common, compared to the techniques mentioned above, and are the only type of GRIT that allows family beneficiaries.

Transfer your residence to a QPRT while continuing to live there for a preset term. Only a grantor who outlives his or her QPRT's term will avoid estate taxes. If you fail to survive the QPRT term, the value of the residence is included in your estate. As with GRATs and GRUTs, the longer the term, the lower the value of the retained interest and the smaller the gift in the eyes of the IRS.

At the end of the fixed term, the residence passes to the Trust's beneficiaries, usually your children. If you wish to continue living in the house, you must lease the residence from them at the prevailing market rate, depleting more of your estate in the form of rent. Real estate taxes and mortgage interest are still deductible on your income tax return.

For gift-tax purposes, because beneficiaries receive no benefit from the gift during the term of the QPRT, the QPRT transfer is made at a discount from the residence's existing value. Once the residence is placed in the QPRT, any appreciation accrues outside your estate.

During the QPRT term, you can sell the residence and either replace it with a new property or convert the sale proceeds to an annuity. While they are triggered by the sale, capital gains on residences receive highly preferential tax treatment. Roll over any gain from the sale into a new residence or use your $250,000 exclusion ($500,000 if married) as often as every two years to avoid the tax. The IRS allows two QPRTs per person, so it is possible to do one for both a principal residence and a vacation home.

Like GRATs and GRUTs, QPRT beneficiaries receive no basis step-up, which may be why QPRTs remain a weapon in the estate planner's arsenal but are less prevalent in an age of higher estate tax thresholds. For this reason, based purely on my own experiences and discussions with other estate-planning lawyers, I would guess that as many people have unwound them in the last decade as have established them during that time.

Asset Protection Offered by FLPs and FLLCs

FLPs and FLLCs are established for reasons other than estate tax planning. They are alternatives to sole proprietorships, traditional corporations, and general partnerships.

Perhaps the biggest non-tax benefit of FLPs and FLLCs is protection from creditors. A properly established and operated entity is not subject to lien, only to a "charging order," allowing a creditor access only to the income paid to you as a limited partner of the FLP or member of the FLLC. In theory, as a control partner or a shareholder, you can decide not to distribute any income, leaving nothing for your creditors to collect. It may be years before a creditor is paid, if at all, putting you in a better negotiating position.

But be careful. In some jurisdictions, retaining full control over the FLP's or the FLLC's assets may convince a judge that the protection is unfair to the creditor, and the court can order distributions. This is particularly true for sole-member FLLCs.

One of the best uses for an FLLC is owning investment property. Liability arising from FLLC-owned real estate, absent any personal negligence and provided all "T"s are crossed and "I"s dotted, is limited to the net value of the real estate and does not bleed over to your personal assets.

Pearls of Wisdom

I got a taste of some non-charitable techniques used by very wealthy people to reduce or eliminate estate taxes. FLPs and FLLCs are also established for asset protection.

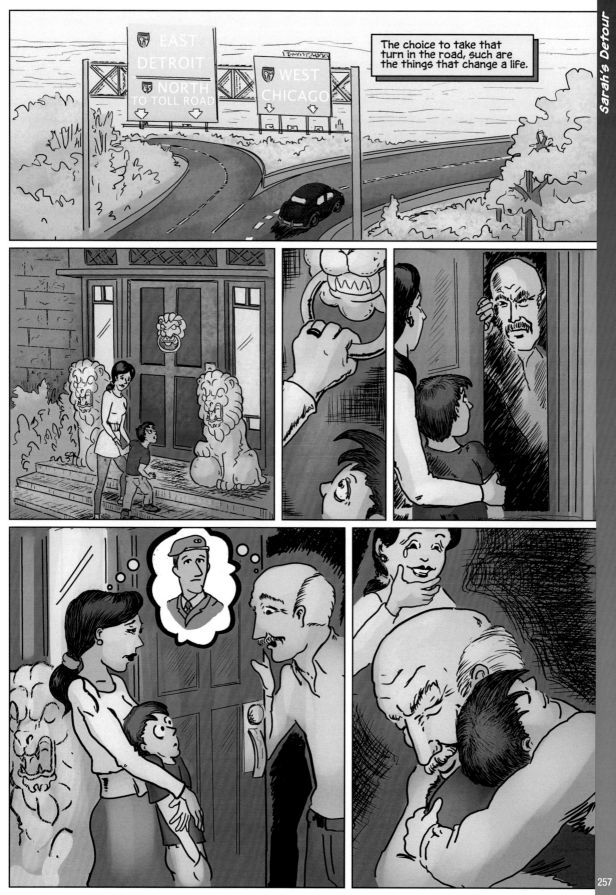

Sarah's sudden detour didn't change everything. Sarah still married Coach.

....and of course, Don still met Libby.

Bump!

The biggest impact was on Jack. Sarah's care and a grandson to love kept his heart open and beating.

He founded charities to support playgrounds and community gardens where he would've previously poured concrete.

He discovered a love of parks...

...including one where a young man now sits, awaiting the arrival of his love.

Chapter 23

$$\$ \$ \$ \$$$

What's for Charity?
Part 2

If you haven't any charity in your heart,
you have the worst kind of heart trouble.
- Bob Hope -

In This Chapter...

you'll discover why the world of split-interest planned charitable giving is like a bowl of
alphabet soup. The best use of the items described in this chapter result in win-wins for
everyone. Certain assets are best suited for this type of planning.

Establishing a charitable Trust or a foundation takes a fair amount of work. Unlike the measure of generosity required by outright gifts, they are complex and can require a sustained commitment.

Why bother with something so complicated? Here are seven good reasons:

1. Get an income tax deduction in the amount of the gift.

2. Eliminate taxable income every year.

3. Receive a relatively fixed income stream.

4. Diversify your portfolio, while eliminating capital gains on appreciated assets.

5. Reduce your eventual estate tax liability.

6. Involve family members in the charitable process.

7. Just as names such as Kresge, MacArthur, and Gates live on charitably, yours will, too.

Charitable Remainder Trusts (CRTs)

A charitable remainder Trust is an irrevocable Trust that allows for gifting assets to charity, while getting financial rewards in return. The gift to a CRT is usually made while you're living but can be done after you die.

The optimal CRT receives a valuable asset that has grown in value but does not produce much in the way of current earnings. If the asset is such a significant part of your overall net worth that transfer constitutes a vulnerability to your overall finances, then a CRT may be the key to properly diversifying. CRT assets can include a portfolio of securities, real estate, or private businesses.

A CRT can then sell the donated assets with no capital gains tax consequence; the full value is reinvested by the charity in (presumably) higher-earning investments. You or your family members receive the income over designated lifetimes or a term of up to 20 years. A CRT can continue in perpetuity, but on termination, remaining assets are distributed for charitable purposes. A CRT enjoys 501(c)(3) status, so others can make tax-deductible donations to it.

As trustee, you can control CRT investments and the yearly income stream to the non-charitable beneficiaries, as long as at least 5 percent and no more than 50 percent is paid to them yearly.

CRT income received by non-charitable beneficiaries is taxable according to a "tiered" system: ordinary income first and usually predominant, followed by capital gains, then "exempt" income, and finally return of principal.

The amount of the income tax deduction you receive when making the gift is based on a number of factors:

1. The present value of the gift (the higher the value, the bigger the deduction).

2. The anticipated wait before the charity receives the donated assets outright (if tied to age, the shorter the life expectancy, the larger the deduction).

3. The income stream selected (a higher potential income paid to non-charitable beneficiaries means a smaller deduction).

4. The applicable federal rate, tied to U.S. Treasuries, published by the IRS each month and used, among other purposes, to establish present values of future interests.

5. No income tax deduction is available if the anticipated remainder going outright to charity is worth less than 10 percent of the present interest.

Enjoy all of the financial benefits of CRTs, but try not to lose sight of your prime charitable directive. If you are too aggressive in accumulating the benefits you or other interested individuals receive, IRS penalties may disrupt your scheme.

Different types of CRTs are tailored to maximize the benefits you seek:

CRATs, CRUTs, SCRUTs, NI-CRUTs, NIM-CRUTs, and FLIP-CRUTs

CRATS

A charitable remainder annuity Trust (CRAT) provides consistency by fixing income payments to non-charitable beneficiaries for the term of the Trust. They never vary, even if the assets increase or decrease in value. However, assets cannot be added to an existing CRAT. So while it provides the most income certainty, a CRAT is the most conservative, least flexible type of CRT. CRATs are best created when interest rates are high.

In the current environment of historically low interest, many CRATs fail the 10 percent rule, allowing for a tax deduction, unless the annuitant is very old already.

CRUTS

A charitable remainder Unitrust's (CRUT) income to the non-charitable beneficiary fluctuates yearly, based on the value of the Trust's assets. Because the CRUT's flexibility may produce more income to the non-charitable beneficiary, meaning a lower present donation value, the initial income tax deduction from a CRUT is usually less than that of a CRAT. CRUTs must be revalued on a yearly basis, and you can expect income to grow if inflation results in higher interest rates. You can also add assets to an existing CRUT whenever you want.

A variety of CRUTs, designed to give varying degrees of flexibility over the non-charitable income payments, can be tailored to your assets and goals.

- SCRUTs. More than half of all CRUTs are standard charitable remainder Unitrusts that mandate a minimum payment, regardless of the Trust's earnings.

- NI-CRUTs. Each year, the net income only charitable remainder Unitrust pays the lesser of the net income or a set percentage (at least 5 percent) of the net fair market value of the asset. It does not allow for depletion of principal. This works well if you do not want the income to be paid to you or other non-charitable beneficiaries soon, if ever. A NI-CRUT is usually funded by non–income producing assets that are expected to grow in value, such as vacant land.

- **NIM-CRUTs.** The net income with makeup charitable remainder Unitrust (NIM-CRUT) also pays a fixed amount, either 5 percent annually or the income, whichever is less. The difference between it and a NI-CRUT is that if the NIM-CRUT's yearly income is insufficient to pay the fixed percentage, the deficiency accumulates in a "make-up account" to eventually pay later. Like the NI-CRUT, NIM-CRUT principal cannot be depleted by the lifetime non-charitable beneficiary. While increasing in value, assets that pay little or no current income work well. They can be converted to a higher-earning investment when you retire, boosting your income when you need it. If you don't need an immediate cash flow but might later, a NIM-CRUT may fit you.

- **FLIP-CRUTs.** The flip charitable remainder Unitrust (FLIP-CRUT) starts out like a NIM-CRUT, delaying any income to the non-charitable beneficiary, but turns into a SCRUT when triggered, perhaps by one of the following:

  o A specific calendar date, either arbitrary or meaningful, such as a 70th birthday.

  o An event whose timing you can approximate but that is not controlled or known with certainty: a child's marriage or graduation, birth of a grandchild.

  o An event with unknown timing, but presumably within some measure of control, such as the sale of a closely held business interest or other illiquid Trust asset.

James Brown. May 3, 1933 – December 25, 2006

Left fortune to needy kids' charities, but family (both proven and possible) cannot accept the Godfather of Soul's wishes and have been fighting for a slice.

Pooled Income Fund CRT

A pooled income fund CRT requires little in the way of sophisticated set-up. You simply donate assets to charity via a preexisting Trust, avoiding much legwork. As with other CRTs, gifts of appreciated assets work best because of the full-value income tax deduction; the absence of capital gains, if and when the charity sells the asset; and the usually higher income. You then receive rights to a percentage of the income until your death.

Pooled income funds allow for diversification of assets during your lifetime, while benefiting a charity at your death without the legal cost of establishing a Trust. Smaller investors, who may want to donate only $5,000 or $10,000, can take advantage of charitable Trust techniques that are generally available only to those giving $100,000 or more. They are comparatively hassle-free and are offered by many charities.

CLTs

A charitable lead Trust (CLT) is an approach opposite to that of a CRT. Let's say, you don't need the income from certain assets, and your estate will likely be subject to estate taxes. Per the CLT, a donor who doesn't need the income from certain assets and whose estate is likely facing estate taxes irrevocably lends income-producing assets to a charity at the applicable federal rate (AFR), an interest benchmark published monthly by the IRS. Similar to most interest rates, the AFR has been relatively low since the beginning of the millennium, making CLTs more attractive.

The charity receives the income for a term of years or for your lifespan. When the term expires or you die, your heirs receive the CLT assets, including any growth, at a discount, outright or in trust, saving or eliminating estate taxes. As long as the CLT assets perform better than the AFR, your individual beneficiaries should receive something. If the investment assets perform worse than the applicable rate, however, your children may get nothing (although they may receive more of your estate by virtue of reduced taxes).

CLTs can be highly advantageous to high net-worth individuals for whom lowering estate taxes is of greater concern than receiving additional life income.

Like CRTs, CLTs are drafted in different flavors to maximize benefits, based on the situation. There are grantor and non-grantor CLT's, and there are CLATs and CLUTs.

Grantor CLT versus non-grantor CLT. This distinction determines the income stream's tax treatment.

- A gift to a grantor CLT comes with a partial income tax deduction on the gift when made, but the income is taxed yearly.

- In the case of a non-grantor CLT, you get no income tax deduction. The Trust itself is taxed on yearly earnings, but any income transferred to the charity gets a deduction, so no income tax is due.

Charitable Lead Annuity Trust (CLAT). CLATs pay the same amount to the charity year after year.

Charitable Lead Unitrust (CLUT). CLUTs pay a fixed percentage of the fluctuating asset value each year.

CLTs are among the most sophisticated charitable Trusts, mostly used by those worth at least $10 million who can fund them with $1 million or more. Because the idea is to remove the growth from your estate, optimal CLT assets both produce income for charity and have great growth potential.

Private Family Foundations

A private family foundation (PFF) is a hands-on approach to planned giving, often with your and your beneficiaries' continuing involvement. Although the substantial financial commitment makes it most appropriate for very wealthy families ready to commit more than $1 million, the IRS estimates that there are more than 14,000 PFFs worth less than $100,000.

Create a PFF as a Trust, controlled by the trustees, or as a corporation, by the board of directors, during your lifetime or following your death. On one hand, the inflexibility of a Trust ensures the continuity of your charitable vision well into the future; on the other, the Trust can lose step with future changes, to which corporations are generally better suited to adapt.

Either way, a PFF can exist in perpetuity, investing and distributing money according to a mission statement, written with the help of your attorney. Submitted to the IRS in order to obtain tax-exempt status, the mission statement serves as a roadmap for the PFF.

A typical PFF established during your lifetime involves appointing a board of directors (or trustees, if established as a Trust), often made up of you and your family, who decide how money is invested and disbursed. PFFs can be a substantial time commitment, which is typically spent reviewing and following up on grant applications.

At least 5 percent of a PPF's value must be paid out each year to recognized charities or other grant-seekers (such as those applying for college scholarships) to qualify as tax-exempt. The PFF can employ your children, but excessive family compensation or other potential self-dealing can force the IRS to pull the plug, sending your PFF down the drain. The IRS demands filings every year, which determine continuing charitable eligibility.

PFFs can provide a forum for family members to discuss and work toward a common goal; a tool to unite your heirs in a shared charitable vision, perpetuating your family's commitment to philanthropy. A PFF can also sow discord if the family members in control are unable to agree on the disbursements necessary to remain tax-exempt. Most problems can be eliminated by careful drafting. For instance, put each child in control of his or her own foundation. Or, to keep them corralled together, refer dispute resolution to a third party.

As with CRTs, donations to PFFs enjoy many tax advantages. Funding them with appreciated assets eliminates capital gains taxes when they are sold or transferred to the charities in the form of grants. Because the PFF is a type of charitable organization, income is only subject to an "excise" tax of 1 to 2 percent each year. You can get an income tax deduction on donated assets, but the deduction is less than that for other types of charitable donations.

A PFF is also another way to provide for the long-term needs of charitable organizations, while mitigating estate taxes. Structured properly and invested wisely, principal can grow and impact generations to come. On the flip side, existing in perpetuity requires following complicated rules to terminate a foundation without resulting in a punitive "termination" tax.

Donor Advised Funds (DAF)

Used on a smaller scale than a regular PFF, but sharing some characteristics, a donor advised fund is the PFF equivalent of a pooled income fund CRT. A DAF allows you to be involved with a favorite charity at relatively low cost, without hiring an attorney to do the paperwork. You get a tax deduction, and although you may recommend to the recipient how to disburse the funds, the charity is not obligated to follow your directions.

Your Museum-Quality Collection

Your charitable gift may be tangible personal property, such as art and other collections. A classic legacy enhancer, displaying it at a museum with the knowledge that other aficionados will appreciate your fine taste is priceless.

A gift made during your own lifetime requires a fresh appraisal in accordance with IRS rules before you take a tax deduction. For estate tax purposes or when you take an income tax deduction, the value of the gift is affected by any substantial restrictions put on it (i.e., it must be displayed in a certain place and/or can never be sold). Over-valuing assets to take a larger-than-warranted tax deduction can invite severe IRS penalties.

Although some museums are well-endowed, many can barely keep their doors open. When shopping for the right museum to receive your gift, consider a conversation with potential recipients. Do they really want your gift? How would your collection be displayed? Investigate their overall financial stability and, depending on the circumstances, consider a monetary gift dedicated to ensuring that your tangible personal property donation will be used and conserved in accordance with your vision.

Finally, regarding any of the split-interest entities discussed in this chapter, keep in mind that if you or your individual beneficiaries retain a measure of control, it comes with a fiduciary duty to avoid self-dealing. If it smells like self-dealing, it probably is. A gift that benefits you or your family members more than it does the charity or the charitable purpose may not pass the smell test.

Pearls of Wisdom

A plethora of tax-advantaged techniques are available to me if I want to donate to charity but retain part of the value of the gift. Some are complicated, others are relatively easy.

Chapter 24

At Last

Death is a distant rumor to the young.
- Andy Rooney -

In This Book...
As you and our hero Don both know by now, practically everyone needs some degree of estate planning. Whether you are rich or poor; twenty-something or elderly; married, partnered, or single, as your life changes, estate planning can be tailored and altered to fit your needs.

Different Stages of Life Typically Address Different Planning Needs

YOU AT:

18	• Have minimal assets or even a negative net worth. • Are still in college or dependent on parents. • Need power of attorney for health care and HIPAA authorization. • Maybe add power of attorney for property (finances) for such things as tax filings, credit cards, and leases.
30	• Are still single but own a few assets. • Add on a simple Will.
35	• Married but no children. • Update your Will to ensure that your spouse and family share your assets, as desired.
40	• With minor children, name a guardian who decides where your children live and other lifestyle issues, if something happens to you (and spouse, if still married). • Add a Trust so that your insurance money and other assets will be properly used for your children's benefit if you (and spouse, if married) die, but they won't get the whole pie when they become legal adults (18 or 21).

55	• Have some significant assets. • The estate plan you wrote when your children were minors needs to be updated. • Name your children in fiduciary capacities, instead of your siblings or elderly parents.
60	• Are sandwiched between generations, so your Trust should consider your parents' needs, as well as your children's.
70	• Are balancing your desire to divest assets to save taxes and help your children with the need to control your own financial future (yes, you are now very wealthy in this fantasy timeline).
80	• Are juggling your desire to leave an inheritance for your children and grandchildren, maintain control over your money, and make intra-family gifts now, because if you don't, taxes may be significant (not the worst thing) or your entire nest egg may be spent on assisted living (bummer).

If you have finished doing as much planning as you want or need, congratulations. Don't neglect the follow-up work that's necessary to make your documents as efficient as they can be. Review your plan as circumstances—yours and those of the important players in your life—change.

Don't end up a joke like the fictional Jane Doe, who died without a Will:

Last Will and Testament of Jane Doe

I, Jane Doe, of Anywhere Spring Falls, Illinois, hereby do make this my Last Will and Testament. Let my family decide where to bury me or whether I should be cremated.

Article 1
My Family

My husband is John Doe. I have two children now living, namely, Peter (age 6) and Patrick (age 4).

Article 2
Distribution of My Financial and Personal Assets

I give my husband one-half (1/2) of the assets I own, and I give my children the remaining one-half (1/2), to be divided equally between them, regardless of their circumstances.

Included in my assets is a very special diamond-and-sapphire necklace, which has been a family heirloom for several generations. My husband may give the ring to his next wife, who in turn can either give it to her daughter from a previous marriage or sell it, as she wishes.

Another important asset of mine is a vacation cottage that has been in my family for three generations. I have very fond memories of this place and had hoped that my children and their children would build memories of their own. Unfortunately, since my husband would rather have cash, he can sell it if he wants, depriving my descendants of this important link to their past. Prior to sale, the property must be probated in the State of Michigan, incurring legal costs that will unnecessarily deplete my estate.

When my children reach age eighteen (18), they shall have full rights to withdraw and spend all of the money that they inherit from me. They may spend this money in any way that they see fit, including, but not limited to: gambling, drugs, motorcycles, and endless parties. No one shall have any right to question my adult children about how they spend their money.

Should my husband remarry and also die without a Will, his second wife shall be entitled to one-half (1/2) of everything my husband owns, including the assets he inherited from me.

My husband's second wife shall not be bound to spend any part of her share on my children's behalf, even if they need the money for their health, education, or support.

After my husband's second wife dies, in her Will she shall be able to give the money she inherits from my husband, who inherited it from me, to whomever she wishes, to the exclusion of my children.

Article 3
Guardian of My Children

My husband, if he is still living at the time of my death, is appointed as guardian of our children. Although I love my husband and absolutely trust that he will care for our children, until they attain the age of majority my husband will be required to provide an accounting of how, why, and where he spent the money necessary for the proper care of our children.

My husband shall be required to post a costly surety bond each year to guarantee that he exercises proper judgment in the handling, investing, and spending of the children's money.

In the event that both my husband and I die before our children reach the age of eighteen (18), rather than nominate the guardian of my preference, I direct my relatives and my deceased husband's relatives to get together and try to reach a consensus on the best guardian. I trust that the court will make the proper decision without any input from me. I further accept the fact that the court may send my children to live in separate homes and that if the children are sent to my husband's sister Trudy, she may make it difficult for my parents to visit with them.

Article 4
Personal Representative

I decline to exercise my right to choose an executor to wind up my affairs. Although the job of executor may be critical to the efficient administration of my probate estate and I know several people who would do a good job, I trust that the probate court will make the proper selection of a personal representative. I also accept that the probate court may, in fact, choose a bank I never worked with or a person whom I despise.

Article 5
Taxes, Costs, and Legal Fees

Under existing tax law, there are certain legitimate avenues open to me to lower federal estate taxes. Since I prefer to have my money used to pay down the government deficit, rather than for the benefit of my husband and children, I direct that no effort be made to lower taxes.

During the entire course of the probate and guardianship proceedings, my surviving family will hire a lawyer to handle the various court proceedings and prepare a good number of documents. I recognize that these legal fees will come straight out of my estate and, in fact, shall be given priority and paid in full prior to making any distributions to the beneficiaries.

By the State of Illinois,
on behalf of Jane Doe, who died without a Will.

Pearls of Wisdom

Perhaps I know the difference between the applicable exclusion amount and the annual exclusion amount; between powers of attorney and powers of appointment; between living Wills and living Trusts. One thing I know for sure is that estate planning applies to me, whether I am 18 or 80 years old, healthy or feeble, materially rich or poor. Sometimes the unexpected happens, so I must plan for contingencies. Above all, my estate-planning wishes, simple or complex, must be in writing!

Glossary

"Be nice to your kids, they'll choose your nursing home."
- Seen on bumper sticker -

501(c)(3) organizations—Refers to the IRS code that confers status on certain types of organizations, such as charities and houses of worship, that enjoy favorable tax treatment and to whom people can donate money and receive tax breaks.

accounting—Detailed analysis of income, gains, losses, transactions, and assets that may be required of a *trustee* or an *executor* or an *agent* acting in a *fiduciary* capacity.

administration—Management and settlement of an estate in *probate court*. Similar in usage to one of the meanings of the term *probate*.

administrator—Person appointed by the *probate court* to act as *personal representative* of a *decedent's estate administration* when there is no *Will* or where the *executor* or executors named in the Will are not serving.

advance directives—Collectively, a living Will and a power of attorney for health care allow you to communicate your philosophy for end-of-life care and select the person who will make health decisions when you are unable to communicate.

agent—Under a *power of attorney,* the person who is granted the legal right to act on behalf of the *principal*. The agent, also sometimes referred to as a *proxy* or an attorney-in-fact, under a *durable power of attorney for property* controls assets in a *fiduciary* capacity without owning them. An agent may also be acting under a *power of attorney for health care*, making personal decisions for the *principal*.

alternate valuation date—As part of the *estate tax* return, the *executor* can choose to value an estate by its fair market value on the *decedent's* date of death or on the alternate valuation date, six months after the date of death. If the assets have declined in value, use of the alternate valuation date can reduce estate tax liability.

ancillary jurisdiction—Jurisdiction outside the state where the *decedent* officially resided. If a *decedent* owns real estate in more than one state, his or her estate may be subject to *probate* in each state where the real estate is located. There are various methods you can use to avoid multiple ancillary probates, which include establishing a *revocable living Trust* and re-titling each piece of real estate into the *Trust*.

annual exclusion amount/gift—Each person may *gift* up to $14,000 per year (in 2017) to any other person without incurring any *gift tax*. Gifts in excess of $14,000 will result in a partial or full use of the maximum *applicable exclusion amount* and require a gift-tax filing. There is no limit on the number of $14,000 gifts you can make to different people in a year. To qualify for this exclusion, the gift must be of a present interest, meaning that the recipient can enjoy the gift immediately. You can use an annual exclusion gift aggressively to deplete large *estates*.

applicable exclusion amount—The amount that you can leave to your designated heirs (other than your spouse, in most cases, who can be left unlimited amounts outright if he or she is a U.S. citizen) without incurring any estate tax or gift tax. After more than a decade of uncertainty, the issue was permanently settled (until it changes again) at the stroke of midnight on January 1, 2013. The applicable exclusion amount is $5.49 million per person in 2017.

applicable exclusion amount shelter Trust—See *shelter Trust*.

applicable federal rate—A federal tax rate tied to U.S. Treasury bonds, notes, and bills. Its use includes determining the value of assets transferred to charity using charitable Trusts.

ascertainable standards—Language describing how *Trust income and/or principal* can be used by a *trustee* for a *beneficiary* that confers a *limited power of appointment*, rather than a *general power of appointment*. If a trustee has a general power of appointment, that person has legal ownership, and the underlying assets are subject to the holder's creditors and other attacks. A common example of ascertainable standards is the authority to distribute for "health, education, maintenance, and support" (HEMS).

basis—Acquisition cost of an asset, used to calculate gains and losses. Also see *stepped-up basis*.

beneficiary—The person or the charity who receives a *gift,* whether from a lifetime transfer or a *testamentary* one from a *Will*, a *Trust*, or contractually from insurance, IRAs and other retirement plans, annuities, or transferable-on-death accounts.

bequest —A *gift* made to a *beneficiary* under a *Will* or a *Trust*.

bond—A guarantee by an insurance company or a bonding agency to repay any loss due to negligence or theft by an *executor*, an *administrator*, or a *trustee*. A *Will* or a *revocable living Trust* can waive bond requirements.

buy-sell agreement —A contractual agreement among partners or shareholders of a business that specifies the terms for buying out one partner's or shareholder's share upon his or her retirement, death, or disability. Often funded by insurance policies.

capital gain—The profit on the sale of an asset that has grown in value. It is the difference between the *basis* of an asset and the net proceeds from the sale of the asset. If the asset is sold for a lower price than its acquisition cost, a capital loss may be reported.

capital gains tax—The tax paid upon realization of a capital *gain*.

charging order—If the owner of a *family limited partnership (FLP)* incurs debt, the creditors cannot place a lien on the FLP assets or force any distributions to pay it. They can only get a charging order that takes a portion of FLP distributions. However, the managing partner(s) may decide not to make any distributions at all, leaving the creditors without a means to reach the FLP assets. The assets of the FLP are best protected in this manner if the FLP is properly established, operating as a functioning business, and correctly maintained.

charitable remainder Trust—A structure for the donation of an asset to a charity, in which the *donor* reserves the right to use the property or receive income from it for a specified period of time, perhaps years or even one or more lifetimes. When the agreed-on period is over, the property belongs to the charity.

codicil—A document that amends or supplements a *Will*. It must be executed with the same degree of formality as a Will.

community property—Community-property states (currently, Arizona, California, Idaho, Louisiana, Nevada, New Mexico, Texas, Washington, and Wisconsin) provide that a husband and a wife each own a one-half interest in the other's assets and earnings during the course of the marriage. States that are not community-property states provide for separate property rights during the course of the marriage. In most community-property states, the only separate property is that which is owned exclusively by one of the spouses prior to the marriage and never commingled with community property and assets received by *gift* or inherited at any time.

conservator—A type of *guardian* appointed by a *probate court* to manage the affairs of a mentally incapacitated adult.

contingent beneficiary—The person or the charity that receives a *gift,* whether from a lifetime transfer or a *testamentary* one from a *Will*, a *Trust*, or contractual property such as insurance, qualified plans, annuities, or transferable-on-death accounts upon the death of the *beneficiary.*

contingent fiduciary—The backup to the successor *trustee, executor, guardian,* or *agent*, should the previous selection be unable or unwilling to act.

corpus—See *principal.*

cost basis—See *basis.*

credit shelter Trust—See *shelter Trust.*

Crummey power—When a *donor* makes a *gift* to an *irrevocable Trust*, the *trustee* must notify the *beneficiary* of rights to withdraw some or all of the value of the gift in the year made. The right to withdraw—typically not exercised—is required for the donation to the Trust to be a gift of a present interest and thereby removed from the donor's estate.

custodian—A person or an organization managing assets for minor children or adults deemed incompetent.

DAPT (domestic asset protection Trust)—An *irrevocable Trust*, available in some states, that allows a *grantor* to transfer assets out of his or her *estate*, putting the assets beyond the reach of creditors, while remaining a potential future beneficiary of the assets

DB—See *designated beneficiary.*

death probate—The process of legally validating a *Will* or an *intestate* estate. It involves collecting assets, paying bills, and eventually *re-titling* the assets under the supervision of the *probate court*. For a living probate, see *guardianship*. Many types of *probate* can be substantially avoided and their costs minimized though proper estate planning.

decanting—Some states allow a *trustee* to transfer assets from an existing *Trust* to a new trust that better serves the *beneficiaries* (including *remainder* beneficiaries), due to changed circumstances or poor Trust planning.

decedent—A person who has died.

descendant—A person who is a relative in a direct vertical generational line from another person: children, grandchildren, great-grandchildren, and so forth. A line going in the other direction leads to ancestors. Spouses are not descendants.

designated beneficiary (DB)—An individual who may take (stretch) the RMD of an IRA or another retirement plan, based on his or her life expectancy.

disclaimer—A person inheriting assets can refuse to accept any or all of those assets. Disclaimers can be useful in certain situations, especially if they have been anticipated and planned for. An effective disclaimer is "qualified" and governed by strict state and federal laws. Among other things, a disclaimer must be in writing and made within nine months of a person's death. The use of disclaimers is akin to postmortem estate planning.

domicile—The state or the county where a person primarily resides, determining tax and *probate* jurisdictions.

donee—A person who receives a *gift* or a *bequest* or to whom a *power of appointment* is given.

donor—A person giving a *gift*. If the gift is made to a *Trust*, see *grantor*, also referred to as *settlor*.

DSUEA—*Deceased spouse's unused exclusion amount*, used when calculating the shortfall in a first-to-die spouse's estate for maximum *portability*, potentially minimizing estate taxes upon the surviving spouse's death.

durable power of attorney for property—See *power of attorney for property*.

escheat—The process by which assets of a person who dies *intestate* (without a *Will*) and without *heirs* go to the state.

estate—What you own.

estate tax—The *transfer* tax that the federal government and some states assess on the distribution of assets to others occurring because of your death. Sometimes referred to as the "death tax" or, incorrectly, as *inheritance tax* (although a few states also have inheritance tax, assessed on the *beneficiary*).

executor—The person, bank, or Trust company designated in your *Will* to administer your estate upon your death, under the supervision of the *probate court*. More than one executor can act together as co-executors. Along with an *administrator*, an executor is referred to in some states as a *personal representative*.

FLLC, family limited liability company—An entity created by state statute that combines aspects of partnerships and corporations. FLLCs are flexible regarding operation, record keeping, and tax treatment. They are owned by members, one or more of whom are managers. Unlike corporations, there is no requirement for officers or a board of directors. An FLLC can have a single member/manager. FLLCs are created to operate a business or own property and offer significant creditor protection. They may be used as a vehicle to transfer assets at a discount to next-generation members and can provide significant creditor protection; some states' statutes are more protective in that regard than others. Though not required in all states, an FLLC operating agreement is recommended for various reasons.

FLP, family limited partnership—An entity whose ownership is composed of general partners, who control the underlying enterprise, and limited partners, who do not. Sometimes, the controlling parents own 1 percent as general partners, and share ownership of the remaining 99 percent with their children as non-controlling limited partners. Limited non-controlling interests can be gifted over time at a discount, shifting money to following generations to minimize transfer tax. The asset is then further discounted by its lack of marketability and control by the partners. FLPs can provide major asset protection, subjecting their assets only to a *charging order*.

fiduciary—A person in a position of trust and responsibility, subject to heightened legal and ethical standards, including, among others, *trustees*, *executors*, *guardians*, and *agents*.

general power of appointment—A grant of full authority over assets given to a *beneficiary* in a *Trust*. It may expose assets to the *beneficiary's* creditors. Appointing to yourself using a general power of appointment is the same as withdrawing an asset from the Trust. Some general powers of appointment may be exercised during your lifetime, and others are exercisable only testamentarily, at death. See also *limited power of appointment*.

generation-skipping transfer (GST) tax exempt Trust—An additional *transfer tax* assessed on *gifts* and *bequests* in excess of the *applicable exclusion amount* to grandchildren, great-grandchildren, or anyone other than a spouse, at least two generations or 37½ years younger than the *donor*. Language allocating and preserving the $5.49 million exemption from the GST tax can be included in a GST tax exempt Trust as part of your overall *Trust* or *Will*.

gift—Voluntary transfer of property by a *donor* to a *donee*, made without receiving something of equal value. A completed gift, which removes an asset from a *donor's* estate, must be of a present interest and without any conditions. The federal government will assess a gift tax when the value of the gift exceeds the *annual exclusion amount* and the lifetime overage exceeds the *applicable exclusion amount*.

grantor—In estate-planning matters, one who transfers assets to a Trust. Also known as a *donor*, a *trustor*, and a *settlor*.

grantor Trust—A *Trust* in which the *grantor* retains control of the assets or income. The income from a grantor Trust is taxable to the grantor, rather than to the *beneficiary*, although the grantor and the beneficiary may be the same person.

GST tax—generation-skipping transfer tax – An additional *transfer tax* assessed on *gifts* and *bequests* in excess of the *applicable exclusion amount* to grandchildren, great-grandchildren, or anyone other than a spouse, at least two generations or 37 1/2 years younger than the *donor*.

GST tax exempt Trust—see generation-skipping transfer (GST) tax exempt Trust.

guardian—A person appointed by a *probate court*, often designated in your *Will*, to be responsible for your children or an incompetent adult. In the case of the incompetent adult, also known as a *conservator*.

guardianship—*Probate court* process of administration or management of the property or person of minor children and incompetent adults, a type of living *probate*. Guardianships of incompetent adults can generally be avoided though the use of *Trusts* and *durable powers of attorney*, if signed while the *principal* is still competent.

heirs—Persons who receive your assets if you die intestate and also others who are *legatees* of a *Will* or *beneficiaries* of a *Trust*.

HEMS—Health, education, maintenance, and support. See *ascertainable standards*.

HIPAA—The federal Health Insurance Portability and Accountability Act of 1996, which exists primarily to protect the confidentiality and security of health-care information.

HIPAA Authorization—Allows designated people to access your health-care information.

holder —A person who possesses a *power of appointment*.

incidents of ownership—Any element of control or ownership rights. This concept often relates to insurance policies. To remove insurance from a gross estate for *estate tax* purposes, you must give up all incidents of ownership and live at least three years.

ILIT—Sounds like "eye-lit." See *irrevocable trust*.

income—Interest, dividends, rent, and other earnings of a *Trust*, as opposed to *principal*. *Capital gains* may also be considered income, depending on the terms of the Trust.

incompetence—Inability of a person to function and take care of his or her own affairs, sometimes referred to as a legal disability or incapacity.

inheritance tax—A tax levied by some states on the right of *heirs* to inherit assets. An inheritance tax is imposed on the *heir*, rather than on the estate.

intentionally defective grantor Trusts (IDGTs)—A type of irrevocable living Trust that is intended to remove assets from an estate, often by partial *gift* and partial sale. In all IDGTs, the *grantor* pays income taxes on earnings and capital gains, even if those earnings and capital gains are paid to the *beneficiaries*.

inter vivos Trust—See *revocable living Trust*.

intestate—Dying without a valid *Will*. When a person dies *intestate*, the *probate court*—following state intestacy laws—will determine who is to receive *probate assets*. The probate court will also select the **administrator** and determine who will act as *guardian* for minor children.

inventory—A list of all assets in a *probate estate*. A probate estate inventory is a matter of public record, available for examination by anyone who cares to request it at the courthouse.

individual retirement account (IRA)—A type of tax-deferred savings account.

irrevocable Trust—A *Trust* that cannot be amended or revoked by its *grantor*. Like corporations, these are tax entities. Irrevocable Trusts are used in estate planning to place assets outside of a person's *estate*. One common irrevocable Trust is an irrevocable life-insurance Trust (ILIT), intended primarily to prevent insurance death benefits from being included in your taxable estate. Irrevocable Trusts may be *living Trusts* or *testamentary Trusts*.

joint tenancy with right of survivorship (JTWROS)—A shared ownership between two or more people, with the survivor(s) owning the property after the death of one or more fellow joint tenants. Compare with *tenancy in common*.

legacy—Property transferred by your *Will*. The person receiving the gift is the *legatee*.

legatee—Someone who receives a *gift* under provisions of a *Will*.

letters of office—A court order that provides the authority to an *executor* to act for the estate of a deceased person. Also referred to as *letters testamentary*.

limited power of appointment—Within a *Trust*, also known as a "special" power of appointment, it protects the Trust asset from being includable in a *beneficiary's* estate for tax purposes. The holder of such a power can never appoint to himself or herself, his or her creditors, his or her estate, or his or her estate's creditors, further protecting the Trust asset from the beneficiary and the beneficiary's creditors. Some limited powers of appointment may be exercised during your lifetime, and others are exercisable only testamentarily, at death. See also *general power of appointment*.

living Trust—A Trust created during a person's lifetime. A living Trust can be revocable or irrevocable.

living Will—A written statement of philosophy regarding your wishes to discontinue treatment in the case of extreme injury or illness if the procedures in question are only going to delay the dying process and you are unable to effectively communicate.

marital Trust—Takes advantage of the *unlimited marital deduction* in the form of a *general power of appointment* marital Trust or, if the surviving spouse's authority is limited, it is called a *QTIP Trust*. All marital Trusts must unconditionally pay all income to the surviving spouse for the remainder of his or her life.

MRD—See *required minimum distribution.*

non-contest clause (in terrorem)—A clause in some *Wills* and *Trusts* that purports to disinherit any person attempting to attack the validity of such Will or Trust. Does this work? Sometimes, depending on the court and the equities involved. Is a *beneficiary* completely disinherited? If so, he or she may have nothing to lose by contesting. Consider giving the beneficiary a gift large enough that he or she will not want to potentially jeopardize it, giving the person pause before contesting the document.

payable-on-death (POD) account—A type of bank, brokerage, or mutual fund account that avoids *probate*. If a person has a limited net worth, few *beneficiaries*, no real estate, and no other complicating factors, PODs can be used to completely avoid probate without the trouble of establishing a *Trust*. Also referred to as a *transfer-on-death (TOD) account*.

per capita—Distribution made equally to a number of persons without regard to generation. A distribution to "all my descendants equally and per capita" would result in children, grandchildren, and great-grandchildren each receiving the same amount. This is generally a less prevalent distribution pattern than *per stirpes* distributions.

per capita at each generation—Hybrid of *per stirpes* and *per capita*. The share of a deceased person is divided into equal shares among those *heirs* living and the number of heirs at the same level who are survived by descendants. When looking to the next level, another equal division is made the same way.

per stirpes—Latin for "by the branch," a method of dividing assets among descendants so that descendants as a class take the share that a deceased ancestor would have been entitled to take had the ancestor survived.

> *Per stirpes, per capita, and per capita at each generation.*
> Example: An unmarried person dies leaving three children, named: A, B, and C.
> A has two children (d & e).
> B is deceased, leaving three children (f, g & h).
> C is deceased, leaving one child (i).
>
> *Per stirpes distribution:*
> A gets 1/3rd.
> f, g & h each get 1/9th (B's share).
> i gets 1/3rd (C's share).
>
> *Per capita distribution:*
> A, d, e, f, g, h & i get 1/7th shares, making no distinction between members of different generations.
>
> *Per capita at each generation:*
> A gets 1/3rd
> d, e, f, g, h & i each get 11.11 percent (an equal share of 2/3s).

personal representative—See *executor* and *administrator.*

planned giving—a gift or series of gifts made to charity, during lifetime or upon death, via a will, trust or beneficiary designation, outright or subject to simple or complex provisions. It is often associated with complex tax planning.

portability—A procedure that allows a surviving spouse, after the death of a first spouse to die, to shelter assets from estate taxes via an estate tax return that preserves any unused estate tax and lifetime gift exclusions *(DSUEAs)* of the first-to-die spouse.

pour-over Will—A Will used in conjunction with a *revocable living Trust*, stating that all remaining assets are to be transferred ("poured over") to the *Trust*. The Trust is therefore the *legatee* of the Will. Even where there is a fully funded Trust, you should have a pour-over Will to pick up the crumbs of your estate.

power of appointment —The right of a *Trust beneficiary* to transfer Trust assets. A power of appointment can be general or limited. If the power is general, the assets are essentially owned by the person who has the power and subject to claim by that power holder's creditors. A *limited power of appointment* limits the authority of the person holding the power to transfer assets to a particular class, such as to the descendants of the original *donor* or to charities. A *general power of appointment marital Trust* (as opposed to a *QTIP marital Trust*) gives the surviving spouse the authority to withdraw as much of the Trust principal as he or she desires whenever he or she wants by allowing the spouse to appoint to him- or herself.

power of attorney—See *power of attorney for health care* and *power of attorney for property*.

power of attorney for health care—Document allowing your *agent (proxy)* to direct your health care and other personal matters if you are unable to do so, letting you avoid being assigned a *guardian*.

power of attorney for property—A document in which you grant an agent the authority to handle financial matters on your behalf, immediately or upon your incapacity. Often referred to as *durable* because it survives the *principal's* incapacity. Used to avoid an estate *guardianship* proceeding in *probate court*.

precatory language—Language in a *Will* or a *Trust* that expresses your sentiments or preferences but is not binding.

principal—(1) Assets that make up a *Trust*, sometimes referred to as the *corpus*. Many Trusts provide for separate treatment of principal and income derived from the principal. (2) Person who confers authority on an *agent with a power of attorney*. If you have trouble spelling it, remember that just as in elementary school days, "the principal is your pal."

probate —See *death probate*.

probate asset—An asset owned by an individual at death.

probate court—State court where probate estates are administered. In some jurisdictions, a magistrate's court or a surrogate court handles probate functions.

proxy—See *agent, power of attorney for health care*, and *durable power of attorney for property*. The agent acting under the powers of attorney and the authority granted under the powers are referred to as proxies.

qualified domestic trust (QDOT or QDT)—A *Trust* that allows a non-citizen spouse to qualify for a *marital deduction*, deferring estate taxes.

qualified personal residence Trust (QPRT: sounds like "cue pert")—A type of *irrevocable Trust* used to reduce your taxable *estate*, whose assets consist of your principal residence and up to one other property.

qualified S corporation Trust (QSST)—A *Trust* that is permitted to own S corporation stock.

qualified terminable interest in property Trust (QTIP)—A type of *marital Trust* that qualifies for the *unlimited marital deduction* but limits a surviving spouse's *powers of appointment* so that the assets are preserved for one or more specific *beneficiaries* at the surviving spouse's subsequent death. As with any marital Trust, a QTIP requires that the surviving spouse receive all of the Trust's income during his or her lifetime. The surviving spouse can, if specified in the Trust, be paid principal for *ascertainable standards (HEMS)*, but distributions cannot be made to any other person. The surviving spouse who is beneficiary of a QTIP marital trust may also, if specified in the Trust, be given a limited testamentary power of appointment but cannot have any lifetime power of appointment, limited or general. QTIPs are often used in blended families, where the grantor wishes to protect the children from a previous marriage, while benefiting the surviving spouse during his or her lifetime. Contrast the QTIP Trust with a *general power of appointment* marital Trust.

RBD—See *required beginning date*.

remainder interest—Assets remaining in an estate for a secondary *beneficiary* after a previous beneficial interest has terminated.

required beginning date (RBD)—The date when you must start withdrawing IRA funds.

required minimum distribution (RMD)—The amount of IRA or other retirement plan assets that must be withdrawn on an annual basis. Commonly referred to as *RMD* or *MRD*. Failure to withdraw RMD results in income tax penalties.

residuary estate—Assets remaining in an estate after all specific transfers of property are made and all expenses are paid. When a *pour-over Will* is being used, the residuary estate is ordinarily transferred to a *Trust*.

re-titling—(1) The process that legally transfers ownership of property from the *grantor* to the *revocable living Trust*. Without re-titling assets, a revocable living Trust is unfunded and will not work efficiently as a means to avoid *probate*. (2) The portion of the probate process that, at the court's direction, transfers ownership of assets from the *decedent* to the *heirs* or *beneficiaries*.

reverse QTIP Trust (see qualified terminable interest in property Trust (QTIP))—A type of *QTIP Trust*, the "reverse" is a confusing misnomer, as there is nothing reverse about it. In fact, like all QTIP Trusts, a reverse QTIP Trust is a type of *marital Trust*, created by an election made on an estate tax return that additionally preserves the ability of the surviving spouse to convert the QTIP Trust of the first-to-die spouse's Trust into a *generation-skipping* transfer (GST) *tax exempt* Trust for the benefit of *contingent beneficiaries*.

revocable living Trust—A *Trust* established by the *grantor* during his or her lifetime. A revocable living Trust can be amended (changed) or revoked (canceled) at any time during the grantor's lifetime. Sometimes called an *inter vivos* (Latin for "while living") Trust, although some living Trusts are irrevocable.

RMD—See *required minimum distribution*.

Rule against Perpetuities—A medieval common-law principle that prevents a person from reaching out from the grave to control his or her assets forever. A *Trust* interest must vest not more than "twenty-one years plus a life in being." In recent years, some states have, by statute, enacted laws enabling people to set up their estates so as to opt out of this deceptively complicated rule. The rule is an important piece of at least two good movies: *Body Heat* and *The Descendants*.

S corporation—A corporation whose income is taxed to its shareholders, thus avoiding a corporate tax. If a *Trust* owns S-corporation shares, it must contain *qualified S corporation Trust (QSST)* language.

Section 2503(c) Trust—An *irrevocable Trust* established for minor children. *Gifts* to such Trusts are deemed gifts of a present interest and thus can qualify for the *annual exclusion amount*. The *trustee* manages the Trust assets and, at his or her discretion, may distribute income or *principal* to a *beneficiary* until the beneficiary reaches age 21. At that point, the beneficiary has the right either to withdraw the Trust assets or to leave it intact until a later date. This type of Trust is generally more flexible than a Uniform Transfers to Minors Act (UTMA) account and is a good choice for removing assets from a grantor's estate in favor of a minor.

self-declaration of Trust—A type of *revocable living Trust*, in which the *grantor* is also the *trustee* and therefore controls the assets of the Trust.

settlor—Also *settler*; see *grantor*.

shelter Trust—A *Trust* designed to protect the *applicable exclusion amount* that each person may *gift* or bequeath to *heirs* other than spouses. It is often referred to as a *bypass Trust* because its assets, more or less, bypass the surviving spouse/beneficiary and are not included in his or her estate. Still, the surviving spouse/beneficiary can have certain rights in the Trust during his or her lifetime. It is also referred to as the "B" Trust in an *A-B* Trust, *an applicable exclusion amount shelter Trust*, or a *credit shelter Trust*.

special power of appointment—See *limited power of appointment*.

spendthrift provision—A clause in a *Trust* that prevents a *beneficiary* from spending an inheritance without restraint and also may prevent creditors from reaching the beneficiary's interest in the Trust.

split gift—By filing an IRS gift tax return, a husband and a wife may double the annual exclusion amount gift to a single individual beneficiary without splitting their assets first.

spray power—See *sprinkle power*.

springing power—The provision that activates the authority of a successor *agent* or *trustee* to act from a previously dormant capacity, usually triggered by disability of the *principal* or the *grantor*. It may also be used to activate *HIPAA* authority.

sprinkle power—The *trustee's* right to distribute income or principal amounts among a class of *beneficiaries*. Such a power gives the trustee the discretion to distribute money according to the relative needs of the beneficiaries. Also called a *spray power*.

stepped-up basis—An IRS principle that makes an *heir's* cost basis equal to the value of the asset at the date of the *grantor's* death–or, alternatively, six months later–rather than its original cost. If a *gift* of an appreciated asset is made during the *donor's* lifetime, the *donee* takes the donor's original carryover *basis*, and there is no step-up. The stepped-up basis avoids a *capital gains* tax on the appreciation that occurred during the donor's lifetime, upon a sale.

successor trustee—Under a *self-declaration of Trust*, the backup to the *grantor*, who is the initial *trustee*. Also, any contingent trustee of any other type of Trust. The same holds true for other *fiduciaries*, such as *executors* and *agents*. The Trust document can provide for successor trustees to act individually or collectively.

survivorship insurance—A life-insurance policy that insures a couple, instead of an individual. The cost of the policy, also sometimes referred to as *second-to-die*, can be less expensive than individual insurance policies on the same two people. Its common purpose is to provide liquidity to pay the *estate taxes* that arise after the death of the surviving spouse, especially for large estates that are predominantly composed of assets difficult to readily convert to cash, such as real estate or a family corporation. In order to be properly utilized, the policy should be owned outside the insured's estate, possibly in an *irrevocable Trust*.

tangible personal property—Movable property such as jewelry, clothing, automobiles, and so on, as opposed to real property (land and buildings) or intangibles such as stocks, bonds, and bank accounts or fungible cash. "Stuff."

tenancy by the entirety—Special type of *joint tenancy* available in some states for a husband and a wife to own real estate, often allowable only for their principal residence. It protects the residence from creditors and liability claims against one of the spouses, because it cannot be unilaterally dissolved.

tenancy in common—Undivided interest in property. Unlike joint tenancy interest, there is no right of survivorship to the remaining tenants in common if one of the tenants dies. Different types of entities, such as Trusts, may also be tenants in common. If the tenant in common who dies is an individual, there may be a need to probate.

testamentary—At death.

testamentary Trust—Trust that activates upon death pursuant to a *Will* or a *revocable living Trust*. Unlike a revocable living Trust, it is not used to avoid *probate*.

testator—Person who creates and executes a valid *Will*.

transfer tax—Tax imposed on lifetime and *testamentary gifts*.

transferable-on-death (TOD) account—See *payable-on-death (POD) account*.

Trust—A legal written arrangement in which one or more *trustees* hold and manage assets for the benefit of one or more *beneficiaries* under a *fiduciary* relationship.

trustee—A person or a company acting in a *fiduciary* capacity, managing and administering Trust assets for the benefit of one or more *beneficiaries*.

trustor—See *grantor* and *settlor*.

unified credit—See *applicable exclusion amount*.

Uniform Transfers to Minors Act (UTMA)—Method of holding property for the benefit of a minor. It is simple to set up but less flexible than a 2503(c) or a *Crummey Trust* (both described in Chapter 21).

unlimited marital deduction—Spouses who are U.S. citizens may transfer unlimited assets to each other, while alive or after death, without any gift, income, or *estate tax* implications. Overuse of the *unlimited marital deduction* may lead to a loss of the *applicable exclusion amount* of the first spouse to die.

Will—A legal document completed in accordance with state law that establishes how your assets will be distributed on your death. The *Will* appoints an *executor* to administer your estate. It may establish *Trusts* for children and recommend *guardians* for minor children.

Will contest—A legal challenge to a *Will* made by one or more disgruntled *heirs*, which can result in great expense to the *estate* and tie it up for some length of time. Will contests are usually based on allegations that the Will was improperly executed or that the *decedent* lacked proper mental capacity at the time he or she created the Will or that someone exerted undue influence on the decedent.

Index

401Ks, 213
403Bs, 213
529 plans, 243–244
2503(b) Trusts, 241
2503(c) Trusts, 241–242

abuse, 182
accumulation Trusts, 210–213
administration costs, 32
advance directives. *See* HIPAA authorizations; living Wills; powers of attorney for finances/property; powers of attorney for health care
advancements, 120
affidavits, 33, 70
AFR (applicable federal rate), 264
agents, 9
airline miles, 192
almsgiving, 189
amendment, 9, 70, 97, 98
American Pet Product Manufacturers Association National Pet Owners Survey, 164–165
American Taxpayer Relief Act (ATRA) of 2012, 222
ancillary probate, 32
animals. *See* pet Trusts
applicable exclusion amount, 126, 140, 220
applicable exclusion amount shelter Trusts, 126–131
applicable federal rate (AFR), 264
appraisals, 47, 182
ascertainable standard Trust distributions, 111–112, 141
assets. *See also* tangible personal property
    basis for, 129, 182, 192, 244
    charitable giving and, 194
    commingling of, 100, 122, 141–142
    digital assets, 48, 192
    hidden assets, 41
    inventories of, 31–32
    marshalling of, 31–32
    pooled assets, 155
    probate assets, 28, 29, 69
    protection of, 99, 103
    segregation of, 122
    types of, 46–48
assisted living, 183
Astor, Brooke, 89
ATRA (American Taxpayer Relief Act) of 2012, 222
attorneys. *See* lawyers
attorneys-in-fact, 82

balancing estates, 128–129
Baldyga, Scott, 75
banks, 178–179
Banks, Ernie, 175
basis
    defined, 129, 192, 244
    QTIP trusts and, 133
    record keeping and, 182
    stepped-up basis, 129, 131, 244
beneficiaries
    defined, 29, 55, 95
    discussing estate plans with, 181
    mojo and, 21–22
    powers of appointment, 109–112
beneficiary designations, 29, 35, 97, 207–214

bequests, 69
bills. *See* debts
blended families
    disclaimer Trusts and, 145
    intestacy and, 33
    QTIP trusts and, 133
    real estate and, 204
    testamentary Trusts and, 123
boarding services for pets, 166
bond premiums, 31
Brown, James, 263
Buddhism, 190
Buffet, Warren, 190
Burger, Warren, 59
Bush, George W., 87, 222
business succession planning, 47–48, 178, 205–206
buy-sell agreements, 206
bypass Trusts, 126–131

capacity, 70
capital gains, 129, 192, 244
capital gains taxes, 129, 133, 192, 244
capital losses, 129
carryover basis, 129
cats. *See* pet Trusts
charging orders, 254
charitable giving. *See also* gifts
    asset selection for, 194
    donor advised funds, 266
    IRAs and, 194, 209
    mojo and, 21–22
    reasons for, 260
    selection of, 191–192
    spirit of, 188–190
    testamentary donations, 194
    Trusts for, 261–264
charitable lead annuity Trusts (CLATs), 264
charitable lead Trusts (CLTs), 264
charitable lead Unitrusts (CLUTs), 264
charitable remainder annuity Trusts (CRATs), 262
charitable remainder Trusts (CRTs), 261–263
charitable remainder Unitrusts (CRUTs), 262–263
charitynavigator.org, 191
children
    college savings for, 240–241, 243–245
    disabilities, special-needs Trusts and, 151–152, 155–157
    godchildren, 21
    grandchildren, 139–142, 176
    GST Trusts, 139–142
    guardianship for in Wills, 72–74
    as underaged beneficiaries, 120
    updating of estate plans about, 176
Christianity, 189
citizenship. *See* non-citizens
civil unions, 128
Clancy, Tom, 112
CLATs (charitable lead annuity Trusts), 264
clients, identification of, 185
CLTs (charitable lead Trusts), 264
CLUTs (charitable lead Unitrusts), 264
codicils, 70
Cohen, Claudia, 204

college savings, 240–241, 243–245
commingling of assets, 100, 122, 141–142
common-law marriage, 128
communication, 173, 179–180
community property, 34, 177
comparable properties, 47
competency, 55, 84
conduit Trusts, 210
conflict reduction, 40–42
conflicts of interest, 180
conformed copies, 174
contingency planning, 11, 70
contractual designations, 29
control, 10
control Trusts, 112
corporations, revocable living Trusts compared, 99.
   See also family businesses
cost basis, 129, 182, 192, 244
co-trustees, 178–179
couples. *See* spouses
CRATs (charitable remainder annuity Trusts), 262
creditors' claims, 31, 100–101, 214
CRTs (charitable remainder Trusts), 261–263
Crummey Trusts, 242–243
CRUTs (charitable remainder Unitrusts), 262–263
custodians, 240

DAF (donor advised funds), 266
dāna, 190
DAPTs (domestic asset protection Trusts), 103
death, 6–7, 90
death benefits, 46. *See also* life insurance
death notices, 31, 100–101
death probate. *See* probate
Death Tax Repeal Act, 222
death taxes. *See* estate taxes
death-delaying procedures, 83, 86–88
death-tax insurance, 203
debts
   creditors' claims, 31, 100–101, 214
   death notices and, 31
   domestic asset protection Trusts and, 103
   FLPs and FLLCs, 254
   GST Trusts and, 141
   payment of, 32
   piercing the corporate veil and, 99
decanting, 156
deceased spouse's unused exclusion amount (DSUEA),
129–130, 145
decision makers, 41–42
designated beneficiaries for IRAs, 207–210
digital assets, 48, 192
disabled people. *See* special-needs Trusts
disclaimer Trusts, 113, 144–147
disincentives, 122
dispute resolution, 40–42
divorce, 100, 175
Do Not Resuscitate (DNR), 86–87
document storage, 174–175
dogs. *See* pet Trusts
domestic asset protection Trusts (DAPTs), 103
domestic partnerships, 128
donations. *See* charitable giving
donor advised funds (DAF), 266
DSUEA (deceased spouse's unused exclusion amount),

129–130, 145
durable powers of attorney for finances/property, 9, 80,
90–91
durable powers of attorney for health care, 83
dynasty Trusts, 142

elder abuse, 182
elder law, 182–185
email accounts, 48
embarrassment avoidance, 40
engagement letters, 173
escheat, 34
estate planning
   discussing with beneficiaries, 181
   documents needed for, 9
   fear and, 7
   financial planning and, 185
   generation-skipping transfer (GST) taxes, 221
   issues to consider, 5, 8, 10, 20
   life stages and, 276–277
   review of, 175–177
   satisfaction of completing, 11
   unintended consequences of failure to make, 9,
   277–278
estate planning mojo, 18–22
estate planning questionnaires, 56–58
estate taxes. *See also* IRAs
   applicable exclusion amount, 126, 220
   charitable giving, 191, 192
   history of, 222
   ILITs and, 102
   life insurance proceeds, 203
   non-resident non-citizens, 223
   state tax, 223
   Sunset Provision, 127, 222
   as unified system, 221
   unlimited marital deduction and, 126–129, 131–132,
   221
ethical Wills, 20
executors/personal representatives, 30–31, 41–42, 71–72

family allowances, 32
family businesses, 47–48, 204–206, 253, 254–255
family limited liability companies (FLLCs), 253, 254–255
family limited partnerships (FLPs), 253, 254
fear, 7
fiduciaries
   bond premiums and, 31
   defined, 29, 55
   discussing estate plans with, 181
   split-interest gifts, 266
   time tracking by, 30
financial institutions, 178–179
financial planning, 185
first-party payback special-needs Trusts (OBRA '93),
155–156
Five Wishes documents, 86
529 plans, 243–244
flip charitable remainder Unitrusts (FLIP-CRUTs), 263
FLLCs (family limited liability companies), 253, 254–255
FLPs (family limited partnerships), 253, 254
401Ks, 213
403Bs, 213
fractional withdrawals, 121
freeze techniques, 252–255

Frozen (Johnson & Baldyga), 75
funeral services, 18–19, 74

Gandolfini, James, 240
general lifetime powers of appointment, 110
general powers of appointment, 110, 112
general testamentary powers of appointment, 110
generation-skipping transfer (GST) tax exempt Trusts, 112, 139–142
generation-skipping transfer (GST) taxes, 140, 221
Genius Award, 195–196
gifts. *See also* charitable giving
    529 plans, 243–244
    2503(b) Trusts, 241
    2503(c) Trusts, 241–242
    basis issues and, 244
    big lifetime gifts, 244
    Crummey Trusts, 242–243
    disclaimers compared, 144
    education and health care exception to limits on, 245
    as estate-depletion technique, 239–240
    lifetime gifts, 40, 220
    to non-citizen spouses, 128
    non-resident non-citizens, 223
    to non-spouses, 128
    present interest requirement, 240
    private family foundations for, 265
    split gifts, 239
    split-interest gifts, 252–254, 260–266
    taxes on as unified system, 221
    Uniform Transfer to Minors Act accounts, 240–241
godchildren, 21
government assistance, 182–185. *See also* special-needs Trusts
grandchildren, 139–142, 176
grantor CLTs, 264
grantor-retained annuity Trusts (GRATs), 253
grantor-retained income Trusts (GRITs), 253
grantor-retained Unitrusts (GRUTs), 253
grantors, 9, 95
GST (generation-skipping transfer) tax exempt Trusts, 112, 139–142
GST (generation-skipping transfer) taxes, 140, 221
guardianship
    overview of, 84
    of children in Wills, 72–74
    discussion of plans about, 181
    income for, 120
    of person versus estate, 72–74
    powers of attorney to avoid, 80, 84, 90

half relatives, 33
handwritten Wills, 70
Health, Education, Maintenance in reasonable comfort, and Support (HEMS), 111–112, 141
health care, 83. *See also* HIPAA authorizations; powers of attorney for health care
heir finders, 34
heirs, 28, 69
Helmsley, Leona, 42, 167
hidden assets, 41
Hinduism, 190
HIPAA authorizations
    overview of, 80–82
    availability of, 89

    defined, 9
    need for, 79–80
    springing powers, 91
holders of powers of appointment, 110
holographic Wills, 70
horses, 167. *See also* pet Trusts
houses. *See* real estate
hybrid beneficiary designations, 213
hybrid life insurance, 203

ILIT (irrevocable life insurance Trust), 102, 242–243
in terrorem (non-contest) clauses, 71
incentives, 122
income taxes. *See* taxes
incompetence, 84
informational estate tax returns, 129–130
initial consultations, 55
insurance, 183–184. *See also* life insurance
inter vivos Trusts. *See* irrevocable living Trusts; revocable living Trusts
intestacy
    avoidance of, 35
    defined, 28
    probate and, 30
    probate assets, what constitutes, 29
    rules about succession, 33–34
intestate heirs, 28
intestate succession, 33–34
inventory of assets, 31–32
investment policy statements (ISP), 180–181
IRAs
    as asset, 48
    beneficiary designations, 207–214
    as charitable donation, 194, 209
    creditors' claims and, 214
    trusteed IRAs, 211–212
    Trusts and, 207–214
irrevocable life insurance Trust (ILIT), 102, 242–243
irrevocable living Trusts, 9, 96, 103
Islam, 189
ISP (investment policy statements), 180–181

Jackson, Michael, 192
Jainism, 190
John D. and Catherine T. MacArthur Foundation, 195–196
Johnson, Larry, 75
joint tenancy with right of survivorship (JTWROS), 28, 29
Judaism, 189

King Lear, 31
Kmart, 193
Kresge, Sebastian S., 193
Kresge Foundation, 193

land. *See* real estate
law, spirit versus letter of, 9
lawsuits, 101
lawyers
    client identification, 185
    initial consultations with, 55
    need for, 59
    residence changes and, 177
    selection of, 172–174
    storage of documents by, 174
    as successor trustees, 178

Lear, King, 31
legacies, 19–20. *See also* mojo
legacy insurance, 203
legatees, 29, 69
Letters (Testamentary/Office/Administration), 31, 72
life insurance
    as asset, 46
    beneficiary designations, 200–201
    business succession planning and, 206
    irrevocable life insurance Trusts and, 102, 242–243
    purposes for, 200
    searches for, 175
    types of, 201–203
life-sustaining treatment, 83, 86–88
lifetime gifts, 40. *See also* gifts
limited powers of appointment, 110–112
liquid portfolios, 46
lives in being, 142
living probate. *See* guardianship
living Trusts, 9, 96, 103. *See also* revocable living Trusts
living Wills, 83, 89
long-term care insurance, 183–184
look-back period for Medicaid, 183–184

MacArthur, John D., 195–196
MacArthur Fellows Program, 195–196
Maimonides, 189
marital Trusts, 131–134
Marshall, J. Howard, 130, 140
"may" versus "shall", 112
McCartney, Linda, 253
Medicaid, 182–185. *See also* special-needs Trusts
Medical Information Bureau (MIB) Solutions, 175
medical issues. *See* HIPAA authorizations; powers of attorney for health care
Medicare, 183
mental capacity, 70
Mental Health Treatment Preference Declarations, 82
metal detectors, 41
minimum required distributions. *See* required minimum distributions (RMDs)
minors. *See* children
mitzvot, 189
mojo, 18–22
Monroe, Marilyn, 40
museums, donations to, 266
Muslims, 189

National Pet Owners Survey, 164–165
net income only charitable remainder Unitrusts (NI-CRUTs), 262–263
net income with makeup charitable remainder Unitrusts (NIM-CRUTs), 263
non-citizens, 128, 133–134, 223
non-contest (in terrorem) clauses, 71
non-grantor CLTs, 264
nursing homes, 183

Obama, Barack, 222
OBRA '93 Trusts, 155–156
online accounts, 48
oral Wills, 70
organization, 54, 56–58
original documents, 174–175

parents, guardianship of children and, 72
Patient Self-Determination Act, 89
payback Trusts, 155–156
per capita, 208
per stirpes, 208
perfection, 59–60
permanent life insurance, 201–203
perpetual Trusts, 142
personal property. *See* tangible personal property
personal representatives/executors, 30–31, 41–42, 71–72
pet Trusts, 42, 164–167
PFFs (private family foundations), 265
Physicians Orders for Life Sustaining Treatment (POLST), 87
piercing the corporate veil, 99
pooled assets, 155
pooled income fund CRTs, 263
pooled Trusts, 155
portability, 129–130, 131, 145
powers of appointment, 109–112
powers of attorney for finances/property, 9, 80, 90–91, 177
powers of attorney for health care
    overview of, 83–85
    agents for, 84–85
    availability of, 89
    defined, 9
    end-of-life philosophies in, 86–88
    limits in, 88
    need for, 79–80
    residence and, 177
    springing powers, 91
prenuptial agreements, 100
principals, 82
privacy, 32. *See also* HIPAA authorizations
private family foundations (PFFs), 265
probate
    overview of, 30
    advantages of, 100–101
    avoidance of. *See* Trusts
    defined, 29
    inventory of assets, 31–32
    lawsuits and, 101
    notification of heirs, creditors, public, 31
    payment of bills and taxes, 32
    personal representatives, 30–31
    as public, 32
    small estate affidavits instead of, 33
probate assets, 28, 29, 69
procrastination, perfection and, 59–60
public policy, Trust incentives and, 122

QDOT (qualified domestic Trusts), 133–134, 223
QTIP (qualified terminable interest in property) Trusts, 132–133
qualified personal residence Trusts (QPRTs), 253–254
qualified retirement plans. *See* retirement plans
quiet title, 101

real estate
    ancillary probate for, 32
    appraisals for, 182
    as asset, 47
    decision making about, 203–204
    Medicaid eligibility and, 183–184
    qualified personal residence Trusts for, 253–254
    quiet title, 101
    vacation homes, 147, 204, 254

reciprocal Trust doctrine, 103
record keeping, 30, 182
required beginning dates (RBDs), 206
required minimum distributions (RMDs), 194, 206–207, 210–213
residence, 177
residuary, tangible personal property, 41–42
restatement of Trusts, 98
retirement plans
    as asset, 48
    beneficiary designations for, 206–210
    creditors' claims and, 214
    IRAs, 48, 194, 207–214
    rollovers of, 213
reverse QTIP Trusts, 133
revocable living Trusts
    amendment of, 98
    defined, 9
    funding of, 97
    incapacity planning with, 99
    irrevocable living Trusts compared, 96
    pets and, 165
    pour-over Wills and, 101
    prenuptial agreements compared, 100
    probate avoidance with, 96–98
    single-owner corporations compared, 99
    Wills compared, 96
revocation
    defined, 9
    powers of attorney for health care, 83
    Trusts, 97
    of Wills, 70, 174
Rivers, Joan, 83
Robert Wood Johnson Foundation, 86
Roosevelt, Theodore, 222
Rule Against Perpetuities, 142

safe-deposit boxes, 174
same-sex marriages, 128. See also spouses
Schiavo, Terri, 87
scrapbooking, 41
SCRUTs (standard charitable remainder Unitrusts), 262
secondary probate, 32
second-to-die insurance, 203
segregation of assets, 122
self-dealing, 180
self-declaration living Trusts, 96
self-proving affidavits, 70
self-settled Trusts, 155–156
SEPs, 213
"shall" versus "may", 112
shareholder agreements, 48
shelter Trusts
    overview of, 126–131
    defined, 112
    disclaimer Trusts compared, 145–146
    for non-spouses, 132
    QTIP trusts and, 133
    state estate taxes and, 223
Sikh teachings, 190
single-owner corporations, revocable living Trusts compared, 99
small estate affidavits, 33
Smith, Anna Nicole, 70, 130, 140
social networking accounts, 48

sound minds, 70
special-needs Trusts, 113, 151–152, 155–157
spending down, 183–184
split gifts, 239
split-interest gifts, 252–254, 260–266
spouses. See also marital Trusts; shelter Trusts
    disinheriting of, 70
    divorce and, 100, 175
    as health-care agent, 85
    IRAs and, 207
spray Trusts, 120, 140
springing powers, 91
sprinkle Trusts, 120, 140
standard charitable remainder Unitrusts (SCRUTs), 262
standard universal life insurance, 202
Steinbrenner, George, 222
step relatives. See blended families
stepped-up basis, 129, 131, 244
stickers, 41
storage of documents, 174–175
succession planning, 47–48, 178, 205–206
Sunset Provision, 127, 222
survivorship life insurance, 203

tangible personal property
    conflict reduction for, 40–42
    donation of, 266
    intestacy and, 29
    resolution methods for, 41–42
    specificity about, 39–40
    updating of estate plans about, 176
Tax Act of 2001, 222
taxes. See also charitable giving; estate taxes; gifts
    commingling of assets and, 100
    payment from estate of, 32
    residence and, 177
    as unified system, 221
    unlimited marital deduction and, 126–129, 131–132, 221
term life insurance, 201
testamentary Trusts. See also control Trusts; disclaimer Trusts; generation-skipping transfer (GST) tax exempt Trusts; pet Trusts; shelter Trusts; special-needs Trusts
    overview of, 108–109
    commingling of assets, 122
    "may" versus "shall", 112
    powers of appointment, 109–112
    reasons to use, 41, 120–123
testators, 69
third-party special-needs Trusts, 151–152, 156
Tikkun olam, 189
timeshares, 147
tithes, 189
traditions, 22
transfer taxes. See estate taxes
trusteed IRAs, 211–212
trustees
    being named as, 179–180
    co-trustees, 178–179
    defined, 29, 95
    selection of, 178–180
    tangible personal property and, 41–42
Trusts. See also irrevocable living Trusts; revocable living Trusts; specific types of Trusts
    decanting of, 156
    defined, 29, 95

IRAs and, 207–214
for pets, 42
Rule Against Perpetuities and, 142
testamentary Trusts, 41
types of, 96
2503(b) Trusts, 241
2503(c) Trusts, 241–242
tzedakah ladder, 189

Uniform Probate Code, 177
Uniform Transfer to Minors Act (UTMA) accounts,
240–241
universal life insurance, 202
unlimited marital deduction, 126–129, 131–132, 221
U.S. Constitution, 177

vacation homes, 147, 204, 254. *See also* real estate
vacation timeshares, 147
valuation formulas, 48
variable universal life insurance, 202

whole life insurance, 202
Williams, Robin, 121
Williams, Ted, 75
Wills
    benefits of, 30
    defined, 9, 28, 69
    disinheriting people in, 70–71
    elements of, 70
    ethical Wills, 20
    funeral wishes in, 74
    guardians for children in, 72–74
    lack of. *See* intestacy
    living Trusts compared, 96–97
    pour-over, 101
    Rule Against Perpetuities and, 142
witnesses, 70

Young, Neil, 10

zakat, 189

Bibliography
and recommended reading

The Illinois Institute for Continuing Legal Education is my main source for drafting estate plan documents. I credit IICLE and IICLE contributors for much of my knowledge base.

My legal knowledge has been enhanced by the Greater North Shore Estate and Financial Planning Council for many informative seminars presented by titans in the legal field.

I have learned a great deal from instructors who teach continuing legal education under the auspices of the Chicago Bar Association, BMO Harris Bank, Northern Trust, JP Morgan, Thompson West, LexisNexis, and Cannon Teleconferencing.

I am happy to be a member of the National Association of Elder Law Attorneys (NAELA), Illinois Chapter, whose members are incredibly generous in sharing their perspectives and work product.

Regarding IRA beneficiary designations, I recommend:
Life & Death Planning for Retirement Benefits, by Natalie Choate
(Ataxplan Publications, 2011, or a later edition)

About the Author

When I was about 10, I attended a friend's uncle's graduation from the John Marshall Law School in Chicago. I was duly impressed with the vaulted ceilings, wood paneling, fancy graduation gowns, and pomp and circumstance, and a seed grew within my brain that culminated with me deciding to become a lawyer.

I graduated from JMLS in 1978 but realized midway through my law school years that courtrooms would be my personal purgatory. Beyond that, I have no taste for litigation, intense negotiations, or excessive legal research. In other words, I discovered that I did not want to be a lawyer in the classic sense of the profession.

I passed the bar exam that summer and became licensed, but my career path led me away from the practice of law.

In June 1990, having neither worked in a law firm nor found true enlightenment in my work life (and married to a woman who refused to allow me to be a stay-at-home-dad), I hung out my shingle and started a solo law practice on a shoestring. From the get-go, I concentrated my practice on estate planning. I acquired the requisite forms, attended seminars, and discovered my calling.

My mantra has been to make the process of estate planning as transparent and understandable as possible to regular people who need it but are not necessarily super-wealthy or particularly enamored of lawyers. In furtherance of this goal, I wrote The Procrastinator's Guide to Wills and Estate Planning (Penguin Group USA/NAL, 2004).

With the help of my able colleagues and staff at Matlin Law Group, P.C.. I have written estate plans for thousands of families, for people and families ranging from having a negative net worth to those worth well over $10 million.

Lawyer, philosopher, aspiring estate-planning guru to both the affluent and the masses, I humbly share my estate-planning expertise. If I can explain it in ways you find relevant and can understand, then I have done my job. My goal is to gently but earnestly prod you through what (at first glance) may seem like a depressing endeavor. No cattle prod needed!

Check the NDY website, www.notdeadyetbook.net
for book updates and related material.

I welcome emails to ndy@ericmatlin.com
with comments, criticisms, and general goodwill.

My law firm website is www.matlinlawgroup.com.
Matlin Law Group, P.C. practice is limited to Illinois and Wisconsin.

Sales of NDY support various charities, including one of which I am a board member, namely The Josselyn Center, located in Northfield, Illinois. For over sixty years, The Josselyn Center has provided high quality interdisciplinary outpatient mental health services for children, adolescents, adults and families, fostering better community health through clinical services, wellness support programs, education and advocacy. The Josselyn Center strives to keep costs of service affordable for all clients by offering a sliding fee scale. If you are in a giving mood, please consider making a donation today to your favorite charity and/or The Josselyn Center: www.josselyn.org.

· ·

My own song list for a memorial party someday, as follows:

"In My Life" (John Lennon)
"Gloria" (Shadows of Night)
"Stand by Me" (Ben E. King)
"Three Little Birds" (Bob Marley)
"Let's Live for Today" (Grassroots)
"It's So Easy to Fall in Love" (Buddy Holly)
"All You Need is Love" (Beatles)
"Ripple" (Jerry Garcia acoustic version)
"After the Gold Rush" (Neil Young)
"Sunrise/Sunset" (Fiddler on the Roof)
"By the Rivers of Babylon" (The Melodians)
"Exodus" (Bob Marley)
"Time Has Come Today" (The Chambers Brothers—long version)
"Hallelujah" (Leonard Cohen)

· ·